Macmillan Building and Surveying Series

Series Editor: **IVOR H. SEELEY**

Emeritus Professor, The Nottingham Trent University

Advanced Building Measurement, secon-
Advanced Valuation Diane Butler and
Applied Valuation Diane Butler
Asset Valuation Michael Rayner
Building Economics, third edition Ivor H

...erleaf

Introduction to Building Services, second edition Christopher A. Howard and Eric F. Curd
Introduction to Valuation, third edition D. Richmond
Marketing and Property People Owen Bevan
Principles of Property Investment and Pricing, second edition W.D. Fraser
Project Management and Control David Day
Property Valuation Techniques David Isaac and Terry Steley
Public Works Engineering Ivor H. Seeley
Resource Management for Construction M.R. Canter
Quality Assurance in Building Alan Griffith
Quantity Surveying Practice Ivor H. Seeley
Recreation Planning and Development Neil Ravenscroft
Resource and Cost Control in Building Mike Canter
Small Building Works Management Alan Griffith
Structural Detailing, second edition P. Newton
Urban Land Economics and Public Policy, fourth edition P.N. Balchin, J.L. Kieve and G.H. Bull
Urban Renewal – Theory and practice Chris Couch
1980 JCT Standard Form of Building Contract, second edition R.F. Fellows

Construction Law

Michael F. James
BSc (Econ), LLB (Wales), MSc (London)
Lecturer in Law, University of Surrey

MACMILLAN

First published 1994 by

THE MACMILLAN PRESS LTD
Houndmills, Basingstoke, Hampshire RG21 2XS
and London
Companies and representatives
throughout the world

ISBN 0–333–59450–9

A catalogue record for this book is available
from the British Library

Typeset by
Richard Powell Editorial and Production Services
Basingstoke, Hants RG22 4TX

Printed and bound in Great Britain by
Mackays of Chatham PLC, Chatham, Kent

Contents

Preface

The term 'Construction Law' is used in three senses:

(i) the principles which govern the duties and liabilities of the parties involved in the construction process and which arise out of that process;
(ii) the law which affects the construction industry; and
(iii) the rules governing the administration of a construction contract.

It is only the first of these senses which is Construction Law proper. Under this definition, Construction Law is that body of law which governs civil liability for the construction of defective buildings. The second two senses are not Construction Law properly defined. Thus, (ii) above would cover a range of subjects going beyond the scope of Construction Law in the first sense; it would, for example, include torts affecting the use of land, employment law and health and safety law. (iii) above is concerned with the application of the standard form contracts, such as the JCT and the ICE, to the running of a construction project and the resolution of disputes which may arise out of the project. This, in my view, is more properly referred to as 'construction contract administration' and is essentially a matter for quantity surveyors rather than lawyers.

This book is concerned with Construction Law in the first of the senses defined above. Essentially it examines three questions:

(1) Who can be sued if a building is defectively constructed?
(2) Who can sue – building owner, tenant, subsequent owner, etc.?
(3) What damages are recoverable?

This book is not, therefore, concerned with liability for matters which may arise *in the course* of building works. Rather it examines the position *after* the work is complete, and the building has been taken over.

There are, I think, three reasons why Construction Law thus defined is worthy of study as a separate branch of the law. In the first place, construction and building cases have been, and continue to be, a source of important developments in the common law. The famous (or infamous) advance and retreat of the tort of negligence and economic loss have involved largely this category of case. Secondly, liability for buildings is an important matter for the individual consumer. For the most part, buildings liability is looked on as of import for construction companies or their professional advisers. Indeed it is, but it is too often forgotten that the victim of defective building works or of unsound advice in relation thereto is an individual. To this extent, Construction Law is an aspect of consumer law. Thus, the recent retreat in the law of negligence has had particularly serious effects for the consumer; it is contract which is now the major source of liability for defective buildings, but in many cases concerning domestic buildings the purchaser will not have a contract with the builder or designer. Thirdly, many recent and forthcoming developments in Construction Law now emanate from the EC. These developments have as their aims the promotion of competition throughout the Community and the protection of the consumer.

The major sources of the general law of construction are common law, statute, private law (i.e., the provisions of any of the standard form building and engineering contracts which may apply to a particular contractual relationship) and, as mentioned in the previous paragraph, EC law. There is no shortage of books on the standard form building and engineering contracts and no independent chapters are devoted to that aspect of Construction Law. Instead, attention is devoted to the relationship between contract and tort and the effect of changes in that relationship upon liabilities in the construction industry and its related professions. Thus, a separate chapter is devoted to collateral warranties and buildings insurance as a result of the impact of the decision in *Murphy v. Brentwood DC* Throughout the book the need for the law to find a balance between professional and consumer interests in the area of civil liability for defective buildings is kept uppermost in mind.

The parameters to Construction Law, as in other areas of law, are set by the appellate courts in the landmark cases. But how those parameters are applied falls usually to the judges at first instance. In the field of Construction Law these judges are known as Official Referees. They are High Court judges with a specialist knowledge of this subject, and it is one of the purposes of this book to examine carefully their most important decisions.

One final point by way of introduction needs to be made. This is not intended to be a book for a beginner. It is intended principally for use by students reading Construction Law as a specialist subject in the later stages of their degree. As such, it assumes a knowledge of the principles of contract and tort. (It is worth stressing at this point the importance of mastering these subjects, without which more specialist areas of law cannot hope to be understood. Not for nothing are contract and tort among the 'core' legal subjects demanded by the Law Society and the Bar

Council!) Nor is this intended to be a practitioner's work, though it is hoped that some practitioners will find in it stimulation to debate further the problematical issues raised by this subject.

The law is as stated at 1 March 1994.

Swansea/University of Surrey M.F.J.

Acknowledgements

The author wishes to thank the following for permission to quote or otherwise use material from the sources indicated:

Butterworths, *The All England Reports*
Estates Gazette, *Estates Gazette Law Reports*
Professor M.P. Furmston (ed.), *Construction Law Reports*
Jon Holyoak and David Allen, *Civil Liability for Defective Premises*, Butterworths, 1982
Incorporated Council of Law Reporting for England and Wales, *The Law Reports* and *The Weekly Law Reports*
Longman Group UK, *Building Law Reports*
Monitor Press, *Building Law Monthly*
J.R. Spencer, *The Defective Premises Act 1972 – Defective Law and Defective Law Reform* [1974] CLJ 307.
Tolley Publishing Co. Ltd, *Professional Negligence*
C.C. Turpin (ed.), *Cambridge Law Journal*

Thanks are due to Stephen Bickford-Smith for reading a draft of Chapter 1 and for making some very helpful suggestions for its improvements. Stephen also made some valuable comments on a synopsis of the text, and the definition of Construction Law contained in the preface owes much to his insight into that synopsis.

Special thanks are due to Valerie Anthony for her word processing. She handled a chaotic manuscript with great patience and skill and with meticulous attention to detail. I know that she was helped in this task by her husband, Roy, who is the Senior Classics Master in Bishop Gore School, Swansea.

I should like to thank the Department of Management Studies of the University of Surrey for defraying some of the expenses involved in preparing this manuscript. I must also thank Sue Kitching of the Department for her secretarial assistance in the word processing of two of the chapters and of the preliminaries.

Jean Simpkins prepared the index and the tables of cases and UK and European legislation. The prepress editorial and typesetting stages were overseen by Richard Powell and Brendan Pender.

Dr Barbara Prentis, writer, retired journalist and author of *The Brontë Sisters and George Eliot*, published by The Macmillan Press in 1988, gave me a good deal of general advice and encouragement of the kind which is so valuable to any first-time author.

Finally, but by no means least, I was a secondment to the Faculty of Law of the University of Leicester in 1991/92 and the Faculty Office – in particular, Ann Hall – provided me with secretarial assistance in submitting the proposal for this book to The Macmillan Press.

Abbreviations

AC	Law Reports, Appeal Cases
ACE	Association of Civil Engineers
ALR	Australian Law Reports
All ER	All England Reports
B	Baron
BLM	Building Law Monthly
BLR	Building Law Reports
CBNS	Common Bench Reports, New Series, 20 vols, 1856–65
Ch	The Law Reports, Chancery Division
CILL	Construction Industry Law Letter
Cl&F	Clark and Finnelly's Reports, House of Lords, 12 vols, 1831–46
CLJ	Cambridge Law Journal
CLY	Current Law Year Book
Cmnd/Cmd	Command Paper
Co Litt	Coke on Littleton (1 Inst)
Con LR	Construction Law Reports
Const. LJ	Construction Law Journal
DC	District Council
DoE	Department of the Environment
DTI	Department of Trade and Industry
EC	European Community (sometimes referred to as the EEC – European Economic Community)
EG	Estates Gazette
EGCS	Estates Gazette Case Summaries
EGLR	Estates Gazette Law Reports
Ex.	Exchequer Reports
ICE	Institution of Civil Engineers
ICR	Industrial Cases Reports
ISVA	Incorporated Society of Valuers and Auctioneers
J.	Justice
JCT	Joint Contracts Tribunal
KB	The Law Reports, King's Bench Division
Law Com.	Law Commission Report
LBC	London Borough Council

L.J. & L.J.J.	Lord Justice, Lord Justices
LQR	Law Quarterly Review
LR Ex	Law Reports, Exchequer Division, 5 vols, 1875–80
MBC	Metropolitan Borough Council
MLR	Modern Law Review
MR	Master of the Rolls
M&W	Meeson and Welsby's Reports, Exchequer, 16 vols, 1836–47
NILR	Northern Ireland Law Reports
NLJ	New Law Journal
NZLJ	New Zealand Law Journal
OJ	Official Journal of the European Communities
OJC	Official Journal of the European Communities: Information and Notices
OJL	Official Journal of the European Communities: Legislation
PN	Professional Negligence
QB	The Law Reports, Queen's Bench Division, 1952–
RIBA	Royal Institute of British Architects
RICS	Royal Institution of Chartered Surveyors
SI	Statutory Instrument
SLT	Scots Law Times
Stark	Starkie's Reports, Nisi Prius, 3 vols, 1814–23
UDC	Urban District Council
US	United States Reports
WLR	The Weekly Law Reports

Table of Cases

Note: Page numbers ending with an 'n' indicate that the case appears in an endnote on the page in question

Table of UK and Commonwealth Legislation

Note: Page numbers ending with an 'n' indicate that the title of the legislation appears in an endnote on the page in question

Table of EC Legislation

Note: Page numbers ending with an 'n' indicate that the title of the legislation appears in an endnote on the page in question

Part I

The Common Law

1 Builders' Liability in Contract

INTRODUCTION

Before examining in detail the potential liability of a builder for defective premises two things must be made clear: the complexity of many building projects and the nature of the contract entered into by the builder.

A building project, especially a large one, involves a number of parties and, consequently, a network of contractual relationships. The person who commissions the work, usually on land over which he has rights of occupation or ownership, and who acquires the building when it is completed, is referred to as the building owner or the employer, or sometimes the client. The person who undertakes the work is referred to as the builder or the contractor, or the building contractor. In a large building project the legal relationship between the building owner and the contractor is known as the main contract. If a builder builds on land which he owns and then sells the building, he is known as a vendor/builder. In addition, it is usual for a number of other parties to be involved in a large project. Firstly, an architect or engineer will be employed by the building owner to design the project. The important point to note here is that such architect or engineer is in a contractual relationship with the building owner, not the contractor. In some cases the contractor will design as well as build the works or subcontract the design to an architect or engineer. The legal relationship between the building owner and contractor is then known as a design and build contract. Secondly, it is usual for the contractor to subcontract parts of the work to specialist firms. These subcontractors each have a contract with the main contractor; they do not have a contract with the building owner unless they provide him with a warranty, e.g. as to the quality of the works. Thirdly, there are suppliers, who supply the contractor with materials and components. The relationship between the contractor and each of his suppliers is that of a contract for the sale of goods. In order to retain control over the cost and quality of the works the building owner may retain the power under the main contract to direct the contractor to employ particular subcontractors and use particular suppliers. In these circumstances the subcontractors and suppliers are referred to as nominated subcontractors and suppliers.

The above network of relationships is that which obtains in a traditional building project. However, an increasingly common feature of the building industry is the use of what is known as a management contract. The main feature of this kind of contract is that there is a management contractor who carries out little or no construction work himself but subcontracts it, and organises and co-ordinates the work of the subcontractors. Architects or engineers will be engaged by the employer as in the conventional procedure.[1]

It is important to note that the first purchaser or lessee of a building may not be in contract with the builder, e.g. where a developer has employed a building contractor to develop a particular site and then leased the completed building. In these circumstances it is the builder who is in contract with the developer. Where a person buys land and a building from a vendor/builder, he will have a contract with the builder. Such a contract is known as a contract for the sale of land and it is based on the principle of *caveat emptor*. That is, there is no warranty as to quality implied on the part of the builder and the purchaser must satisfy himself as to the condition of the building through a surveyor's inspection.[2]

This chapter, however, is not principally concerned with contracts for the sale of completed buildings; rather it is concerned with contracts for the erection of works, e.g. a contract for the erection of a supermarket or a house on land already owned by the employer. The essence of this sort of contract is that the contractor agrees to supply work and materials for the erection of a building or other works for the benefit of the employer. It is an example of a type of contract known as a contract for work and materials.

Building contracts impose a wide range of obligations on the contractor. It must be emphasised that this chapter is concerned only with contractual liabilities for defects in the building; other aspects of construction contracts such as delay, frustration, etc., are outside its scope.[3] In other words, the subject matter of this chapter is the contractual obligations of the builder for the quality and safety of the works he constructs. We shall also be concerned with the remedies available to the employer in the event of the contractor being in breach of those obligations and whether or not the contractor can effectively exclude or limit his liability for such breach.

THE CONTRACTOR'S OBLIGATIONS

The contractor's obligations for the quality and safety of the building can be found in: (1) the express terms of the contract; and (2) the implied terms.

Express terms

Express terms are the terms agreed upon by the parties to the contract. Such terms may be oral, written or partly oral and partly written. Contracts in the construction industry generally involve complex arrangements with many difficult points of procedure which have to be provided for. As a result the contractual terms will invariably all be set down in writing. Indeed the industry has gone one stage further and has evolved standard forms of contract for use in large projects. The one most frequently used for building projects is the standard form of building contract published by the Joint Contracts Tribunal (the JCT).[4] The standard form of contract most frequently used for engineering projects is the one published by the Institution of Civil Engineers (the ICE).[5] Essentially, these contracts are bodies of private law governing the relationships of the parties to them. They are enforceable in the courts in that it is a basic principle of English contract law that, subject to certain exceptions, the parties to a commercial project may make any arrangement they wish governing that project, without regard to fairness or equity.

The provisions of the JCT and ICE relating to the contractor's obligations for quality and safety are to be found in the clauses on workmanship and materials and the statutory obligations of the contractor in relation to design.

Workmanship and materials

Under clause 2 of the 1980 JCT form the contractor's principal obligation is to erect the building in such a way as to correspond with the Contract Drawings and descriptions in the Contract Bills. He must use such materials and adopt such standards of workmanship as are specified, subject to the approval of the architect.[6] Under the provisions of clause 8 the contractor may be called upon by the architect to vouch that this obligation has been complied with. Clause 8 further provides that the architect can demand that completed work be uncovered and inspected or that tests be carried out on the materials used in the works to assess their quality. If the work or materials are below the standard required by the contract then the contractor will have to pay for them; in other cases the cost is added to the contract price. In the event of default the architect can order removal of work or materials that fail to meet contractual specifications and at any time he may reasonably order the dismissal of any person or firm employed on the site.

The provisions of the ICE relating to workmanship and materials are contained in clauses 36–39. Under the provisions of clause 36 (1) all materials and workmanship must be of the kind described in the contract and in accordance with the engineer's instructions. The engineer has the power to order that tests be carried out, either at the place of manufacture or on site. Clause 38 (1) states that no work may be covered up without the consent of the engineer and the contractor must allow the engineer to examine and measure any work which is about to be covered up.

Clause 38 (2) permits the engineer to order uncovering of work and provides for apportioning the cost. Under the provisions of clause 39(1), if the materials used are not in accordance with the contract, the engineer has the power to order their removal from the site and he can require the contractor to substitute materials which are in accordance with the contract. If the contractor defaults on the obligations, then under the provisions of clause 39 (2) the employer is entitled to employ other persons to carry them out and recover the cost of so doing from the contractor.

Design

The liability of the builder under the general law for defects in the design is still not entirely clear, though it is probable that he has a duty to bring to the attention of the architect or engineer any obvious errors in the design of which he has actual knowledge.[7] The duties of the builder under the JCT form in this regard are somewhat clearer.[8] Firstly, under the provisions of clause 2.3 he has an express duty to give the architect written notice of any discrepancy or divergence between the Contract Drawings, the Contract Bills and other documents issued by the architect. Secondly, under the provisions of clause 6.1 he must comply with the Building Regulations.[9] This imposes a heavy onus on him, but it is alleviated by saving provisions in clause 6.1. Under these provisions, if the builder does find any divergence between the Building Regulations and the contractual specifications then he must give written notice to the architect.[10] The architect then has seven days from receipt of this notice to issue instructions regarding the works to be varied accordingly.[11] Clause 6.1 goes on to state that provided that the contractor has complied with its provisions he is not liable if the works do not comply with the Building Regulations.[12]

Implied terms

The common law has always implied a number of terms into a contract for building works:

(1) that the contractor will carry out this work in a good and workmanlike manner;
(2) that any materials supplied by him will be of good quality and reasonably fit for their purpose; and
(3) that in the case of a dwelling house, it will be fit for human habitation.

These terms are imposed on the parties by law, regardless of whether they intend them to be included in the contract. The implied terms relating to work and materials are now in statutory form, and are contained in the Supply of Goods and Services Act 1982. It should be noted that this Act does not replace the common law obligations, and the case law on this subject is therefore still of great importance.

Workmanship

As a general rule, there is an implied duty of care and skill imposed on the contractor requiring him to exercise the skill and competence required of an ordinarily competent building contractor.[13] In addition, it appears that there is an implied term that the completed building will be reasonably fit for any purpose for which the contractor knew it would be required. Fitness for purpose is a greater obligation than the duty of reasonable care and skill; it is an obligation of strict liability.

Authority for an implied term of fitness for purpose is to be found in two cases, *Greaves & Co. (Contractors) Ltd v. Baynham Meikle and Partners*[14] and *IBA v. EMI Electronics Ltd and BICC Construction Ltd.*[15]

In *Greaves* contractors agreed to design and construct a warehouse and office for a company who intended to use the warehouse as a store for oil drums. The oil drums were to be kept on the first floor and moved into position by fork-lift trucks. The contractors engaged structural engineers to design the structure of the warehouse and they told the design engineers the purpose for which it was required. The engineers in their design did not take into account the effect of the vibrations from the fork-lift trucks. The result was that, when the warehouse was completed, the floor cracked under the weight of the oil drums and the trucks. The building contractors sued the engineers for breach of an implied warranty that the floor would be fit for the purpose for which they knew it was required. The Court of Appeal held that the engineers were liable. In the course of his judgement Lord Denning discussed the obligations of the building contractors. He said:

> The owners made known to the contractors the purpose for which the building was required, so as to show that they relied on the contractor's skill

> and judgement. It was therefore the duty of the contractors to see that the finished work was reasonably fit for the purpose for which the building was required. It was not merely an obligation to use reasonable care.[16]

IBA v. EMI & BICC concerned a contract to erect a TV mast. *EMI* was the main contractor; *BICC* were subcontractors responsible for the design of the mast. In bad, though not exceptional, weather conditions the mast collapsed, after just three years in service. The Court of Appeal held that there was an implied term in the contract that the mast should be fit for its intended purpose, i.e. that it should be able to withstand likely weather conditions in the area where it was built. The House of Lords upheld this finding on the ground that EMI's obligations to IBA extended to the design of the mast. The fact that BICC had been negligent in the design of the mast was no defence.

These two cases have attracted a great deal of comment and a word of caution about their effect is necessary. Both cases arose on particular facts and they did not involve the commonly found relationship between designers, contractors and employers. In *Greaves* the contract was a design and build contract; in *IBA v. EMI & BICC* it was the subcontractor who carried out the design. Neither case can be taken as authority for the general imposition of an implied term as to fitness for purpose into contracts for work and materials. In other words, such a term arises only in fact, not in law.[17] This view of the law was confirmed by the Court of Appeal in *George Hawkins v. Chrysler (UK) Ltd and Burne Associates.*[18] Further, the Law Commission has concluded that no immediate reform in this area of the law is necessary.[19]

Materials

The common law

At common law a person contracting on the basis of work and materials impliedly warrants that the materials will be of good quality and reasonably fit for their purpose, unless he can show that the purchaser did not rely on his skill and judgement. Authority for the implication of these warranties in building contracts is provided by the cases of *Young & Marten Ltd v. McManus Childs Ltd*[20], and *Gloucestershire County Council v. Richardson.*[21]

In *Young & Marten* building contractors subcontracted roofing work and specified that the subcontractors were to use a particular kind of tile known as 'Somerset 13'. The tiles had a latent defect which caused them to disintegrate within a few years. The House of Lords held that the subcontractors were liable in damages for breach of the implied warranty that the materials supplied be of good quality, even though the person to whom they had supplied them had nominated the source of supply. There was, however, no implied warranty as to fitness in this case because the materials were chosen by the main contractors and therefore they did not rely on the skill and judgement of the subcontractors in that respect.

In *Gloucestershire County Council v. Richardson* under a contract to build an extension to a college, the contractors were obliged to obtain concrete columns from suppliers nominated by the employer. The columns suffered from latent defects. The House of Lords held that the contractors were not liable for these defects. There were two particular factors which influenced their Lordships in coming to that decision. Firstly, very detailed specifications were laid down by the employer. Secondly, the contractor was obliged by his contract with the employer to purchase materials on terms which excluded certain of the manufacturer's normal liabilities. This decision does appear to be an exception to the general rule that the contractor will be held liable in most instances for defects in the materials which he supplies, even when they are not of his choosing. The opening statement of Lord Pearce's speech can be taken as authority for this view:

> ... the contractor in any particular field of business, when he engages to do certain work and supply materials, impliedly warrants that the materials will be of good quality, unless the particular circumstances of the case show that the parties intended otherwise.[22]

Liability for breach of the warranties as to quality and fitness is strict; it is no defence for the builder to say that he took all reasonable care. This point is well illustrated by *Hancock v. B.W. Brazier (Anerley) Ltd.* In that case the defendant developed an estate of houses. Within four years of completion three of the houses developed serious cracking of the walls and floor. This was found to be due to the presence of sodium sulphate in the hardcore. When exposed to moisture, this expands, causing the concrete to crack. At first instance, it was held that although this characteristic of sodium sulphate was known at the time when the estate was developed, it was not thought as likely to happen in the ordinary course of building a house. The builder was therefore not negligent. None the less, he was held to be in breach of the implied terms of quality and fitness.

The imposition of these implied terms may seem rather harsh on the builder. The House of Lords explained their rationale in *Young & Marten* by saying that the subcontractor could sue his supplier under what is now section 14(2) of the Sale of Goods Act 1979 for breach of the implied term as to merchantable quality under their contract of sale. That supplier could then sue his supplier under this provision. He was probably the manufacturer of the tiles, so that by this chain of contractual litigation liability would ultimately come to rest upon the party at fault.[23] This is the classic contractual model of product liability. It may be thought that it would be more efficient to allow the party at the end of the chain to sue the manufacturer direct. That is possible, following the decision of the House of Lords in *Donoghue v. Stevenson*[24], where the defect in the product has led to personal injury or damage to other property. But where the loss suffered is simply to have acquired a poor quality product, one whose actual value is less than the price paid for it, the courts have clung rigidly to the classic model of litigation, saying that to allow otherwise would be to circumvent the doctrine of privity of contract. In practice, the chain of product liability may break down because of insolvency or the existence of a valid exclusion clause in one of the contracts.[25]

The Supply of Goods and Services Act 1982

The implied obligations of the contractor in relation to the materials used are now contained in Part I of the Supply of Goods and Services Act 1982 ('the 1982 Act'). The common law obligations in this respect are very similar to, if not identical with, the obligations imposed upon the seller in a contract for the sale of goods.[26] However, it was felt that from the point of clarity of the law and in order to put the matter beyond doubt, the obligations should be cast in statutory form to conform as near as possible to those in a contract of sale.[27] It is the purpose of Part I of the 1982 Act to do that. Part I does not merely apply to contracts for work and materials; it extends to a whole range of contracts where goods are supplied but which are not contracts of sale in the strict meaning of that term.[28] It is based on the concept of a contract for the transfer of property in goods. These are defined by the 1982 Act as contracts under which one person transfers or agrees to transfer to another the property in goods (section 1(1)). Contracts for the sale of goods, hire-purchase agreements and contracts for the sale of land are excluded from this definition (section 1(2)). A normal building contract is clearly within the scope of this definition because the builder transfers the property (i.e. ownership) of the materials he uses to the building owner.

The obligations imposed upon the supplier are contained in sections 2–5 of the 1982 Act. They are as follows:

(a) *An implied condition relating to title.* The transferor has the right to transfer the property in the goods (section 2(1)), and he impliedly warrants that the goods are free from charges or encumbrances not disclosed or known to the transferee before the contract is made and that the transferee will enjoy quiet possession of the goods (section 2(2)).

(b) *An implied condition relating to description.* The goods transferred must correspond with their description (section 3(2)). If the transferor transfers or agrees to transfer the property in the goods by sample as well as by description, it is not sufficient that the bulk of the goods correspond with the sample if the goods do not also correspond with the description (section 3(3)). There is still a transfer by description if the goods are selected by the transferee (section 3(4)).

(c) *Implied conditions relating to quality and fitness.* By section 4(2) where the transferor transfers the property in goods in the course of a business, there is an implied condition that the goods supplied under the contract are of merchantable quality. Section 4(3) states that there is no such implied condition

 (i) as regards defects specifically drawn to the transferee's attention before the contract is made; or
 (ii) if the transferee examines the goods before the contract is made, as regards defects which that examination ought to reveal.

There has been a great deal of uncertainty over the precise scope of this implied term and there is now a statutory definition of merchantable quality. It is contained in section 4(9) of the 1982 Act. Goods are of merchantable quality if they are fit for the purpose or purposes for which goods of that kind are commonly supplied as it is reasonable to expect having regard to any description applied to them, the price (if relevant) and all the other relevant circumstances.[29] This definition has not stayed pressure for a further statutory (and more detailed) definition of this concept.[30]

Where the transferor transfers the property in goods in the course of a business and the transferee, expressly or by implication, makes known to the transferor any particular purpose for which the goods are being acquired, there is an implied condition that the goods supplied under the contract are reasonably fit for that purpose, whether or not that is a purpose for which such goods are commonly supplied (sections 4(4) and (5)). There is no obligation of fitness for purpose where there was no reliance upon the skill and judgement of the contractor in the choice of those materials (section 4(6)).[31]

(d) *An implied condition relating to sample.* Where the transferor transfers or agrees to transfer the property in the goods by reference to a sample there is an implied condition

(a) that the bulk will correspond with the sample in quality; and
(b) that the transferee will have a reasonable opportunity of comparing the bulk with the sample; and
(c) that the goods will be free from any defect, rendering them unmerchantable, which would not be apparent on reasonable examination of the sample.

A detailed examination of the content of these implied obligations is beyond the scope of this work and the reader is referred to specialist works on the sale of goods for that purpose.[32] However, several points are worthy of mention.

Firstly, the implied obligations in sections 2–5 of the 1982 Act are, with the exception of the obligation in section 2(2), *conditions*. This has an important implication: in the event of the supplier being in breach of one or more of these obligations, *however minor the breach*, the customer can elect either to reject the goods and claim damages or accept the goods and claim damages. In contrast, the implied obligation in section 13 of the 1982 Act is a *term*, i.e. it is not classified as a condition or as a warranty. This means that the question of whether or not breach of section 13 would entitle the innocent party to terminate the contract would depend on how the court interpreted the contract, and whether the breach deprived the innocent party of most of the benefit of the contract.[33] Secondly, liability for breach of the obligations in section 2–5 is strict, i.e. it is not dependent on the supplier failing to exercise reasonable care and skill.[34]

Thirdly, it is generally thought that the implied obligations of quality and fitness apply to the goods supplied *at the time of sale*, and that there is no obligation that the goods remain merchantable, etc., for any period of time after the completion of the contract of sale, i.e. an obligation as to durability. However, there is authority for the view that the obligations as to quality and fitness are of a continuing nature.[35]

An interesting illustration of the points concerning strict liability and the continuing nature of the obligations as to quality and fitness in the context of builders' materials is provided by *Lee v. West.*[36] In that case a builder contracted to provide an electronically operated up-and-over garage door for the plaintiff's garage. For this purpose the builder selected a lintel from a manufacturer's brochure. Some two and a half years after the contract was completed the lintel deflected, damaging the brickwork. Remedial work had to be carried out, and the plaintiff sought the cost of this work from the builder. The Court of Appeal held that even though the builder had not been negligent in selecting the lintel or in attaching it to the garage door, he was liable for breach of the provisions of section 4 of the 1982 Act. Thus far the case is unremarkable. The interesting point raised by it is that the Court of Appeal accepted the fact that the lintel had failed *after two and a half years* as evidence that it was unfit *at the time of sale.* In so doing the appellate judges may well have introduced a concept of durability into the implied obligations of quality and fitness by the back door.[37]

The builder's liability for design

We have seen that in a design and build contract the builder is under a duty to see that the building is fit for any purpose made known to him. We have also seen that, under the conventional JCT form of building contract, where the builder is aware that the design does not comply with the Building Regulations he is under an express duty to bring that fact to the attention of the architect. The question for consideration in this section of the chapter is whether in the conventional tripartite form of building contract there is a duty under the general law on the builder to warn the employer of any defects in the design which he has reason to believe may exist. The cases appear to be in conflict on this matter.

In *Duncan v. Blundell*[38] the plaintiff erected a store in the defendant's shop and laid a tube under the floor to carry off smoke, but the plan failed entirely. Bayley J. said:

> Where a person is employed in a work of skill, the employer buys both his labour and his judgement; he ought not to undertake the work if he cannot succeed, and he should know whether it will or not; of course it is otherwise if the party employing him choose to supersede the workman's judgement by using his own.

In *Lynch v. Thorne*[39] a builder constructed, as specified, a solid brick wall of a house without rendering. This allowed rain to enter the house. The Court of Appeal held that there was no implied term that the walls would be waterproof and that the builder was not liable for the defect. The rationale of this decision was expressed by Lord Evershed in the following terms:

> if two parties elect to make a bargain which specifies in precise detail what one of them will do, then, in the absence of some other express provision, it

> would appear to me to follow that the bargain is that which they have made; and as long as the party doing the work does that which he has contracted to do that is the extent of his obligation.[40]

The *Lynch v. Thorne* approach to the duty to warn issue was not followed in the Canadian case of *Brunswick Construction Ltd v. Nowlan.*[41] In 1962 Brunswick Corporation entered into a contract with Dr Nowlan, for the construction of a house in accordance with drawings and a specification prepared for Dr Nowlan by a firm of architects. The contract contemplated the appointment of an engineer to supervise the execution of the work but no one was appointed to perform that function. After the house had been built and occupied, leaks developed in the roof which required extensive major repairs. The cause of the problem was the design, which did not contain sufficient provision for ventilation of the roof space and timbers, with the result that the house became seriously affected by rot. Ritchie J., giving the majority judgement of the Supreme Court of Canada, held that a company of the experience of Brunswick Corporation should have detected that the design of the house was bad. As the house owner did not appoint an architect or engineer to supervise the works then he must be taken to have relied entirely on the skill of the contractors. The contractors must have known of this reliance and they were therefore under a duty to warn the house-owner of the defects in the architect's design. Ritchie J. then went to say that the contractors' obligation was to carry out work which would perform the intended duty or function, and that obligation overrode the obligation to comply with the plans and specifications. Dickson J., in his dissenting judgement, said that the building contractor could not be expected to have detected the design errors. He thought that there was no warranty implied in the contract that the house be reasonably fit for the purpose for which it was required: namely, human habitation.

With one exception, recent English decisions at first instance have followed the reasoning in *Brunswick* rather than that in *Lynch v. Thorne.* In *Equitable Debenture Assets Corporation Ltd (EDAC) v. Williams Moss Corp Ltd*[42] Judge Newey held that there was an implied term in a contract requiring contractors to inform their employer's architect of any defects in the design of which they knew. In *Victoria University of Manchester v. Hugh Wilson*[43] it was held that this duty extended to defects which the builders believed to exist.

In *University of Glasgow v. William Whitfield & John Laing (Construction) Ltd*[44], however, Judge Bowsher followed the reasoning in *Lynch v. Thorne.* He said that where there is a detailed contract, together with plans produced by an architect, there is no room for the implication of a duty to warn about possible defects in design. He suggested that there are two circumstances in which a term may be implied requiring a contractor to warn a building owner of defects in the design: firstly, where there is a special relationship between the parties so that the contractor knows that the building owner is relying upon him; and secondly, where the builder undertakes to achieve a particular purpose or a function.

In *Lindenberg v. Canning*[45] Judge Newey held that a builder was in breach of his duty of reasonable care and skill in circumstances where he simply obeyed his employer's instructions, which proved defective. The judge, however, reduced the damages awarded to the employer by 75 per cent on the ground of his contributory negligence.

Judge Newey's approach to the duty to warn issue seems, to the author, to be more satisfactory than that of Judge Bowsher. If the employer does give exact specifications to the builder, that surely does not mean that he would not rely on the builder to warn him of any defects in those specifications. It is tentatively suggested that the common law in this area can be summed up as follows:

(1) There is no duty of result imposed upon the builder, except when he enters into a design and build contract with the employer or where he is employed to construct a dwellinghouse, which must be fit for habitation when completed.
(2) The builder is under a duty to warn of defects in the design which come to his attention. However, that duty does not extend to overriding the design without first seeking fresh instructions from the employer or his architect.

Judgements at first instance are, of course, only of persuasive authority and perhaps it is time for the Court of Appeal to take another look at this subject.

EXCLUSION OF LIABILITY[46]

It is common to find a clause in a contract whereby one party who would otherwise be under a certain liability in relation to that contract seeks to exclude or limit that liability. These clauses are frequently found in standard form contracts, though there is no such clause in the JCT or ICE forms. However, it is always open to a contractor to vary those forms to include an exclusion or limitation clause. In a domestic building contract the contractor may well seek to exclude or limit his liability under the contract.

Exclusion and limitation clauses are controlled by both the common law and statute in the form of the Unfair Contract Terms Act 1977 (UCTA).

The common law controls these clauses and notices by requiring that to be effective they must meet certain conditions. In the first place, it must be shown that they have been incorporated into the contract, or in the case of a non-contractual notice, that they have been brought to the attention of the other party. Secondly, assuming that the clause has been incorporated into the contract (or the notice brought to the other party's attention), it must adequately cover the breach of contract or tort in question. The Act does not replace these rules and they continue to be of importance, for two reasons: firstly, because some very important classes of contract are outside the scope of the Act altogether; and secondly, because where the Act provides that an exclusion clause is valid if reasonable, the recipient of the clause may argue:

(a) that it has not been incorporated into the contract; or
(b) that, on its true construction, the clause does not cover the breach in question, in which case it is ineffective even if reasonable.

However, it is UCTA which is now the most important form of control and it is to that Act which most attention must be devoted.

The scope of the Act

The title of the Act is misleading in two respects. Firstly, it is not confined to contractual terms; it imposes limits on the extent to which civil liability for breach of contract and for negligence can be excluded or limited by contract terms or notices. Secondly, it is not concerned with contract terms that may be thought 'unfair', but only with clauses that exclude or restrict liability and indemnity clauses.

The concept of an exclusion clause is given an extended definition by section 13(1) of the Act, and the following types of terms are caught by the Act:

(a) a term making the liability or its enforcement subject to restrictive or onerous conditions;
(b) a term excluding or restricting any right or remedy in respect of the liability, or subjecting a person to any prejudice in consequence of his pursuing any such right or remedy; and
(c) a term excluding or restricting rules of evidence or procedure.

Section 13(1) also prevents the restriction or exclusion of liability by the exclusion or restriction of the relevant obligation or duty. Thus, a disclaimer to the effect that no responsibility is undertaken for, say, the contents of a report would be caught by the Act.[47] The courts, in general, look to the substance and effect of a clause rather than its form in order to determine whether it is an exclusion clause.[48]

The Act covers only business liability, i.e. liability for things done by a person in the course of a business or which arise from his use of premises for business purposes. There is no definition of 'business' in the Act but section 14 provides that 'business' includes a profession and the activities of any government department or local or public authority.

The provisions of the Act

The provisions of the Act are of immense importance for business and for the professions because it imposes severe restrictions on the effective use of exclusion clauses. Under the basic scheme of the Act these clauses can be divided into three categories:

(a) clauses which are not allowed to operate at all;
(b) clauses which, in order to be legally effective, must satisfy a statutory test of reasonableness; and
(c) clauses not covered by the Act.

The detailed provisions of the Act are best examined in relation to the areas of liability which they concern.

Negligence liability

Negligence is defined by section 1 of the Act as the breach not only of a duty of care imposed by the law of tort, but also of one arising out of contract. It also includes the breach of the duty owed by the occupier of premises to his lawful visitors under the Occupiers' Liability Act 1957. Under the provisions of section 2(1) any attempt to exclude liability for death or personal injury is rendered ineffective. Under the provisions of section 2(2) any attempt to exclude liability for 'other loss or damage' is also ineffective, except where the term or notice satisfies the requirement of reasonableness. 'Other loss or damage' includes damage to property and financial loss. It should be noted that if a contractor does seek to rely on a clause or term excluding his liability for negligence, he will not be permitted to argue the doctrine of *volenti non fit injuria*. This is because, under the provisions of section 2(3), a person's agreement to or awareness of such a term cannot of itself be taken as indicating his voluntary acceptance of any risk.

Liability arising in contract

Under the provisions of section 3 of the Act, where a person deals as a consumer or on the other's written standard terms of business the other cannot by reference to any contract term

(a) when himself in breach of contract, exclude or restrict any liability of his in respect of the breach; or
(b) claim to be entitled
  (i) to render a contractual performance substantially different from that which was reasonably expected of him, or
  (ii) in respect of the whole or any part of his contractual obligation, to render no performance at all,

except in so far as the contract term satisfies the requirement of reasonableness in these respects.

There is no definition of 'written standard terms of business' in section 3, or in any other part of UCTA. Further, there is no English appellate authority on the meaning of this concept, though it has been considered by the Scottish Outer House in *McCrone v. Boots Farm Sales Ltd,*[49] and by the High Court (Official Referee's Business) in *The Chester Grosvenor Hotel Company Ltd v. Alfred McAlpine Management Ltd.*[50]

In *McCrone* Lord Dunpark said that although he did not attempt to formulate a comprehensive definition of a standard form contract, its meaning was not difficult to comprehend. In relation to section 17 of the Act, which applies in Scotland, he said:

> the section is designed to prevent one party to a contract from having his contractual rights, against a party who is in breach of contract, excluded or restricted by a term or condition which is one of a number of fixed terms or conditions invariably incorporated in contracts of the kind in question by the party in breach, and which have been incorporated in the particular contract in circumstances in which it would be unfair and unreasonable for the other party to have his rights so excluded or restricted. If the section is to achieve its purpose, the phrase 'standard form contract' cannot be confined to written contracts in which both parties use standard forms. It is, in my opinion, wide enough to include any contract, whether wholly written or partly oral, which includes a set of fixed terms or conditions which the proponer applies, without material variation, to contracts of the kind in question.[51]

In *The Chester Grosvenor Hotel* the plaintiffs, Grosvenor, were the owners of the Chester Grosvenor Hotel, a luxury hotel. They engaged the defendants, McAlpine, as management contractors on two refurbishment contracts in 1984 and 1985. The form of these contracts was devised by McAlpine. One of the questions for consideration was whether McAlpine's management contract fell within the meaning of 'written standard terms of business'. In considering this matter Judge Stannard relied on Lord Dunpark's dictum. He said:

> What is required for terms to be standard is that they should be regarded by the party which advances them as its standard terms and that it should habitually contract in those terms. If it contracts also in other terms, it must be determined in any given case, and as a matter of fact, whether this has occurred so frequently that the terms in question cannot be regarded as standard, and if on any occasion a party has substantially modified its prepared terms, it is a question of fact whether those terms have been so altered that they must be regarded as not having been employed on that occasion.[52]

The judge concluded that the two management contracts in question were entered into on McAlpine's written standard terms of business.

The interesting question for the construction industry is whether the JCT and ICE forms come within the scope of section 3. There is no binding authority on this question and the two leading academic works on Construction Law appear to differ on it. In the view of the editor of *Keating on Building Contracts* the use of a JCT or ICE form would not fall into the category of written standard terms because they are 'compromise' contracts drawn up by bodies representative of all branches of the construction industry, including employers.[53] However, the editors of *Emden's Construction Law* take the view that the provisions of section 3 do not prevent a set of standard terms from coming within their scope merely because they are the standard terms of the other party.[54] The author inclines to the view of *Keating*, for two reasons. Firstly, it is consistent with the general philosophy of UCTA, which is to protect contracting parties from having exclusion clauses imposed upon them; the JCT and ICE forms are freely negotiated contracts. Secondly, it accords with the approach to standard form contracts adopted by the EC Directive on unfair terms in consumer contracts:

> A term shall always be regarded as not individually negotiated where it has been drafted in advance and the consumer has therefore not been able to influence the substance of the term, particularly in the context of a pre-formulated standard contract.[55]

The supply of goods

Where the possession or ownership of goods passes under a contract which is not a contract of sale, then under the provisions of section 7(2), as against a person dealing as consumer, liability in respect of the implied terms of description, quality, fitness and sample cannot be excluded. However, where the supplier deals with a person who is not a consumer, then under the provisions of section 7(3) that liability can be excluded if the requirement of reasonableness is satisfied. Clearly, contracts for the transfer of property in goods as defined in Part I of the Supply of Goods and Services Act 1982, such as a contract for work and materials, are within the scope of section 7. Thus, a builder engaged by a consumer would not be able to exclude his liability for the quality, fitness, etc., of the materials he uses. On the other hand, a builder engaged by another business may exclude such liability if reasonable.

The concept of 'dealing as consumer' is defined in section 12 of UCTA. This section states that a party to a contract 'deals as a consumer' in relation to another party if

(a) he neither makes the contract in the course of a business nor holds himself out as doing so; and
(b) the other party does make the contract in the course of a business; and
(c) in the case of a contract for the sale of goods or hire purchase, or a contract for the supply of goods, the goods passing under the contract are of a type ordinarily supplied for private use or consumption.

This definition has not proved entirely satisfactory, as it is not clear from the wording whether or not it covers the case of the business person who buys an article for use in his business but whose business does not deal in that article. The test adopted by the courts for deciding this question is whether the purchase is an integral part of the buyer's business; if so, then the buyer does not deal as a consumer within the meaning of UCTA. Thus, in *R & B Customs Brokers Co. Ltd v. United Dominions Trust Ltd*[56] the Court of Appeal held that the acquisition of a car for the use of a director of a shipping brokerage did not require the company to be treated as a consumer within the meaning of UCTA. This approach was adopted in *The Chester Grosvenor Hotel*, where the judge had to decide whether Grosvenor had 'dealt as a consumer'. He held that they had entered into the management contracts as an essential part of its business of providing luxury hotel facilities. Therefore, these contracts were an integral part of Grosvenor's business and in entering them it did not 'deal as a consumer'.

The requirement of reasonableness

The one area of doubt in this area of the law is the precise meaning of the requirement of reasonableness. The Act itself provides only limited guidance on this point. Thus, section 11(1) provides that a term will satisfy the requirement of reasonableness if it is a fair and reasonable one to be included in the contract having regard to the circumstances which arose, or ought reasonably to have been known to or in the contemplation of the parties when the contract was made. In the case of a non-contractual notice, section 11(3) states that it should be fair and reasonable to allow reliance on it having regard to all the circumstances obtaining when the liability arose or (but for the notice) would have arisen. Under the provisions of section 11(5) the burden of proving that a contract term satisfies the requirement of reasonableness rests upon the party who claims that it is reasonable.

In relation to contracts for the sale and supply of goods, Schedule 2 to UCTA provides the courts with a (non-exhaustive) list of guidelines to follow when assessing reasonableness. They are:

(a) the strength of the bargaining positions of the parties relative to each other, taking into account (among other things) alternative means by which the customer's requirements could have been met;
(b) whether the customer received an inducement to agree to the term, or in accepting it, had an opportunity of entering into a similar contract with other persons, but without having to accept a similar term;
(c) whether the customer knew or ought reasonably to have known of the existence and extent of the term (having regard, among other things, to any custom of the trade and any previous course of dealing between the parties);
(d) where the term excludes or restricts any relevant liability if some condition is not complied with, whether it was reasonable at the time of the contract to expect that compliance with that condition would be practicable;
(e) whether the goods were manufactured, processed or adapted to the special order of the customer.

The exact meaning of reasonableness in relation to sections 2(2) and (3) of UCTA has been left to the courts to work out. Gradually, a number of guidelines emerged as cases on this issue came before the courts, but it was not until the consolidated appeals of *Smith v. Bush* and *Harris v. Wyre Forest District Council* that the House of Lords had the opportunity to take a more comprehensive view of the matter. There Lord Griffiths identified a range of factors which would be relevant to assessing the reasonableness or otherwise of terms and notices seeking to exclude or limit liability for damage to property or economic loss resulting from negligence. Strictly speaking, these guidelines are concerned with the reasonableness or otherwise of disclaimers in mortgage valuation reports, but there seems to be no reason why they will not be capable of a wider application.

The guidelines are as follows:

(a) the relative bargaining strengths of the parties;
(b) the availability of alternative sources of advice;
(c) the difficulty of the professional task involved; and
(d) the practical consequences of the decision, in particular the effect on insurance.

(a) *Relative bargaining strengths* Where the parties are of unequal bargaining strengths, as in *Smith v. Bush and Harris*, this will point to an exclusion clause or notice disclaiming liability as being unreasonable. Conversely, where the recipient of such a clause or notice is a business, and the parties are deemed to be of equal bargaining power, the courts are much more likely to uphold the clause or notice as reasonable.

(b) *The availability of alternative sources of advice* In *Smith v. Bush and Harris* the House of Lords thought that it would not be fair to require a purchaser of a domestic property at the lower end of the market to pay twice for the same advice, by his having to commission his own independent survey of the property in question. On the other hand, in the case of commercial properties and very expensive houses with very large sums of money at stake, the House of Lords thought that prudence would require a purchaser to obtain his own structural survey and, in such circumstances, it may be reasonable for the surveyors valuing on behalf of a building society or finance company to include or limit their liability to the purchaser. The wider corollary from this would seem to be that where advice is given to a firm or company with a disclaimer attached, reliance on the disclaimer by the adviser may well be reasonable.

(c) *The difficulty of the professional task* Lord Griffiths said that the task of mortgage valuation was not a difficult one, since only defects which are observable by a careful visual examination have to be taken into account. Obviously, therefore, where a professional person undertakes a complex task in the course of his profession, this may be a factor pointing to the reasonableness of any exclusion or limitation of liability in his report.

(d) *The availability of insurance* Lord Griffiths recognised that holding the disclaimers in the mortgage valuation reports concerned to be unreasonable was likely to lead to an increase in surveyors' insurance premiums which would be passed on to the public. However, he felt that it was better to distribute the risk of negligence among all house purchasers through an increase in fees rather than to allow the whole of the risk to fall upon a few unfortunate purchasers.

The upshot of these judicial developments would seem to point to the conclusion that in a non-negotiated contract between a business organisation (even a small-scale builder) and a consumer, an exclusion clause will not pass the reasonableness test. However, that test is much more likely to be satisfied in the case of exclusion clauses contained in freely negotiated contracts made between two business concerns. The matter was expressed by Lord Wilberforce in *Photo Production Limited v. Securicor Limited* in the following terms:

> When the parties are not of unequal bargaining strength, and when risks are normally borne by insurance, not only is the case for judicial intervention undemonstrated, but there is everything to be said for leaving the parties free to apportion the risks as they think fit and for respecting their decisions.[57]

The application of the reasonableness test in a business to business contract is never beyond doubt, however, a point illustrated by *Edmund Murray Ltd v. BSP International Foundations Ltd.*[58] Edmund Murray Ltd (EML), a small firm of piling contractors, ordered a drilling rig from BSP. The rig was manufactured according to EML's special orders and the contract contained express terms that the rig would comply with its specification. The contract also contained clauses excluding the seller's liability if the rig proved 'defective by reason solely of faulty materials or workmanship', limiting the seller's liability to the cost of repairing or replacing the defective rig in the event of faulty workmanship or materials, and prohibiting outright the recovery of damages for consequential loss. The rig proved unsuitable for the specific function for which it was required and which the sellers promised it would perform. The sellers argued that they were protected by the above exemption clauses. The Court of Appeal held that these clauses did not satisfy the statutory test of reasonableness, for the following reasons:

(a) the rig was specially ordered;
(b) the specification contained precise details of required technical standards;
(c) EML made known to BSP the purpose for which they required the rig; and
(d) the guarantee was restricted to faulty workmanship or materials.

The Court of Appeal said that in such circumstances it was not fair or reasonable to allow BSP to deprive EML of all redress for breach of the express terms.

DAMAGES

If a contractor is in breach of his contractual obligations, then the relevant remedy for the employer to seek is damages.

General principles governing an award of damages

Damages are monetary compensation to put the plaintiff in the position he would have been in had the wrong against him not been committed. In contract this means a sum of money to put the plaintiff in the position he would have been in had the contract been performed.

The innocent party will not always be awarded all the loss resulting from a breach of contract; he will only be awarded those damages which are not too remote from the breach. The test for determining which damages are too remote and which damages are not too remote was laid down by Alderson B. in *Hadley v. Baxendale*:

> Where two parties have made a contract which one of them has broken, the damages which the other party ought to receive in respect of such breach of contract should be such as may fairly and reasonably be considered either arising naturally, i.e. according to the usual course of things, from such breach of contract itself, or such as may reasonably be supposed to have been in the contemplation of both parties, at the time they made the contract, as the probable result of the breach of it.[59]

This rule was reformulated by Asquith L.J. in *Victoria Laundry (Windsor) Ltd v. Newman Industries Ltd.*[60] In the course of his judgement he laid down the following three propositions:

(1) In cases of breach of contract, the aggrieved party is only entitled to recover such part of the loss actually resulting as was at the time of the contract reasonably foreseeable as likely to result from the breach.
(2) What is reasonably foreseeable depends on the knowledge then possessed by the parties or, at all events, by the party in breach.
(3) For this purpose, knowledge possessed is of two kinds:
    (i) imputed knowledge, i.e. everyone is taken to know the ordinary course of things and what loss is liable to result from a breach of contract in that ordinary course, and
    (ii) actual knowledge of special circumstances outside the 'ordinary course of things'.

In *Czarnikow Ltd v. Koufos, The Heron II*[61] the House of Lords approved the rule in *Hadley v. Baxendale*, but they disapproved of Asquith L.J.'s criterion of reasonable foreseeability to determine remoteness. They said that the question of whether damages in contract are too remote should be determined by the criterion of whether the probability of their occurrence should have been within the reasonable contemplation of both parties at the time when the contract was made, having regard to their knowledge at that time.

The introduction of different tests for remoteness in contract and tort has led to problems in this area of law. This is illustrated by *H. Parsons (Liverstock) Ltd v. Uttley Ingham & Co. Ltd.*[62] The defendants supplied the plaintiffs, who were pig farmers, with a hopper in which to store nuts. The hopper was not properly ventilated, with the result that the nuts became mouldy. The plaintiff's pigs suffered a rare intestinal disease and 254 of them died. The Court of Appeal awarded them damages for this loss on the ground that the type of loss which occurred (physical loss) was within the parties' reasonable contemplation, even if the full extent of that loss was not.

The measure of damages for defective building work

The actual losses for which damages may be awarded can be divided into three categories:

(1) damages for direct loss, i.e. general damages;
(2) damages for consequential loss; and
(3) damages for mental distress.

General damages

There are three possible bases for assessing general damages:

(a) the cost of reinstatement;
(b) the difference in cost to the builder of the actual work done and the work specified; or
(c) the diminution in value of the work due to the breach of contract.

As a general rule, the owner of a building is entitled to recover such damages as will put him in a position to have the building for which he contracted, and wherever it is reasonable the courts will treat the cost of reinstatement as the measure of general damage.[63] The cost is to be assessed at the earliest date when, having regard to all the circumstances, the repairs could reasonably be undertaken, rather than the date when the damage occurred.[64]

The cost of reinstatement measure was applied by the Court of Appeal in *Minscombe Properties v. Sir Alfred McAlpine & Sons*.[65] In 1976 the parties agreed that the defendants should have the right to dump spoil on the plaintiffs' land during construction of the A34. In breach of contract the defendants overdumped and dumped where they were not entitled to. The defendants contended that the measure of the damage was the diminution in the value of the land (about £800), while the plaintiffs contended that they were entitled to removing the cost of the spoil in order for planning permission to be obtained (about £78 000). The judge held that, as the plaintiffs had a good chance of obtaining planning permission, the measure of damages was the cost of removing the spoil. The Court of Appeal upheld the judge's decision.

There are, however, some exceptions to this general rule. In *Applegate v. Moss*[66] the Court of Appeal said that where a building is so defective as to be incapable of repair the appropriate measure of damages is the value of the building less its value as it stands, i.e. the diminution in the value of the property. In *G.W. Atkins Limited v. Scott*[67] the Court of Appeal said that diminution in value is more appropriate where the proportion of defective work is small in relation to the whole property, where the sale of the property is not in prospect, and where the damage only affects the 'amenity value' of the property.

Damages for consequential loss

This expression refers to further harm, such as personal injury or damage to property, suffered as a result of the breach. Thus, if a garage collapses because of inadequate foundations and causes damage to a car left inside, the builder will be liable not only for the cost of repairing the garage but also for the cost of repairing or replacing the car.

Damages for mental distress[68]

Defective building work involves the building owner, particularly the owner of a dwelling, in much anxiety, and undoubtedly much inconvenience and distress is suffered by such a person while remedial works are carried out. At one time it looked as though the law might award general damages for this inconvenience and distress, but the Court of Appeal in *Watts v. Morrow*[69] firmly rejected this development. This section briefly traces the history of this development.

As a matter of contract law in general, the law traditionally denied recovery from mental distress. In *Addis v. Gramophone Company*

Limited[70] the House of Lords held that where a servant is wrongfully dismissed from his employment the damages for the dismissal cannot include compensation for the manner of the dismissal, for his injured feelings, or for the loss he may sustain because of the fact that the dismissal of itself makes it more difficult for him to obtain fresh employment. This reasoning was applied by the Court of Appeal in *Bliss v. South East Thames Regional Health Authority.*[71] There the regional health authority was held to be in repudiatory breach of contract when it asked one of its consultant surgeons to undergo a psychiatric test after he had written a number of angry and offensive letters to his colleagues. However, Dillon L.J. stated an important exception to this general rule:

> There are exceptions now recognised where the contract which has been broken was itself a contract to provide peace of mind or freedom from distress.[72]

The question for present purposes is whether such exception applies to a building contract. In *Perry v. Sidney Phillips & Son*[73] the Court of Appeal awarded damages for the distress, worry, inconvenience and trouble which the plaintiff had suffered while living in the house he bought, due to the defects which his surveyor had overlooked. Lord Denning said that these consequences were reasonably foreseeable, but Kerr L.J. stated a narrower test:

> [The deputy judge] awarded these damages *because of the physical consequences of the breach, which were all foreseeable at the time* [author's italics].[74]

In *Hayes v. James & Charles Dodd*[75], however, the Court of Appeal rejected this approach and said that damages for anguish and vexation arising out of a breach of contract were not recoverable unless the object of the contract was to provide peace of mind or freedom from distress. Staughton L.J. said:

> It seems to me that damages for mental distress in contract are, as a matter of policy, limited to certain classes of case. I would broadly follow the classification adopted by Dillon L.J. in *Bliss v. South East Thames Regional Health Authority.*[76]

He concluded that damages for distress should not be awarded in any case where the object of the contract was not comfort or pleasure, or the relief of discomfort, but simply carrying on a commercial activity with a view to profit.

The rule concerning damages for mental distress laid down in *Hayes v. Dodd* was applied by the Official Referee in *Victor Jack Michael v. Ensoncraft Limited.*[77] In that case builders negligently caused fire damage to a house. The judge held that the owner was not able to recover damages for inconvenience and annoyance because at the time of the fire the house was let to tenants and he did not live in it.

In *Syrett v. Carr & Neave*[78] the Official Referee, Judge Bowsher, Q.C., said that the plaintiff who suffered a great deal of disruption after buying a defective property in reliance on a negligent surveyor's report was entitled to damages for inconvenience and distress on a scale which is not excessive, but modest.

In *Watts v. Morrow*, however, the Court of Appeal firmly rejected the notion that a house-buyer's contract with a surveyor is a contract to provide peace of mind or freedom from distress as 'an impossible view of the ordinary surveyor's contract'. It said that *Perry v. Sidney Phillips* was authority for the proposition that a plaintiff is entitled to damages for the discomfort suffered through having to live for a lengthy period in a defective house which was not repaired between the time the plaintiff acquired it and the date of the trial. The court was at pains to stress that these damages were limited to distress caused by the physical consequences of the breach. Bingham L.J. stated the position as follows:

> A contract-breaker is not in general liable for any distress, frustration, anxiety, displeasure, vexation, tension or aggravation which his breach of contract may cause to the innocent party .... But the rule is not absolute. Where the very object of a contract is to provide pleasure, relaxation, peace of mind or freedom from molestation damages will be awarded if the fruit of the contract is not provided .... A contract to survey the condition of a house for a prospective purchase does not, however, fall within this exceptional category.[79]

Bingham L.J. did not say whether or not a contract for the carrying out of building works fell outside the above exception, but presumably it does.

The law on damages for mental distress may be summed up as follows:

(1) As a general rule, damages for mental distress resulting from a breach of contract are not awarded.
(2) As an exception to this general rule, damages for mental distress resulting from breach of contract will be awarded where the object of the contract is to provide peace of mind or freedom from distress.
(3) Commercial contracts fall outside this exception. Thus, damages for mental distress will not be awarded in the case of a contract to repair or survey a house used as an income-producing asset.

(4) Contracts to survey a house, and presumably contracts to carry out building work on a house, do not have as their object the provision of peace of mind. However, damages are recoverable for any physical discomfort resulting from breach of this kind of contract, together with any mental distress associated with that discomfort.

NOTES

1. The Joint Contracts Tribunal has produced a standard form of management contract, JCT Management Contract 1987 Edition. This is published in *Emden's Construction Law*, 8th edn, Butterworths, 1990 (Issue 28, February 1993), Binder 3, Division F.
2. See *Hancock v. B.W. Brazier (Anerley) Ltd* [1966], 1 WLR 1317, p. 1324.
3. For an exposition of these aspects of contractual liability see Sir Anthony May, *Keating on Building Contracts*, 5th edn, Sweet & Maxwell, 1991, *passim*, and *Emden's Construction Law*, Binder 1, *passim*.
4. The latest edition of this form was issued in 1980 and is known as the 'JCT '80'. There are various versions of this form and they are published in *Emden's Construction Law*, Binder 2, Divisions A and B.
5. 6th edn, 1991.
6. The powers of the architect in administering a construction project are discussed in Chapter 6.
7. See below (p. 13–15).
8. The Joint Contracts Tribunal uses the term 'contractor', but in this text the terms 'builder' and 'contractor' are used interchangeably.
9. Now the Building Regulations 1991, SI 1991/2768. The liability issues arising out of breach of these Regulations are explored in Chapter 4.
10. Subclause 6.1.2.
11. Subclause 6.1.3.
12. Subclause 6.1.5.
13. Authority for the implication of this term dates from *Harmer v. Cornelius* (1858) 5 CBNS 236. It is now contained in section 13 of the Supply of Goods and Services Act 1982.
14. [1975] 3 All ER 99.
15. (1980) 14 BLR 1.
16. *Supra*, n.14, p. 102
17. The implication of these cases for design professionals is discussed in Chapter 6.
18. (1986) 38 BLR 36. See, further, Chapter 6.

19. Law Com. No. 156, *Implied Terms in Contracts for the Supply of Services* (1986).
20. [1968] 2 All ER 1169.
21. [1968] 2 All ER 1181.
22. *Ibid.*, p. 1184.
23. See, in particular, the speech of Lord Reid, *supra*, n.20, p. 1172.
24. [1932] AC 562.
25. For a critique of the doctrine of privity of contract see Law Commission Consultation Paper No. 121 (1991), in particular pp. 76–78.
26. See now Sale of Goods Act 1979, sections 12–15.
27. See Law Com. No. 95, *Implied Terms in Contracts for the Supply of Goods* (1979).
28. See section 1(1) of the Sale of Goods Act 1979, where a contract of sale is defined as a contract under which the seller transfers or agrees to transfer the property in goods to the buyer for a money consideration called the price.
29. This is the same definition as that contained in section 14(6) of the Sale of Goods Act 1979.
30. Law Com. No. 160, *Sale and Supply of Goods* Cm. 137 (1987).
31. This, of course, is the same as the position under the common law in respect of building contracts: see *Young and Marten v. McManus Childs Limited, supra*, n.20.
32. See, in particular, Guest. A.G. (Ed.), *Benjamin's Sale of Goods*, 3rd edn, Sweet & Maxwell, 1987; and Atiyah, P.S., *Sale of Goods*, 8th edn, Pitman, 1990.
33. This is the innominate term approach to contractual terms: see *Hong Kong Fir Shipping Co. Ltd v. Kawasaki Kisen Kaisha Ltd* [1962] 1 All ER 474.
34. *Frost v. The Aylesbury Dairy Co.* [1905] 1 KB 608.
35. *Lambert v. Lewis* [1981] 1 All ER 1185, p. 1191 (per Lord Diplock).
36. [1989] EGCS 160.
37. The Law Commission has included durability in its proposal for an amended statutory definition of merchantable quality: *supra*, n.30, para. 3.57.
38. (1820) 3 Stark 6.
39. [1956] 1 WLR 303.
40. *Ibid.*, n.39, p. 308.
41. (1974) 21 BLR 27.
42. (1984) 2 Con LR 1.
43. (1984) 2 Con LR 43.
44. (1988) 42 BLR 66.
45. (1993) 62 BLR 147.

46. See, generally, Furmston, M.P., *Cheshire, Fifoot and Furmston's Law of Contract*, 12th edn, Butterworths, 1991, Ch.6, pp. 155–198.
47. See *Smith v. Eric S. Bush; Harris v. Wyre Forest District Council* [1989] 2 All ER 514.
48. See *Phillips Products Ltd v. Hyland* [1987] 2 All ER 620.
49. [1981] SLT 103.
50. (1992) 56 BLR 115.
51. *Supra*, n.49, p. 105.
52. *Supra*, n.50, p. 133.
53. 5th edn, 1991, p. 68.
54. Section 111, para. 575.
55. 93/13/EEC, OJ 1993 L.95/29, Article 3(2).
56. [1988] 1 WLR 321.
57. [1980] AC 827.
58. (1992) *Building Law Monthly*, April; (1993) 33 Con LR 1
59. (1854) 9 Ex. 341.
60. [1949] 1 All ER 997.
61. [1967] 3 All ER 686.
62. [1978] 1 All ER 525.
63. *East Ham Corporation v. Bernard Sunley & Sons Ltd* [1966] AC 406.
64. *Dodd Properties (Kent) Ltd v. Canterbury City Council* [1980] 1 All ER 928, CA.
65. (1986) 279 EG 759.
66. [1971] 1 All ER 747.
67. (1992) Const. L.J. 215. The judgements of the Court of Appeal were given on 15 February 1980.
68. See, generally, Kim Franklin (1992) 8 Const. L.J. 318.
69. [1991] 4 All ER 937.
70. [1909] AC 488.
71. [1987] ICR 700.
72. *Ibid.*, n.71, p. 718.
73. [1982] 3 All ER 705.
74. *Ibid.*, n.73, p. 712.
75. [1990] 2 All ER 815.
76. *Ibid.*, n.75, p. 824.
77. (1991) CILL 653.
78. [1990] 48 EG 118.
79. *Supra*, n.69, pp. 959–60.

2 Builders' Liability in Negligence

INTRODUCTION

This chapter is concerned first with the liability of the builder to a subsequent owner of a building. In such a case there is no contractual relationship between the parties and the basis of the builder's liability under the common law is the tort of negligence. The liability of the builder in negligence may, in certain cases, also be of relevance to the first purchaser. Thus, where a defective house has been purchased from a developer, rather than the builder, and the developer then goes into liquidation, the purchaser's only worthwhile cause of action will be against the builder. Under the common law this will have to be based on tortious negligence, since in such circumstances there will be no privity of contract between the purchaser and the builder. In the event of a purchase of a defective house from a vendor/builder who goes into liquidation, the purchaser's only means of recovery will be against any subcontractor if he has been responsible for the defect. Again, under the common law such recovery will have to be based on the tort of negligence. It must also be remembered that, as we have seen in Chapter 1, the purchaser of a defective building will in any case rarely have an action against his vendor because of the doctrine of caveat emptor, and so he is forced to seek elsewhere for a remedy.

This area of Construction Law gives rise to a number of problematical issues. These issues are where the boundaries of the law of tort should be drawn where the loss suffered is purely economic, the relationship between contract and tort, and whether the law should impose different obligations on a builder from those imposed on a manufacturer of chattels. It is an area of the law which has seen great change during the last twenty years. The pendulum has swung from a position where the law did not permit recovery in tort for a defective building to a position where recovery for such loss could be recovered in the tort of negligence in certain circumstances and then back to its original position.[1] It is the purpose of this chapter to trace these movements of the pendulum and to examine the arguments which the courts have advanced to justify these swings and counter-swings.

THE ORTHODOX VIEW

The orthodox view of liability in negligence for defective buildings, which may be said to have existed up to the period of the 1970s, was clear, if rigid in its application. It was that there was no liability in negligence on the part of the builder for any defective building work which he may have carried out, even if such works led to the death or personal injury of the occupier. Two cases can be cited as authority for that proposition. In *Cavalier v. Pope*[2] the owner of a dilapidated house contracted with his tenant to repair the floor in the kitchen, but failed to do so. The tenant's wife, who lived in the house and was well aware of the danger from the floor, was injured when she fell through it. The House of Lords, although sympathetic to the wife, held that she had no claim for damages against the owner as she was not a party to the contract between the owner and the tenant. In *Bottomley v. Bannister*[3] a firm of builders sold a new house to Mr Bottomley. It was agreed that they would make the house fit for habitation. By agreement Mr and Mrs Bottomley moved in before the house was completed. The boiler in the house was defectively installed in that no flue had been fixed to carry the fumes from it to the air outside, and, shortly after moving in, Mr and Mrs Bottomley were found dead in the bathroom from carbon monoxide poisoning. The administrators of Mr and Mrs Bottomley brought an action in contract and in tort against the builders. The Court of Appeal, rather surprisingly, held that there had been no breach of contract because the boiler was part of the realty and if properly regulated was not dangerous. In relation to the claim in tort, Scrutton L.J. said:

> Now it is at present well established English law that, in the absence of an express contract, a landlord of an unfurnished house is not liable to his tenant, or a vendor of real estate to his purchaser, for defects in the house or land rendering it dangerous or unfit for occupation, even if he has constructed the defects himself or is aware of their existence.[4]

Greer L.J. denied the claim in tort in somewhat wider terms, stating:

> English law does not recognise a duty in the air, so to speak; that is, a duty to undertake that no one shall suffer from one's carelessness .... It seems to

> me that this principle ... applies to the case of a builder or other owner of property, when the question is whether he owes any duty towards people who may with his consent either as purchasers, tenants, or licensees or purchasers or tenants, come on to his property and be damaged by its defective condition.[5]

Some seven months after the judgements in *Bottomley v. Bannister* were delivered the House of Lords handed down their decision in *Donoghue v. Stevenson*,[6] during the course of which Lord Atkin set out his famous neighbour principle for determining when relations give rise to a duty of care in tort.[7] The exact status of that principle is still a matter for debate,[8] and it certainly did not bring about a revolution overnight in the scope of tortious relations. However, for present purposes, it is the importance of the case for the law on liability for defective products that must be considered. The facts of the case are of course extremely well known, but for the sake of demonstrating the seminal importance of the case they are worth repeating. The appellant drank a bottle of ginger-beer manufactured by the respondent, which a friend had bought from a retailer and given to her. She alleged that the bottle contained the decomposed remains of a snail, as a result of which she suffered from shock and severe gastro-enteritis. The bottle was opaque and the remains were not, and could not be, detected until the greater part of the contents of the bottle had been consumed. She did not have a contract with the retailer and she accordingly instituted proceedings against the manufacturer. The House of Lords held, by a bare majority of three to two, that these facts disclosed a cause of action and that the manufacturer of an article owed a duty to the ultimate consumer of it to take reasonable care to see that it is free from defect likely to cause injury to health. This has become known as the narrow rule of the case and it was expressed by Lord Atkin in the following terms:

> A manufacturer of products, which he sells in such a form as to show that he intends them to reach the ultimate consumer in the form in which they left him with no reasonable possibility of intermediate examination, and with the knowledge that the absence of reasonable care in the preparation or putting up of the products will result in an injury to the consumer's life or property, owes a duty to the consumer to take that reasonable care.[9]

There are a number of significant aspects of this narrow rule that need to be noted. Firstly, it created a new duty in the English law of tort (and also the Scottish law of delict) in that it demonstrated that there could be liability in negligence for a defective product independent of a contractual relationship. In this respect it disposed of what became known as the 'privity of contract fallacy', whereby it was said that the manufacturer of a defective product could not owe a duty of care to the ultimate consumer of that product because it would enable that consumer to take the benefit of a contract to which he was not a party. Secondly, the duty created was concerned with safety; that is, it is a duty owed by the manufacturer of a dangerous product, not simply a defective product. There is nothing in the speeches of the majority to suggest that the manufacturer would have been liable if the ginger-beer had been simply flat. Thirdly, the duty has not been confined to food and drink but has been extended to a wide range of products.[10] It has also been extended to include repairers.[11]

Buildings, however, were at first thought to be outside the scope of the rule. Thus, in *Otto v. Bolton*[12] Atkinson, J. stated very firmly that the law as stated by Scrutton L.J. and Greer L.J. in *Bottomley v. Bannister* was not altered by the decision of the House of Lords in *Donoghue v. Stevenson.* He said:

> That was a case dealing with chattels and there is not a word in the case from beginning to end which indicates that the law relating to the building and sale of houses is the same as that relating to the manufacture and sale of chattels.[13]

If the orthodox principle governing this area of Construction Law can be stated clearly, the same cannot be said of the rationale underlying that principle. On examination, a number of factors can be seen to have influenced the courts in this area of the law. First and foremost, the doctrine of privity of contract, that only a person who is a party to a contract can sue on it, has had, and continues to have, immense influence on the development of the law of tortious liability for defective buildings. The question, of course, is why so many of the judiciary have felt bound by that doctrine. The answer lies partly in the fear of creating unlimited liability – a fear which has dominated and continues to dominate the whole law of negligence. The fear was expressed in the following terms by Alderson B. in *Winterbottom v. Wright*:

> If we were to hold that the plaintiff could sue in such a case, there is no point at which such actions would stop. The only safe rule is to confine the right to recover to those who enter into a contract: if we go one step beyond that, there is no reason why we should not go fifty.[14]

As we have seen, that did not deter the majority of the House of Lords in *Donoghue v. Stevenson,* but their decision did not pave the way for the creation of a duty of care in negligence on the part of the builder. The reason for that seems to be that in the case of products the manufacturer does not intend his article to be examined either by the consumer or by any intermediate party. In this way, he is said to bring himself into a direct, or proximate, relationship with the consumer. In the case of buildings, however, it was felt that examination by a purchaser was much more likely, particularly in view of the fact that there is no implied obligation as to quality on the sale of a house.[15]

One final point needs to be made at this juncture on the rationale governing negligence and defective buildings. That is, in the cases so far discussed, the issue has always been liability for death or personal injury. No question has so far arisen of liability for a building – or a product, for that matter – which is defective but not dangerous.

THE ABANDONMENT OF ORTHODOXY

The orthodox view of the duty of care owed by a builder was abandoned in the 1970s and early 1980s when, in a series of decisions, the courts significantly enlarged the builder's liability in negligence. The two most significant of these cases are *Dutton v. Bognor Regis UDC*[16] and *Anns v. Merton LBC.*[17] Both these cases involved claims against local authorities, so that the question of the builder's liability was not before the court. However, in each of these cases the court felt it necessary to consider this issue.

The decisions in *Dutton* and *Anns* were foreshadowed by the High Court ruling in *Sharpe v. E.T. Sweeting & Son Ltd.*[18] The facts of that case are that the defendant company built a number of houses for Middlesbrough Corporation and the plaintiff's husband went into possession, as first tenant, of one of them when it was completed. The plaintiff lived there with him. Over the front door of the house was a reinforced concrete canopy which the defendants had constructed. One evening the plaintiff went outside the door and the concrete canopy fell on her, causing her injury. The cause of its fall was the faulty and negligent reinforcement by the defendant builders of the concrete. The legal issue in the case was whether or not the principle laid down in *Donoghue v. Stevenson* applied to these circumstances. Nield J. held that it did. After considering the decisions in *Bottomley v. Bannister* and *Otto v. Bolton* which he thought were based on the fact that the defendants in those cases were owners, he summarised the law in the following terms:

> ... the fact that the owner is also the builder does not remove the owner's immunity, but when the builder is not the owner he enjoys no such immunity.[19]

It was in *Dutton* and *Anns,* however, that the most significant development in the builder's liability in negligence occurred. These two decisions are almost certainly the most radical in the recent history of tort law and are an integral part of the expansionist and plaintiff-oriented phase of that branch of the law. In *Dutton* a builder developing a housing estate on land owned by him applied to the local council for permission to build a house and for approval under the building by-laws made under the Public Health Act 1936. Permission was granted and one of the council's building inspectors approved the foundations, which were then covered up. The house was completed and sold to C, who nearly one year later sold it to the plaintiff, Mrs Dutton. As the house was almost new, she did not have it surveyed, but it was passed by the surveyor to the building society from whom she had obtained a mortgage. Soon after the plaintiff moved in serious defects developed in the internal structure of the house. Expert investigation revealed that the foundations were unsound because the house was built on the site of an old rubbish tip, and that if the council's inspector had been careful, he would have detected that fact.

The plaintiff began an action against the builder and the council, though her action against the builder was settled for £625 on advice that as the law stood a claim in negligence against him could not succeed. At first instance, the judge held that the neighbour principle in *Donoghue v. Stevenson* applied to land as well as chattels and that accordingly the council were in breach of the duty of care owed to the plaintiff. The council appealed, but their appeal was dismissed by a majority of the Court of Appeal. In considering the position of the builder Lord Denning MR said:

> the distinction between chattels and real property is quite unsustainable. If the manufacturer of an article is liable to a person injured by his negligence, so should the builder of a house be liable.[20]

After referring to the distinction between cases in which the builder was only a contractor and cases in which he was the owner of the house itself, he went on to say:

> There is no sense in maintaining this distinction. It would mean that a contractor who builds a house on another's land is liable for negligence in constructing it, but that a speculative builder, who buys land and himself builds houses on it for sale, and is just as negligent as the contractor, is not liable. That cannot be right. Each must be under the same duty of care and to the same persons.[21]

Lord Denning MR held that *Bottomley v. Bannister* and *Otto v. Bolton* were no longer authority and overruled them. He said that *Cavalier v. Pope* was reversed by the Occupiers Liability Act 1957, section 4(1). The other member of the majority, Stamp L.J., was more cautious in his approach. He simply disapproved of *Bottomley v. Bannister* and *Otto v. Bolton* and said that *Cavalier v. Pope* did not affect the liability of a local authority.

The decision in *Dutton* was approved by the House of Lords in *Anns.* Lord Wilberforce, with whom the other Law Lords agreed, did, however, qualify the reasoning of the majority of the Court of Appeal by saying that a cause of action only arose when the state of the building is such that there is a present or imminent danger to the health of the persons occupying it. With reference to the position of the builder Lord Wilberforce said:

> I agree with the majority of the Court of Appeal in thinking that it would be unreasonable to impose liability in respect of defective foundations upon the council, if the builder, whose primary fault it was, should be immune from liability.[22]

Lord Wilberforce went on to say that the doctrine of *Donoghue v. Stevenson* did apply to realty, and he expressed approval with Lord Denning's judgement in *Dutton* on that point.

Strictly, the *dicta* in *Dutton* and *Anns* as to the legal position of the builder were *obiter* and for that reason those decisions did not completely dispel the doubt as to whether a builder of defective premises did come within the scope of the principle laid down in *Donoghue v. Stevenson.* However, the legal position of the builder arose directly in *Batty v. Metropolitan Property Realisations Ltd.*[23] In that case developers built a house on sloping ground which was subject to subsidence. Part of the garden slipped away, though the house itself was undamaged. However, expert evidence showed that at some point in the following ten years the house was likely to suffer damage. The Court of Appeal held that the developers were liable to the building owner. They said that the damage to the garden could be considered physical loss, and the threatened damage to the house could be considered to come within the scope of Lord Wilberforce's doctrine of present or imminent danger to the occupant.

The implications of *Dutton, Anns* and *Batty* were far-reaching for the whole common law of obligations.

In the first place, the duty established in those cases was owed not just to the first owner or occupier of the defective premises, but to any subsequent owner or occupier who suffered injury or whose health and safety was endangered. Privity of contract was no longer a prerequisite for a successful suit against a negligent builder. The significance of this for the builder was that in an action by a third party he could not rely on any exemption clause in his contract for sale. In other words, establishment of a tortious duty of care circumvented both the doctrine of privity of contract and any contractual exemption clause.

Secondly, the establishment of such a duty provided the first owner or occupier of defective premises with a tortious action as well as a contractual action.[24] This was a significant advantage to him from the standpoint of limitation. In contract a plaintiff has six years from the date of the breach of contract in which to commence an action; in an action for personal injury resulting from negligence the plaintiff has three years from the date when he suffers injury in which to commence an action.[25] In building cases damage invariably takes a great deal longer than six years in which to manifest itself, and a plaintiff in such a case will often be out of time in contract but still in time in tort. Thus, if a builder had built a house with unsafe foundations in 1980 and sold it to the plaintiff in that year and the plaintiff was injured by collapse of the ceiling in 1992, he would of course be out of time in contract but he would have until 1995 in which to bring an action for damages in tort.

The most significant aspect of those decisions, however, lies in the nature of the loss suffered by the plaintiff. In each of these cases a remedy was granted in respect of the cost of remedying *threatened* structural failure. Thus, Mrs Dutton complained not that she had suffered personal injury nor that the defective house had damaged other property, but that a defect in the house had damaged the house itself. Counsel for Bognor Regis UDC argued that the council should not be liable for this loss and that liability would only arise where the defects had caused personal injury or damage to the occupier's chattels. Lord Denning MR, replying to counsel's submission, stated:

> If Mr Tapp's submission were right, it would mean that if the inspector negligently passes the house as properly built and it collapses and injures a person, the council are liable: but if the owner discovers the defect in time to repair it – and he does repair it – the council are not liable. That is an impossible distinction. They are liable in either case.[26]

Lord Denning MR classified Mrs Dutton's loss as physical damage to the house and, in *Anns,* Lord Wilberforce said that the relevant damage was physical, though subject to the qualification that what is recoverable is the amount of expenditure necessary to restore the dwelling to a condition in which it is no longer a danger to the health or safety of the occupants. Arguably, however, the loss in those cases, and in *Batty,* was economic in the sense that the plaintiffs succeeded in tort for a defect in the quality of their premises. This was of great significance in the law of negligence because until those decisions it had been thought that such loss, if resulting from a negligent act, could not be recovered.[27] In the field of product liability, the decision in *Donoghue v. Stevenson* was concerned solely with physical injury. Lord Wilberforce's notion of endangering health and safety seems to bring the building cases within the scope of the narrow rule in *Donoghue* in the sense that the loss suffered in those cases can be regarded as a mitigation of the potential damage, to both persons and other property, that might occur if the premises were left in a dangerous state. Even this test, however, involves a form of economic loss.[28] Thus, Weir states, 'by making a bad thing you do not damage it; you damage a thing by making it worse than it was'.[29]

The extension of tortious liability for defective buildings following *Anns* reached its high water mark in the decision of the House of Lords in *Junior Books Ltd v. Veitchi Co. Ltd.*[30] *Junior Books* (the pursuers) employed contractors to construct a factory, the flooring work being carried out by the defenders as nominated subcontractors. Some two years after it had been laid, the floor developed cracks and it had to be replaced. There was no danger to personal safety but Junior Books sued for the cost of replacing the floor and the consequential economic loss suffered during the period of replacement. The House of Lords held, by a majority of four to one, that where the relationship between the parties was sufficiently close the scope of the duty of care in tort extended to this form of loss. On the assumption that the defective floor resulted from the negligence of the subcontractors, the Law Lords held that there was a sufficient degree of proximity between the parties to give rise to a duty of care and that there were no policy factors negativing that duty. This was a remarkable decision and it seemed to pave the way for a general principle allowing recovery for economic loss in the tort of negligence. There are, in fact, differences of emphasis in the speeches. The most radical in its approach was Lord Roskill's speech, who thought that the question of the scope of the tort of negligence should be determined by considerations of principle rather than policy. He said:

> the proper control lies not in asking whether the proper remedy should lie in contract or instead in delict or tort ... but in the first instance in establishing the relevant principles and then in deciding whether the particular case falls within or without those principles.[31]

It must be emphasised that such a wide approach to the common law of obligations was not echoed in the other speeches. As we shall see, although the decision has not been overruled, it has been confined to its own facts in subsequent cases and today it is most significant for the dissenting speech of Lord Brandon. He argued that there was no sound policy reason for imposing a duty on the subcontractors in these circumstances because it would create contractual obligations between two parties who were not in any contractual relationship with each other. In view of the subsequent approval of Lord Brandon's speech by the House of Lords, his remarks on the matter are worth quoting *in extenso*:

> ... by what standard or standards of quality would the question of defectiveness fall to be decided? In the case of goods bought from a retailer, it could hardly be the standard prescribed by the contract between the retailer and the wholesaler, or between the wholesaler and the distributor, or between the distributor and the manufacturer, for the terms of such contracts would not even be known to the ultimate buyer. In the case of subcontractors such as the appellants in the present case, it could hardly be the standard prescribed by the contract between the subcontractors and the main contractors, for, although the building owner would probably be aware of those terms he could not, since he was not a party to such contract, rely on any standard or standards prescribed in it. It follows that the question by what standard or standards alleged defects in a product complained of by its ultimate user or consumer are to be judged remains entirely at large and cannot be given any just or satisfactory answer.[32]

THE RETURN TO ORTHODOXY

Following the decision in *Junior Books,* the courts have adopted a much more cautious and pragmatic approach to the question of tortious liability for defective buildings. Both the Court of Appeal and the House of Lords have been at pains to emphasise that, despite the decisions in *Anns* and *Junior Books,* the law of negligence ordinarily does not permit recovery for purely economic loss consequent upon negligent acts.

The return to orthodoxy began in 1984 with the case of *Governors of the Peabody Donation Fund v. Sir Lindsay Parkinson & Co. Ltd.*[33] There the House of Lords held that a local authority's statutory powers to approve plans and inspect drainage systems were not intended to protect developers from sustaining economic loss. Their purpose was to safeguard the occupiers of houses built in the area, and members of the public generally, against dangers to their health arising from defective drainage. This new approach was supported by the Australian appeal court in the case of *Sutherland Shire Council v. Heyman.*[34] The facts of that case were similar to those of *Anns* but the court reinterpreted Lord Wilberforce's proximity test as requiring 'a close relationship' and not simply one where there was 'reasonable contemplation of damage'. So defined, there was insufficient proximity because there was no evidence that the occupier had ever relied on the council's approval of the house foundations as assuring that the house would be free of subsidence defects.

The implications of *Junior Books* were considered in *Muirhead v. Industrial Tank Specialties Ltd.*[35] A negligent manufacturer of water pumps was sued by the operator of a lobster farm whose lobsters had died because defects had prevented the pumps circulating adequate supplies of fresh water. In the event, the manufacturer was held liable, as the defect had led to damage to the plaintiff's property (the lobsters). But Goff, L.J. made it clear that the manufacturer would not have been liable for the defect alone. He argued that the key to *Junior Books* seemed to be that the House of Lords through the conceptions of proximity and reliance, was treating the nominated subcontractors as having voluntarily assumed responsibility with respect to the work which arose. However, such an analysis seemed not to fit the facts, as the parties' contractual relationship was so structured as to avoid any direct contractual liability of the subcontractors to the clients. The implication of *Muirhead* was clear, however: *Junior Books* was now to be looked on as establishing an exception to non-liability for defects rather than as a general basis for liability.

Another blow to *Junior Books* was delivered by the Court of Appeal in *Simaan General Contracting Co. v. Pilkington Glass Ltd (No. 2).*[36] A manufacturer supplied a subcontractor with glass panels for the exterior cladding of a building in Abu Dhabi. The glass should have been green but it was alleged that, owing to negligent manufacture, the glass turned red under the Middle Eastern sun. The main contractor, who had to bear the cost of replacing the defective glass, sued the manufacturer in tort. The relationship between the manufacturer and the main contractor appeared very similar to that between the subcontractor and the owner in *Junior Books,* but the Court of Appeal had no hesitation in distinguishing that decision as limited to its particular facts.

This trend culminated in a trilogy of cases: *D & F Estates v. Church Commissioners of England,*[37] *Murphy v. Brentwood DC*[38] and *Department of the Environment v. Bates.*[39] The importance of these cases is that the House of Lords discussed the nature of the damages involved (in *Peabody,* etc., that issue had not been directly addressed). In *D & F Estates* the plastering work in a block of flats had been subcontracted by the builders. The plaintiffs were lessees and occupiers of one of the flats. Fifteen years after construction it was discovered that the plastering had not been carried out in accordance with the manufacturer's instructions, causing peeling from ceilings. The plaintiff sued the builders in negligence for the cost of the remedial work. The House of Lords held that the cost of repairing a defect in a building before the defect had actually caused personal injury or physical damage to other property was not recoverable in negligence from the builder responsible for causing the defect, because the cost of repair was pure economic loss, and pure economic loss was not generally recoverable in the law of tort. The two main speeches were delivered by Lords Bridge and Oliver. Lord Bridge put forward the following view regarding the liability of a builder of a building which is dangerously defective:

> ... liability can only arise if the defect remains hidden until the defective structure causes personal injury or damage to property other than the structure itself. If the defect is discovered before any damage is done, the loss sustained by the owner of the structure, who has to repair or demolish it to avoid a potential source of danger to third parties, would seem to be purely economic.[40]

Both of their Lordships, with whom the other Law Lords concurred, said that defective buildings were to be treated in the same way as defective products. In the case of a defective product where the defect was discovered before it caused injury to persons or other property, the loss was recoverable in contract by a buyer or hirer of the chattel, but was not recoverable in tort by such persons. There was no non-contractual or transmissible warranty of quality attached to the goods.

The problem for the House of Lords was that the decision in *Anns* seemed to imply that there was such a warranty attached to buildings. In order to reconcile this inconsistency their Lordships distinguished between complex and simple structures. In the case of complex structures one element of the structure should be regarded as distinct from another element so that damage to one part of the structure caused by a hidden defect in another part may qualify as damage to 'other property'. In this way, Lords Bridge and Oliver attempted to reconcile *Anns* with *Donoghue v. Stevenson.*

This decision produced a great deal of confusion in this area of law.[41] The complex structure theory seemed tailor-made for litigation. The notion of when different parts of a building may be regarded as 'other property' is by no means clear. The concept of 'other property' has not been without its problems in the field of product liability.[42] Further, the concept of the complex structure did not entirely reconcile *Anns* with *Donoghue v. Stevenson*, because under the *Anns* principle the cause of action accrues when the building 'becomes a present or imminent danger', which means that the plaintiff does not have to wait until damage to the building itself occurs.

The House of Lords were not able to overrule *Anns* under the *Practice Statement* of 1966,[43] because the facts of *D & F Estates* did not raise the issue of local authority liability. That issue did arise in *Murphy* and on that occasion the House of Lords, consisting of seven Law Lords, did overrule *Anns*. The facts of *Murphy* are that in 1970 the plaintiff purchased from a construction company one of a pair of semi-detached houses. The houses were newly constructed on an in-filled site on a concrete raft foundation to prevent damage from settlement. The plan and calculations for the raft foundations were submitted to the local council for building regulation approval and the council approved the design after first referring them to consulting engineers. In 1981 the plaintiff noticed serious cracks in his house and discovered that the raft foundation was defective. In 1986 he sold the house subject to its defects for £35 000 less than its market value in sound condition. He sued the local authority for negligence in approving the plans. The House of Lords held that when carrying out its statutory function of building control, a local authority was not liable in negligence to a building owner or occupier for the cost of remedying a dangerous defect in the building which resulted from the negligent failure of the authority to ensure that the building was designed and erected in accordance with the Building Regulations.[44] Their Lordships advanced two reasons for this ruling. Firstly, the damage suffered by the building owner in *Murphy* was not physical but the purely economic loss of the expenditure occurred in remedying the defect. Secondly, a dangerous defect once known became merely a defect in quality and to permit the building owner or occupier to recover his loss would lead to an unacceptably wide category of claims in respect of defective buildings and products; in effect, it would introduce transmissible warranties of quality into the law of tort by means of judicial legislation. For these reasons their Lordships felt that the decision in *Anns* had not been based on any recognisable principle and consequently they overruled it.

In the course of their speeches, the Law Lords reviewed the complex structure theory, and, no doubt mindful of the criticism to which it had been subjected, rejected the version of it contained in *D & F Estates.* They said that any defect in the structure is a defect in the quality of the whole and that it is quite artificial to treat a defect in an integral structure which weakens the structure as damage to 'other property'. Thus, cracking in walls and ceilings caused by defective foundations cannot be treated as damage to 'other property'. Lord Bridge distinguished between a part of a complex structure which is a danger because it does not perform its proper function of sustaining the other parts and a distinct item incorporated in the structure which malfunctions, thereby causing damage to the structure in which it is incorporated. To illustrate this form of the theory he gave the following example:

> Thus, if a defective central heating boiler explodes and damages a house or if a defective electrical installation malfunctions and sets the house on fire, I see no reason to doubt that the owner of the house, if he can prove that the damage was due to the negligence of the boiler manufacturer in the one

case or the electrical contractor in the other, can recove
Donoghue v. Stevenson principles.[45]

One final point needs to be made on the speeches
decision in *Junior Books* was not overruled; rather it wa
approval in that it was explained in terms of the doctrin
contained in *Hedley Byrne v. Heller.*[46] The relationship the
building owner and the subcontractor in *Junior Books* was so close that the building owner could be said to have relied on the expertise of the subcontractor.

The decision in *Murphy* was applied by the House of Lords to builders in *Department of the Environment v. Bates.* In that case the plaintiffs were the underlessees of the upper nine storeys of an eleven storey office in a building complex constructed by the defendants in 1970–71. It was discovered in 1981 that, because low-strength concrete had been used in the pillars, the building, although capable of supporting its existing load safely, was not capable of supporting its design load. The plaintiffs sued for the cost of carrying out remedial works to strengthen the pillars. The House of Lords held that the loss suffered by the plaintiffs was purely economic and therefore not recoverable at the time when the work was carried out. The building was not unsafe but merely suffered from a defect in quality.

The judicial reasoning underlying *Murphy*, etc.

The general significance of *D & F Estates, Murphy* and *Bates* is that they have re-established the orthodox view of the law regarding recovery for economic loss resulting from negligence. From that point of view, these decisions are good news for builders and local authorities, but they will leave many owners of defective buildings without a remedy. It is because of this last point that they have attracted much comment and criticism.[47]

The reasons given for denying recovery for economic loss are often obscure and it is essential that they be subject to scrutiny. The usual reason given is the floodgates argument, i.e. to permit recovery would open the floodgates to a potentially unlimited number of claims, thereby exposing any particular defendant to the prospect of indeterminate liability. This argument is by no means as straightforward as it seems at first sight.[48] It was not, however, the reason for denying the claims in *D & F Estates* and *Murphy*, etc., because in each of those cases there was only one potential defendant. The arguments put forward by the Law Lords for denying recovery were:

(i) that it would create a large new area of tortious liability and this would amount to judicial legislation which is not a proper exercise of judicial power;[49]
(ii) that consumer protection is best left to the legislature and that this area has received full treatment by Parliament in the form of the Defective Premises Act 1972;[50]
(iii) that to allow recovery in negligence for defective buildings would be to impose a non-contractual and transmissible warranty of quality on builders and local authorities which would be contrary to principle;[51] and
(iv) that to allow recovery for economic loss in English law would be contrary to recent decisions of certain of the Commonwealth courts and the US Supreme Court.[52]

Each of these arguments needs to be examined closely.

In relation to the argument that *Dutton* and *Anns* were judicial legislation, it needs to be remembered that they both gave rise to a new point in law and that the resolution of any such point must be judicial legislation. Even if *Dutton* and *Anns* had been decided to the contrary, that would still have been judicial legislation. To that extent the decisions in *D & F Estates*, *Murphy* and *Bates* all amount to judicial legislation just as much as the decisions in *Dutton* and *Anns*. It would be more accurate to say that the decisions in *Dutton* and *Anns* belonged to an expansionist, plaintiff-oriented and welfarist phase in the law of tort, whereas the *Murphy* line of cases belongs to a phase which is more defendant-oriented and cautious in the creation of new duties.

In relation to consumer protection, the passing of the Defective Premises Act 1972 was a recognition by Parliament that in the case of dwellings the law should have a consumer protectionist role. The existence of that Act was thought by the Law Lords in *Murphy* to preclude the upholding of the decisions in *Dutton* and *Anns*. Further, it may be thought that the duties specified in the 1972 Act, together with the NHBC scheme,[53] make the imposition of a general tortious duty on housebuilders and local authorities unnecessary.[54] Two points can be made in answer to these views. Firstly, section 6(2) of the Act expressly provides that any duty imposed by or enforceable by virtue of any provision of the Act is in addition to any duty a person may owe apart from that provision. In other words, it seems that the intention of the Act is not to put a brake on the development of wider common law duties as circumstances require. Secondly, there are a number of limitations on the legislative duty which have prevented the Act from being as valuable a piece of consumer protection legislation as it might otherwise have been.[55]

The overriding consideration in *D & F Estates, Murphy* and *Bates* was a desire on the part of the Law Lords to re-emphasise the distinction between contractual and tortious obligations and to assert that liability for defective buildings and defective products belong to the domain of contract law. It was in this context that the (dissenting) speech of Lord Brandon in *Junior Books* was expressly approved. This is the argument that the manufacturer of a defective product, or builder of a defective building, cannot be liable to the ultimate consumer or occupier of such product or building because such loss is a form of expectation loss. When a consumer purchases an article, he has certain expectations of the quality of that article based on its price, any description attached to it by the seller, and so forth, and if the quality of the article does not match those expectations, only the immediate seller can be responsible. However, this argument does not explain why such obligations should lie solely in the province of the law of contract. There seems no reason in logic why strict contractual obligations of quality should preclude the existence of a tortious obligation of quality based on reasonable care. To the argument that it would be impossible to define the standard required of the manufacturer or builder in these circumstances it may be said that the law has not found it impossible to define standards of safety in the absence of express contractual obligations. And more to the point, these safety standards are based on a consumer expectations test.[56] Further, this judicial argument seems to ignore the commercial reality that in a modern economy consumers frequently do rely on manufacturers for the quality of their products.

Space does not permit a detailed examination of Commonwealth and US judicial developments in relation to negligence and economic loss. Suffice it to say that the references to these developments by the Law Lords have been heavily criticised as misleading and one-sided. In general, *Anns* has been followed in Canada and New Zealand, though not in Australia. In *East River Steamship Corp. v. Transamerica Delaval Inc.*[57] the US Supreme Court denied recovery for economic loss resulting from negligence in a maritime case.[58]

In short, the speeches in *D & F Estates* and *Murphy* emphasise legal doctrine rather than examine the issues raised by this area of the law from the point of view of policy. Should purchasers of defective buildings – in particular, homeowners – be protected by the law of negligence? In answer to this question, a number of things need to be pointed out. Firstly, many defects in buildings, in particular, dwellings, are not covered by first party insurance.[59] Secondly, it seems wrong to put defective buildings on a par with defective products. The purchase of a domestic dwelling is the most important financial transaction most persons enter into, and, if such a dwelling proves defective, the occupier concerned will almost certainly be unable to absorb the loss. This is in contrast to products, many of which are of trivial monetary value. Moreover, whereas a tortious duty of care extending to quality in the case of products may involve the manufacturer concerned in an indeterminate volume of claims, the same cannot be said of buildings. The courts have accepted that in the event of a negligent survey of a low or moderately priced house the surveyor should be liable in tort to the buyer of the house.[60] There seems to be no sound reason in policy to distinguish between builders and local authorities and surveyors in this context.

SUMMARY AND CONCLUDING COMMENTS

In view of the dramatic changes that have occurred in this area of law, it may be pertinent to summarise its present state. The essential principles are as follows:

(i) Where the defect in a building causes death or personal injury or damage to property other than the defective building itself, the builder will be liable under the *Donoghue v. Stevenson* principle.
(ii) If the defect is simply one of quality and does not render the building a danger to the health or safety of its occupants, then such loss is pure economic loss and not recoverable.
(iii) If the defect does render the building an imminent danger to the health and safety of its occupants, the cost of averting that danger is again economic loss and irrecoverable.
(iv) If an item, such as a boiler, incorporated in the structure malfunctions and damages the structure, then the supplier of that item will be liable for the damage to the structure.

The return to orthodoxy in this area of law has had, and will continue to have, important practical consequences for the construction industry. Most prominently, the shift of judicial emphasis back to contractual obligations has meant increased pressure on architects, engineers and contractors from occupiers for collateral warranties, i.e. guarantees of fitness for use in the absence of any tortious duty.[61] From the standpoint of the occupier of a defective dwelling the decisions in *Murphy*, etc., have led to a renewal of interest in the provisions of the Defective Premises Act 1972 as a means of redress.[62] The principle of reliance, first set out in *Hedley Byrne v. Heller,* is now the only basis of liability in negligence for economic loss and this has meant that in many cases of defective buildings the only chance of a successful suit will lie against the surveyor of the building. One commentator has summed up the common law of defective buildings in the following terms:

> ... the victim often finds himself caught in a pair of pincers, one jaw of which is the doctrine of privity of contract, and the other the tortious principle that there is no liability in negligence for 'purely economic loss'.[63]

For a time the jaws of the pincers loosened their grip on plaintiffs, but now their grip is tighter than ever.

NOTES

1. This has been described in terms of the military analogy of advance and retreat in Farrar, J.H. and Dugdale, A.M., *Introduction to Legal Method*, 3rd edn, Sweet & Maxwell, 1990, Ch. 8.
2. [1906] AC 428.
3. [1932] 1 KB 458.
4. *Ibid.*, n.3, p. 468.
5. *Ibid.*, n.3, p. 476.
6. [1932] AC 562.
7. *Ibid.*, n.6, p. 580.
8. See, in particular, the speeches of their Lordships in *Caparo v. Dickman* [1990] 1 All ER 568.
9. *Supra*, n.6, p. 599.
10. For example, underpants (*Grant v. Australian Knitting Mills* [1936] AC 85); and chemicals (*Vacwell Engineering Co. Ltd v. B.D.H. Chemicals Ltd* [1971] 1 QB 88).
11. See *Haseldine v. Daw & Son Ltd* [1941] 2 KB 343.
12. [1936] 2 KB 46.
13. *Ibid.*, n.12, p. 54.
14. (1842) 10 M & W 109, p. 115, and quoted by Lord Denning in *Dutton v. Bognor Regis UDC* [1972] 1 QB 373, p. 393.
15. See Atkinson J.'s judgement in *Otto v. Bolton, supra*, n.12, p. 58.
16. *Supra*, n.14.
17. [1978] AC 728.
18. [1963] 1 WLR 665.
19. *Ibid.*, n.18, p. 675.
20. *Supra*, n.14, p. 393.
21. *Supra*, n.14, pp. 393–94.
22. *Supra*, n.17, p. 758.
23. [1978] QB 554.
24. This is known as concurrent liability: see *Midland Bank Ltd v. Hett, Stubbs and Kemp* [1978] 3 All ER 571.

25. See sections 5 and 11 of the Limitation Act 1980. These provisions, together with the limitation periods for actions in negligence not involving personal injury, are discussed more fully in Chapter 9.
26. *Supra*, n.14, p. 396.
27. See, in particular, *Cattle v. Stockton Waterworks* (1871) LR 10 QB 453; *Weller v. Foot and Mouth Disease Research Institute* [1966] 1 QB 569.
28. See the remarks of Lord Oliver in *Murphy v. Brentwood DC* [1990] 2 All ER 908, p. 932.
29. *Casebook on Tort*, 4th edn, p. 29.
30. [1983] 1 AC 520.
31. *Ibid.*, n.30, p. 545.
32. *Ibid.*, n.30, p. 552.
33. [1984] 3 All ER 529.
34. (1985) 60 ALR 1 (H.C).
35. [1985] 3 All ER 705.
36. [1988] 1 All ER 791.
37. [1988] 2 All ER 992.
38. *Supra.*, n.28.
39. [1990] 2 All ER 943.
40. *Supra*, n.37, p. 1006.
41. See Ross (1989) 5 PN11.
42. See *Aswan Engineering Establishment Co. v. Lupdine Ltd* [1987] 1 All ER 135.
43. [1966] 3 All ER 77.
44. See, further, Chapter 4.
45. *Supra*, n.28, p. 928.
46. [1964] AC 465. Discussed further in Chapter 7.
47. See Cane (1989) 52 MLR 200; Brown (1990) 6 PN 150; Olowofoyeku (1990) 6 PN 158; Sir Robin Cooke (1991) 107 LQR 46; Wallace (1991) 107 LQR 228; Stapleton (1991) 107 LQR 249; National Consumer Council, *Murphy's Law*, 1991; and Cane, P., *Tort Law and Economic Interests*, Clarendon Press, 1991 (Appendix).
48. See Stapleton, *supra*, n.46, pp. 253–56.
49. Per Lord Keith, *supra*, n.28, pp. 922–23; Lord Bridge, *supra*, n.28 at p. 924; and Lord Oliver, *supra*, n.28, p. 937.
50. Per Lord Bridge, *supra*, n.37, p. 1007; Lord Mackay L.C., *supra*, n.28, p. 912; Lord Keith, *supra*, n.28, p. 923; Lord Bridge, *supra*, n.28, p. 93; Lord Oliver, *supra*, n.28, p. 938; Lord Jauncey, *supra*, n.28, pp. 942–43.
51. Per Lord Keith, *supra*, n.28, pp. 917–20; Lord Bridge, *supra*, n.28, pp. 925–26; Lord Oliver, *supra*, n.28, pp. 934–36; and Lord Jauncey, *supra* n.28, pp. 940–41.

52. Per Lord Keith, *supra*, n.28, pp. 920-22; Lord Bridge, *supra*, n.28, pp. 924–28; and Lord Jauncey, *supra*, n.28, pp. 940–41.
53. The detailed provisions of this scheme are set out in Chapter 3.
54. This has been suggested by Professor J. A. Smilie in [1990] N2LJ 310, p. 314 and quoted by Sir Robin Cooke, *supra*, n.46, p. 69.
55. See Chapter 3.
56. See section 3 of the Consumer Protection Act 1987.
57. (1986) 476 US 858.
58. See, further, Sir Robin Cooke, *supra*, n.47; and Fleming (1990) 106 LQR 525, p. 530; Markesinis (1993) 109 LQR 5; and Todd [1993] 9 PN 2.
59. But see Chapter 8 for a discussion of BUILD.
60. See *Smith v. Bush* [1989] 2 All ER 514, discussed further in Chapter 7.
61. See, further, Chapter 8.
62. See Duncan Wallace [1991] 107 LQR 228, p. 243.
63. J.R. Spencer [1974] CLJ 307, p. 309.

3 The Defective Premises Act and the NHBC Scheme[1]

INTRODUCTION

This chapter examines the liability of the builder under the provisions of sections 1 and 2 of the Defective Premises Act 1972 and the National House-Building Council (NHBC) scheme.

The 1972 Act is based on a report of the Law Commission, *Civil Liability of Vendors and Lessors of Defective Premises.*[2] Its purpose is to provide the purchaser of a defective dwelling house with an additional remedy against the architect who designed it and the builder who built it. At the time of passing of the Act the common law in this area was considered generally to be deficient. In the first place, the sale of houses is governed by the doctrine of *caveat emptor*; the purchaser of a defective house generally has to bear the consequences unless the vendor has undertaken a contractual responsibility for the defects, which is rare. Secondly, this doctrine not only applies to the sale of an existing house by a private seller but extends also to the builder who builds a house on his own land and later sells or lets the house (the case of the vendor/builder). The only exception to this rule would be if the builder is registered with the NHBC, in which case the buyer would be provided with express contractual warranties. Thirdly, if a builder builds a house on another person's land, then he owes certain duties to that person in relation to the standard of workmanship and the quality of the materials provided. These duties provide some measure of protection for the person on whose land the house was built. But that protection does not extend to a lessee or subsequent purchaser of the house; such persons have no privity of contract with the builder, and unless the house is dangerous and causes them personal injuries or damages other property belonging to them, they cannot successfully sue in negligence.

The attempt made by the Act to remedy these deficiencies in the common law has so far proved largely unsuccessful and the provisions of the Act in relation to defective dwellings have been little used by plaintiffs. One of the principal reasons for this was the radical developments which

occurred in the common law shortly after the pass
developments, in the shape of the decisions of the
Dutton v. Bognor Regis UDC[3] and the House of Lord
LBC,[4] extended the builder's liability in tort by allowi
cost of repairing defective building, such loss to the
regarded as the mitigation of personal injury or damage
which could eventually ensue. However, the overruling o ecisions
in *Murphy v. Brentwood DC*,[5] and the ruling in that case that such repair costs are a form of economic loss and as such irrecoverable in the tort of negligence, save where the relationship between the plaintiffs and the builder can be brought within the reliance doctrine, has given the 1972 Act a new importance for plaintiffs who seek redress for defective buildings and who fall outside the scope of the implied contractual obligations imposed on the builder and outside the scope of the NHBC scheme.

THE DEFECTIVE PREMISES ACT 1972

The nature of the duty

The duty in respect of building created by the Act is contained in section 1(1). This states that a person taking on work for or in connection with the provision of a dwelling (whether the dwelling is provided by the erection or by the conversion or enlargement of a building) owes a duty to see that the work which he takes on is done in a workmanlike or, as the case may be, professional manner, with proper materials and so that as regards that work the dwelling will be fit for habitation when completed. These requirements are virtually identical with the obligations implied by the common law to a contract for work and material and to the express warranties contained in the NHBC scheme. However, the duty in section 1(1) is additional to the common law duties (section 6(2)). Further, it cannot be excluded by agreement to the contrary (section 6(3)).

The duty is qualified by the provisions of sections 1(2) and (3) of the Act. Section 1(2) states:

> A person who takes on any such work for another on terms that he is to do it in accordance with instructions given by or on behalf of that other shall to the extent to which he does it properly in accordance with those instructions, be treated for the purposes of this section as discharging the duty imposed on him by subsection (1) above except where he owes a duty

...o that other to warn him of any defects in the instructions and fails to discharge that duty.

This means that a builder will discharge his duty under section 1(1) if he is instructed to build according to a particular specification and follows such instructions. However, if the instructions are defective then he may incur liability under the Act if he fails to warn of those defects. It is not clear when this duty to warn arises.

Section 1(3) states:

> A person shall not be treated for the purposes of subsection (2) above as having given instructions for the doing of work merely because he has agreed to work being done in a specified manner, with specified materials or to a specified design.

The purpose of this subsection is to circumvent the rule in *Lynch v. Thorne*[6] that where a builder builds according to specifications then, in the absence of some other express provision, that is the extent of his obligation under the contract. In other words, under the provisions of section 1(3) of the Act, if a builder is provided with defective specifications, then he is under a duty to warn the employer of those defects.[7]

One of the problematical aspects of the duty contained in section 1(1) is whether it is contractual or tortious in nature. This is not merely an academic issue, since it involves the practical questions of the kind of defects which are covered by the duty, the losses which are recoverable under it and, in particular, the meaning of 'fit for habitation'. In one sense, the duty may be looked on as in essence a contractual warranty which is transmissible to 'every person who acquires an interest ... in the dwelling'. Support for this view can be found in the fact that in the event of the NHBC scheme being in operation rather than the provisions of section 1(1), then the rights under such a scheme are extended to subsequent purchasers. If this is the correct interpretation of section 1(1), then the duty would seem to extend to defects of quality. On the other hand, the Law Commission, in their report which forms the basis of the Act, appear to take the view that the duty is more tortious than contractual in nature.[8] The report draws a firm distinction between defects of quality and dangerous defects. It goes on to state the view that in the law of tort it is only dangerous defects for which a builder should be liable; defects of quality are seen as the sole province of the law of contract. The long title of the Act seems to reflect that view:

> An Act to impose duties in connection with the provision of dwellings and otherwise to amend the law of England and Wales as to liability for injury or damage caused to persons through defects in the state of premises.

The meaning of 'fitness for habitation' has been considered in *Alexander v. Mercouris*[9] and, more recently, in *Thompson v. Alexander.*[10] In *Alexander v. Mercouris* the Court of Appeal said, *obiter*, that 'fitness for habitation' was a measure of the standard to be achieved through the use of proper work and materials, not a separate, third obligation. Thus, Buckley L.J. said:

> The reference to the dwelling being fit for habitation indicates the intended consequences of the proper performance of the duty and provides a measure of the standard of the requisite work and materials. It is not, I think, part of the duty itself.[11]

This *obiter dictum* was relied upon by Judge Esyr Lewis in *Thompson v. Alexander.* In that case three house owners brought proceedings under section 1(1) against the architects and engineers whom they alleged designed and supervised the construction of their houses. The architects and engineers contended that it was an essential ingredient of a cause of action under section 1(1) that, in addition to proving that the defect arose out of a failure to carry out the work in a professional manner or with proper materials, the defect should also render the dwelling unfit for habitation. In respect of many of the defects complained of, the house owners did not contend that they made the dwellings concerned unfit for habitation. However, they argued that section 1(1) imposed three separate obligations. The judge accepted the contention of the architects and engineers. He said that the duty imposed by section 1(1) is intended to ensure that the persons concerned in the design or construction of a dwelling will carry out their work in a manner which will result in the building's being fit for habitation when completed. In other words, before a duty can arise under the Act the dwelling must be rendered unfit for habitation by the defect complained of. The judge then went on to say that it would not be reasonable to construe section 1(1) in a way which would make builders and designers of a dwelling liable to a subsequent purchaser for trivial defects in design and construction. He thought that the existence of such defects would be reflected in the price paid for the dwellings by such a purchaser.

The result of these decisions seems to be that the duty extends only to defects of a major (structural) kind; more minor defects are outside its scope.

When does the duty apply?

The rules concerning the application of the duty in section 1(1) are as follows:

(a) The duty arises when a party to a contract agrees to carry out work and, in any event, not later than the start of the work. This rule was laid down by the Court of Appeal in *Alexander v. Mercouris.* On 20 November 1972 the defendants entered into an agreement with the plaintiff for the sale of a dwelling-house. It was part of that agreement that the defendants would modernise the house and convert it into two flats and they employed a firm of builders to carry out this work. The work was completed in February 1974. It was not satisfactory and the plaintiff brought an action under section 1(1) of the Act. The question for determination was whether or not the Act applied in this case. Under the provisions of section 7(2) the statutory duty applies only if the work was taken on after 1 January 1974. The Court of Appeal held that the duty arose when the work was taken on, i.e. in November 1972. This was before the Act came into force and therefore the defendants owed no duty under its provisions to the plaintiff.

(b) It applies only to the construction, conversion or enlargement of a *dwelling.* It does not extend to industrial or commercial premises. This limitation is based on the Law Commission's view that in such cases the parties are generally able to protect their own interests.

(c) It imposes liability for *nonfeasance* as well as *misfeasance.* In *Andrews v. Schooling*[12] the defendant company acquired, in 1986, two adjacent Edwardian semi-detached houses and employed sub-contractors to convert them into flats. One of these flats was on the ground floor and included a cellar. The subcontractors did not put a damp-proof course into this cellar, but merely pointed the walls. In 1987 the defendants leased the ground floor flat to the plaintiff. Shortly after moving in she complained that the flat suffered from penetrating damp coming from the cellar and she sued the defendants for breach of the duty imposed by section 1(1) of the Act. The defendants argued that this provision only applied to liability for misfeasance and they could not be liable, therefore, for *omitting* to put in a damp-proof course. The Court of Appeal rejected this argument. They held that the provisions of section 1(1) applied as much to a failure to carry out the necessary work as to the carrying out of such work badly.

(d) It does not apply to building works covered by an approved scheme. This is the effect of section 2, which provides that the duty contained in section 1(1) is not applicable if at the time of the first sale or letting an 'approved scheme' conferring rights in respect of defects in the dwelling was in operation. The only scheme to have obtained such approval is that operated by the NHBC and since almost all new dwellings are covered by this scheme this meant that in practice section 1(1) applied only to extensions and improvements. Thus Spencer in his article on the Act comments:

> Section 1 gets all dressed up, and section 2, by excluding any case where the NHBC scheme applied, leaves it with virtually nowhere to go.[13]

That view is no longer correct. After 31 March 1979 the NHBC scheme was no longer officially approved and it seems that section 1(1) does apply to *all* new dwellings erected since that date.[14] In other words, dwellings covered by the 1985 and 1992 editions of the NHBC scheme do come within the scope of the section 1(1) duty.

Who owes the duty?

The duty in section 1(1) is imposed upon those who take on work in relation to the provision of a dwelling. It is beyond doubt that this includes builders, subcontractors, architects and engineers. The subsection, however, is wider than simply imposing a duty on the actual person who carried out the work; section 1(4) provides that the duty extends to a person who in the course of a business or in the exercise of a statutory power arranges for another to take on work for or in connection with the provision of a dwelling. In other words, the statutory duty covers developers and local authorities.

To whom is the duty owed?

Under the provisions of section 1(1) the duty is owed to:

(a) the person who orders the building; and
(b) every person who acquires a legal or equitable interest in the dwelling.

In other words, the statutory duty extends to both the first purchaser of the dwelling and every subsequent owner.

Limitation

Section 1(5) provides that the limitation period for the statutory duty is normally six years *from the time when the dwelling was completed.* This is a much more unfavourable limitation period to the plaintiff than in a common law action for negligence, where the basic rule is that the limitation period is six years *from the date when the damage occurred*[15].

THE NHBC SCHEME

The NHBC was founded in 1936. It is a private company limited by guarantee and registered under the Companies Acts in England and Wales. The council consists of nominees of all the main bodies concerned with new housing, including the professions (RIBA, RICS, ICE, Law Society, etc.), the Building Societies Association, the Consumers Association and local authority bodies. The chairman is nominated by the Secretary of State for the Environment. In effect it is the consumer protection body of the house-building industry.

The NHBC serves two particular functions. Firstly, it keeps a National Register of approved house-builders, who are entitled to build houses either for sale direct to the public or for developers, and developers, who are not entitled to build houses themselves but must employ a registered house-builder as a main contractor. Most builders are registered with the NHBC; they have a strong, if not overwhelming, commercial incentive to register, since building societies and banks are reluctant to lend on the security of new houses not guaranteed by the NHBC. Secondly, the NHBC inspects new houses under construction in order to ensure that the NHBC's standards are being met and in order to see that the Building Regulations are being observed.

The NHBC scheme, known as 'Buildmark', is in essence a method of self-regulation on the part of the building industry of setting minimum standards for the construction of new dwellings. The scheme began in 1936 and by 1969–70 98 per cent of new private sector housing was covered by it.[16]

Under the Buildmark scheme builders who are members of the NHBC have a threefold duty to the NHBC when building new dwellings:

(i) a duty to comply with the NHBC's requirements;
(ii) a duty to offer the purchaser of the dwelling the House Purchaser's Agreement (Form HB5); and
(iii) a duty to complete the work to a standard sufficient to obtain the Council's Notice of Insurance Cover (Form HB7).

If a builder fails to apply for the inspection of a dwelling and/or to offer the Buildmark, NHBC may take disciplinary action under its Rules. The ultimate sanction is deletion from the Register.

The House Purchaser's Agreement

This is nominally a separate contract made between the vendor and the purchaser, for the benefit of which the purchaser provides a consideration of 5p. It is the rights conferred by this agreement that form the primary remedy for the purchaser of a defective new dwelling-house.

Under the agreement the builder warrants to the purchaser that the dwelling has been or will be built:

(a) in accordance with the NHBC's requirements; and
(b) in an efficient and workmanlike manner and of proper materials and so as to be fit for habitation.

(b) above is, of course, virtually identical with the obligations imposed on a builder by the common law. The rights conferred by the House Purchaser's Agreement are, however, additional to the common law rights.[17]

Under the Agreement there are two guarantee periods:

(i) the initial guarantee period; and
(ii) the structural guarantee period.

The initial guarantee period

During this period the builder warrants that he will put right *any* defects which are:

(i) due to non-compliance with the NHBC's Technical Requirements; and
(ii) which occur within two years of the date of the Notice of Insurance Cover.[18]

During this period the Council acts as underwriter of this obligation, i.e., if the vendor does not satisfy an award or judgement made against him for breach of this undertaking, the Council will do so. The liability of the Council in this respect is limited to the purchase price of the dwelling, subject to a maximum of three times the national average purchase price. These limits are increased in line with inflation, up to a maximum of 12 per cent per annum compound from the date of purchase.

The structural guarantee period

This runs from the third to the tenth years after the Notice of Insurance Cover has been issued. During this further eight-year period the NHBC will pay the cost of putting right any 'major damage' which first appears and is reported to the NHBC before the end of the period. 'Major damage' is defined as damage which is:

(a) caused by a defect in the structure; or
(b) caused by subsidence, settlement or heave affecting the structure.

The liability of the NHBC during the structural guarantee period is subject to the same financial limits as during the initial guarantee period.[19]

Subsequent purchasers[20]

The rights under the House Purchaser's Agreement extend to subsequent purchasers of the dwelling. That is, second and subsequent purchasers are safeguarded against new defects which appear after they bought the dwelling. However, this aspect of the NHBC scheme suffers from the doctrine of privity of contract, that no one who is not a party to a contract can take the benefit of it. The House Purchaser's Agreement is a contract made between the vendor and the first purchaser and confers rights on no one save the first purchaser. The fact that Form HB5 is expressed to be for the benefit of subsequent purchasers is no help in this matter, firstly, because it is not under seal, and secondly, because a subsequent purchaser will not have provided consideration for it. In order to ensure that a subsequent purchaser does take the benefit of the Agreement, it must be assigned to him under the provisions of section 136 of the Law of Property Act 1925. In this way the problem of privity of contract can be overcome.

The NHBC has a rule forbidding its members from taking the privity point in litigation. However, if the HB5 form was not validly assigned and the builder chose to ignore that rule, then a subsequent purchaser could well find that he did not have the benefit of the Buildmark scheme.

SUMMARY

By way of summary the following points can be highlighted.

In the case of the first purchaser of a defective new dwelling the principal course of action will be under the NHBC scheme. But that scheme does not cover extensions or improvements to existing dwellings. In those cases a plaintiff will have to seek a remedy either under the

Defective Premises Act or for breach of the common law implied obligations.

It is the case of the subsequent purchaser of a defective dwelling, however, to which attention needs to be drawn. He is still at a disadvantage in respect of the rules governing privity of contract and economic loss. The privity rule may operate to the effect that the benefits of the NHBC scheme are not available to him. Further, following the decision in *Murphy* he will have no remedy in tort against the builder. This means that section 1 of the Defective Premises Act may well be a last straw for him to clutch. But that section does not appear suited to play this role; the duty contained in it is subject to too short a limitation period, and, moreover, it is not clear as to whether this duty covers economic loss. The courts are not at present in the mood to take a liberal view of this last factor!

NOTES

1. See, generally, J.R. Spencer (1974) CLJ 307; and Holyoak, J.H. and Allen, D.A., *Civil Liability for Defective Premises*, Butterworths, 1982, pp. 93–106 and 116–18.
2. Law Com. No. 40 (1970).
3. [1972] 1 QB 373.
4. [1978] AC 728.
5. [1990] 2 All ER 908.
6. [1956] 1 WLR 303.
7. See *Lindenberg v. Canning* (1992) *Construction Law Digest* (May) p. 21; and (1993) 62 BLR 147.
8. *Supra*, n.2. The courts, of course, must ignore Law Commission reports when construing the provisions of an Act of Parliament.
9. [1979] 1 WLR 1270.
10. (1992) 59 BLR 77.
11. *Ibid.*, n.9, p. 1274
12. [1991] 3 All ER 723.
13. *Supra*, n.1, p. 320.
14. See *Keating on Building Contracts*, 5th edn, 1991, pp. 362–363 and I.N. Duncan Wallace (1991) 107 LQR 228, pp. 242–243.
15. See *Anns, supra*, n.4; and *Pirelli v. Oscar Faber* [1983] AC1. Limitation is a problematic issue in Construction Law and it is an important enough topic to merit its own chapter, Chapter 9.
16. The latest edition of the NHBC scheme was published in 1992. Copies can be obtained from NHBC, 58 Portland Place, London, W1N 4BU.

17. This point is recognised in the NHBC's Explanatory Notes to Form HB5.
18. Defects due to normal shrinkage or drying out are excluded, and purchasers must notify defects in writing to the vendor as soon as practicable after they appear.
19. It should be noted that the Buildmark booklet provides a list of items for which the builder will *not* be liable under the scheme during the initial guarantee period and a list of items for which the NHBC will *not* be liable under the scheme during the structural guarantee period.
20. This section of the chapter is based on J.R. Spencer's analysis, *supra*, n.1

4 The Building Regulations[1]

ORIGINS AND PURPOSE OF THE BUILDING REGULATIONS

The Building Regulations are a comprehensive set of rules which provide a detailed system of quality control for all stages of building work. They cover a wide range of matters including drains, sewage and sanitary conveniences, foundations and building materials. They were originally model by-laws which were made under the Public Health Act 1875 and which many local authorities adopted with modification. The Public Health Act 1961 replaced these by-laws by the Building Regulations, which came into effect in 1966.

Historically, the Regulations have been seen as a cornerstone of the maintenance of general standards of public health. The need for such detailed controls was created by the very poor housing conditions which were all too common a feature of the industrial towns which grew so rapidly in the nineteenth century. This public health role was emphasised by the House of Lords in *Anns v. Merton LBC*.[2] Lord Wilberforce pointed out that the purpose of the Regulations is to provide for the health and safety of owners and occupiers of buildings, including dwelling-houses, by setting standards to be complied with in construction and by enabling local authorities to supervise and control the operations of builders.[3] Lord Salmon expressed this point as follows:

> The Public Health Act 1936 and the building byelaws made under it confer ample powers on the council for the purpose, among other things, of enabling it to protect the health and safety of the public in its locality against what is popularly known as jerry-building.[4]

To say that the Building Regulations are an aspect of public health is to say that a poorly constructed building may well have harmful effects, not just for the occupiers of the building, but on the environment of the locality in which it stands. In other words, poor-quality buildings may well subject their locality to what economists refer to as external diseconomies, i.e. they may impose costs, not just on their occupiers, but on the community at large. The principal purpose of the Regulations, therefore, is to eliminate or at any rate reduce these externalities.

The more controversial question is whether the Regulations have a wider consumer protection role. Clearly they provide protection for the person who employs a builder to build on land which he, the employer, owns; at the very least the building must come up to the standards prescribed by the Regulations. But what of the subsequent purchaser of such a building or the person who buys or leases a building from a developer? The key issue in those circumstances is whether the building control authority in whose area the building was erected can be said to owe a duty in tort to these persons to adequately enforce the Regulations. In *Anns* the House of Lords said that there was such a common law duty, but in the more recent case of *Murphy v. Brentwood DC*[5] *Anns* has been overruled and the House of Lords has said that such a duty cannot be founded on principle. The Law Lords in *Murphy* strenuously denied that the courts had any such consumer protection role. Lord Jauncey put this point bluntly:

> Parliament imposed a liability on builders by the Defective Premises Act, a liability which falls far short of that which would be imposed on them by *Anns*. There can therefore be no policy reason for imposing a higher common law duty on builders, from which it follows that there is equally no policy reason for imposing such a high duty on local authorities. Parliament is far better equipped than the courts to take policy decisions in the field of consumer protection.[6]

Given the much more conservative approach of the present Judicial Committee of the House of Lords to the creation of new tortious duties, it is clear that any broader consumer protection role for the Building Regulations must await another day. None the less, it cannot be denied that the Building Regulations were, and still are, an important part of that governmental paternalism to the protection of the industrial environment which grew up in the nineteenth century. This philosophy has been summed up as follows:

> The Building Regulations may be seen as a classic example of the increase in governmental control over day-to-day living where a small initial degree of intervention has burgeoned into a comprehensive panoply of what may, depending on one's political viewpoint, be regarded as useful controls or excessive interference. They also illustrate the ever increasing tendency to place the responsibility for state intervention in the hands of central, rather than local government. The history of the Regulations is in essence a gradual realisation during the nineteenth century that Britain's housing conditions were often intolerable – inadequately constructed houses surrounded by

> squalor in unhygienic surroundings were the norm for many in newly industrialised towns and cities.[7]

The present government plainly sees the Regulations more in the nature of 'excessive interference' than 'useful controls', and much of the detail of the Regulations is now contained in approved documents, with the Regulations themselves providing a broad framework of control. However, is is hard to imagine building work ever being entirely free of detailed quality control in some form or other.

SCOPE OF THE BUILDING REGULATIONS

The present system of building control is based on the Building Act 1984. Section 1 of that Act empowers the Secretary of State to make regulations with respect to the design and construction of buildings and the provision of services, fittings and equipment in or in connection with buildings for the following purposes:

(a) securing the health, safety, welfare and convenience of persons in or about buildings and of others who may be affected by buildings or matters connected with buildings;
(b) furthering the conservation of fuel and power; and
(c) preventing waste, undue consumption, misuse or contamination of water.

The Building Regulations 1985 were made under these powers and they operated from 11 November 1985 until 31 May 1992. They revoked and replaced the Building Regulations 1976. The 1985 Regulations differed in form from those they replaced in that they were expressed in broad functional terms and the technical details contained in the 1976 Regulations were replaced by approved documents. The Building Regulations 1991 revoked and replaced the 1985 Regulations with effect from 1 June 1992; they bring into effect a major review of technical and procedural requirements.

The Building Regulations apply throughout England and Wales. At first the Inner London boroughs remained outside their scope and were subject instead to the London Building Acts. However, they have now, for the most part, been brought within the national system.[8]

Under Regulation 4 of the 1991 Regulations, building work must be carried out so that it complies with the requirements set out in Schedule 1. These requirements are in 13 parts, and are as follows:

Part A (Structure)
Part B (Fire Safety)[9]
Part C (Site Preparation and Resistance to Moisture)
Part D (Toxic Substances)
Part E (Resistance to the Passage of Sound)
Part F (Ventilation)
Part G (Hygiene)
Part H (Drainage and Waste Disposal)
Part J (Heat Producing Appliances)
Part K (Stairways, Ramps and Guards)
Part L (Conservation of Fuel and Power)
Part M (Disabled People)
Part N (Glazing – Materials and Protection)[10]

'Building work' is defined in Regulation 3 of the 1991 Regulations as:

(a) the erection or extension of a building;
(b) the provision or extension of a controlled service or fitting in or in connection with a building;
(c) the material alteration of a building, or a controlled service or fitting;
(d) work relating to material change of use;
(e) the insertion of insulating material into the cavity wall of a building; and
(f) work involving the underpinning of a building.

Certain buildings are exempted from the Building Regulations by section 4 of the Building Act 1984. They are educational buildings and buildings belonging to statutory undertakers, the United Kingdom Atomic Energy Authority, the British Airports Authority, and the Civil Aviation Authority. Under the provisions of section 5 of the 1984 Act certain public bodies – in particular, local authorities – are exempt from the procedural, as opposed to the substantive, requirements of the Regulations.

Finally in this section, some comment must be made upon the nature of the 'approved documents'. They were first introduced in 1985 and are a key feature of the modern system of building control. Prior to 1985 the Building Regulations contained much technical detail; now they provide the broad framework of control and the approved documents provide the technical detail and the guidance as to how to comply with the Regulations. The argument for these documents is that they are a better way of accommodating technical information than the Regulations themselves which are published by way of statutory instrument; in particular, they can be updated much more easily than statutory instruments.

The legal status of these approved documents is evidentiary rather than substantive. Compliance with their provisions is not mandatory; under the provisions of section 7 of the Building Act 1984 a failure to comply with any of the provisions of these documents does not of itself render a person liable to civil or criminal proceedings, but in any such proceedings a failure to comply may be relied on as tending to establish liability. This means that if, say, a builder does not comply with the requirements of an approved document, then he will not be liable under the 1984 Act if he can show that he has complied with the requirements of the Regulations themselves by another, and equally satisfactory, method.

SUPERVISION OF THE BUILDING REGULATIONS

There are now two methods by which a builder or architect can have the building work supervised: (1) by a local authority, or (2) by an approved inspector.

Local authority control

Under local authority control, two options are available. The first option is the deposit of full plans, together with the prescribed fee. Local authorities have no discretion when considering such plans; under the provisions of section 16 of the Building Act 1984 they must approve the plans unless they are defective or in contravention of the Regulations. They have five weeks in which to pass or reject the plans, although this period can be extended, by agreement, to two months. The second option, which is available essentially for small scale domestic work, involves the applicant serving a 'building notice' on the local authority together with the prescribed fee. The notice must contain a short description of the work, the site, size and use of the building, proposals for drainage and a block plan of the new building or extension. The local authority does not issue any approval of the work, but it has powers to seek additional information and to check work in progress.

Approved inspector control

This form of supervision was introduced by Part II of the 1984 Act, though the detailed procedures are set out in regulations.[11] In broad terms Part II provides that responsibility for ensuring compliance with the Building Regulations may, if the person intending to carry out the work so chooses, [illegible] proved inspector rather than a local authority. The [illegible] also enable approved public bodies to approve their

[illegible] ethod of supervision the developer and the approved [illegible] serve an 'initial notice' describing the proposed work on the lo[illegible]rity. This notice can only be rejected by the local authority on very limited grounds. On acceptance the local authority's powers to enforce the Regulations are suspended and the approved inspector becomes responsible for inspecting the plans and the work and for issuing the final certificate on completion.

At present the only approved inspector is the National House-Building Council (NHBC). No other bodies seem likely to be approved in the near future because of the difficulties of obtaining professional indemnity insurance for this work.

ENFORCEMENT

Under the provisions of section 35 of the Building Act 1984 contravention of the Building Regulations is a criminal offence. Under the provisions of section 36 a local authority may serve a notice (known as a section 36 notice) on an owner requiring the building work to be pulled down or altered if it does not comply with the Regulations. If the owner fails to comply with such a notice, the local authority may pull down the work itself and recover the cost from the owner.

CIVIL LIABILITY

Builders

Section 38 of the Building Act 1984 provides that breach of a duty imposed by the Building Regulations shall, if it causes damage, be actionable except in so far as the Regulations provide otherwise. However, this section has not yet been brought into force. If it is eventually brought into effect, then it would have a number of advantages for a plaintiff. Firstly, *vis-à-vis* an action in negligence, there would be no need for a duty of care to be established by the plaintiff, since the statute spells this out. Secondly, and more importantly, the obligations imposed by the Building Regulations are clear, concise and comprehensive; in this respect section 38 has the potential to render redundant the provisions of section 1 of the Defective Premises Act 1972.

There appears to be no common law liability for breach of statutory duty independent of the provisions of section 38. In *Anns* Lord Wilberforce, in considering this matter, said:

> ... since it is the duty of the builder to comply with the byelaws, I would be of the opinion that an action could be brought against him, in effect, for breach of statutory duty by any person for whose benefit or protection the byelaw was made.[12]

These remarks were *obiter* and they have not been applied in subsequent cases. In *Murphy* Lord Oliver said:

> There is nothing in the terms or purpose of the statutory provisions which support the creation of a private law right of action for breach of statutory duty.[13]

Apart from an action for breach of statutory duty, a builder who builds in contravention of the Building Regulations may be in breach of an *express* term of his contract with the employer. Thus, under the provisions of clause 6 of the JCT '80 the contractor must comply with all statutory requirements and is therefore in breach of contract if he builds the works in contravention of the Building Regulations. There appears to be no *implied* obligation imposed upon the builder that he will construct the works according to the Building Regulations. However, a contravention of the Building Regulations may well be strong evidence that the builder was in breach of his implied obligation to construct the works in a workmanlike manner, using reasonable care and skill.

If the design is in breach of the Building Regulations and the builder builds according to that design, then, if he knew of the contravention, he may well be liable for failing to use reasonable care and skill.[14] It seems that in the circumstances his duty is to warn the architect or the employer of the contravention.[15]

Local authorities

Section 91 of the 1984 Act imposes on local authorities the general duty of implementing the Act and enforcing the Building Regulations in their area. In 1972 the Court of Appeal in *Dutton v. Bognor Regis DC*[16], and in 1978 the House of Lords in *Anns*, held that, in addition to this statutory duty, local authorities had a common law duty to take reasonable care to see that the Building Regulations were complied with.

In *Dutton* the foundations of a house were inspected and approved by one of Bognor Regis DC's building inspectors. In fact they did not comply with the by-laws because the house was being built on an old rubbish tip, a fact which a competent inspection would have revealed. The plaintiff, Mrs Dutton, bought the house as a second owner. It subsided and serious cracking in the walls occurred. Cusack J. at first instance held that the council owed Mrs Dutton a duty of care and that they were liable for breach of that duty. His decision was upheld by the Court of Appeal. Lord Denning, MR said that the Public Health Act 1936 and the by-laws made under it conferred on the local authority a control so extensive over building work and the manner in which it was performed that it carried with it a common law duty to exercise that control with reasonable care. That duty was owed to everyone who the inspector knows or ought to know is relying on his plaintiff.

The decision in *Dutton* was approved, subject to certain modifications, by the House of Lords in *Anns.* In 1962 the local council approved building plans for a block of flats, the construction of which was completed that year. In 1970 structural movements led to walls cracking and other damage. In 1972 the lessees commenced proceedings against the council, alleging that they had either negligently inspected the foundations or not inspected them at all. The House of Lords held that where an inspection was made there was a common law duty to take reasonable care to secure compliance with the building by-laws. The main speech was given by Lord Wilberforce and in its implications it was one of the most radical in the modern history of tort law. He said that the damages recoverable included damages for personal injury, damage to property and damage to the dwelling-house itself. He added:

> If classification is required, the relevant damage is in my opinion material, physical damage, and what is recoverable is the amount of expenditure necessary to restore the dwelling to a condition in which it is *no longer a danger to the health or safety of persons occupying* ... [author's italics][17]

Lord Wilberforce also considered the legal position if a local authority decided not to inspect. He said that it can still be challenged in the courts; although councils are under no duty to inspect, they are under a duty to give proper consideration to the question whether or not they should inspect. Essentially this means that before a local authority can be liable in negligence for an omission to inspect, that omission must be *ultra vires.* Lord Wilberforce emphasised that a local authority has to strike a balance between the claims of efficiency and thrift and that they are entitled not to inspect in certain circumstances. In other words, as long as a decision not to inspect is a properly taken policy decision, then a local authority cannot, it seems, be liable in negligence.

The decisions in *Dutton* and *Anns* were a radical development for the tort of negligence in general and for the duties of building control authorities in particular. They were controversial decisions, representing as they did the potential for further radical developments in the scope of this tort.[18] Not surprisingly, it was not long before the appellate courts began to place limitations on the extent of these decisions.[19] In these (subsequent) cases the issue for consideration was whether or not a local authority in exercising their building control duties owed a common law duty to the original building owner or developer. This issue came before the House of Lords in *Governors of the Peabody Donation Fund v. Sir Lindsay Parkinson & Co. Ltd.*[20] The plaintiffs in that case were developers. Their architects submitted plans for the construction of a flexible system of drainage to the local authority concerned. These plans were approved. However, the plaintiffs' contractors, on instructions from the architect, installed a rigid system of drainage. This fact came to the attention of the local authority but they took no action. The drains proved defective and had to be reconstructed, causing delay and substantial loss to the plaintiffs. They sued the local authority for negligence in carrying out their building control duties. The House of Lords held that the plaintiffs as owners of the building site were responsible for seeing that the drainage scheme conformed to the design approved by the local authority. The fact that they suffered loss because they were in breach of that duty did not make it reasonable or just to impose on the local authority a liability to indemnify the plaintiffs.

The principle in *Peabody* was applied by the Court of Appeal in *Investors in Industry Commercial Properties Ltd v. South Bedfordshire DC.*[21] The Court said that the purpose of the supervisory powers of the building control authorities is to protect the occupiers of buildings and members of the public generally against dangers to health or personal safety. It is not to safeguard the building developer himself against economic loss.

In *Richardson v. West Lindsey DC*[22] the Court of Appeal reiterated that view. They said that it is the duty of a building owner who intends to develop his building to observe the provisions of the Building Regulations. They also said that the local authority owed no common law duty to the building owner himself to ensure that he complied with the Regulations, *whether the loss he suffered was physical or economic.*

Clearly these decisions put significant limitations on the *Anns* principle. But it was not until *Murphy* that the House of Lords confronted the crux of that principle, the nature and classification of the loss suffered by the occupier of a building which is *potentially* dangerous. The facts of *Murphy* are as follows. In 1970 the plaintiff purchased from a construction company one of a pair of semi-detached houses newly constructed on an in-filled site. They were supported by a concrete raft foundation to prevent damage from settlement. The plans and calculations for the foundations were submitted to the local council for approval. The council approved them after referring them to consulting engineers for checking. In 1981 the plaintiff noticed serious cracks in his house and investigation showed that the foundation was defective. In 1986 he sold the house subject to its defects for £35 000 less than its market value in sound condition. The plaintiff sued the council for negligence and the judge at first instance held that the council were liable for the consulting engineers' negligence. The judge's decision was upheld by the Court of Appeal. The council then appealed to the House of Lords, who upheld their appeal.

The House of Lords held that when carrying out its building control functions, a local authority was not liable in negligence to a building owner or occupier for the cost of remedying a defect in the building which resulted from the negligent failure of the local authority to ensure that the building was constructed in accordance with the Building Regulations. The Law Lords were at pains to emphasise that such loss was not physical damage but economic loss. They said that once a dangerous defect became known it was a defect in quality. If a duty to avoid such loss was to be imposed on the local authority, then a similar duty would have to be imposed on the builder. There would be no grounds in principle for not extending such liability to the manufacturer of a chattel and that in turn would lead to an exceedingly wide field of claims involving the introduction of a transmissible warranty of quality into the English law of tort. *Dutton* and *Anns* were overruled.

There is no doubt that the decision in *Murphy* has ended a period of great uncertainty in this area of law as to the true extent of the *Anns* doctrine. The underlying reasoning of these two seminal decisions has been extensively examined in Chapter 2. Suffice it to say here by way of summing up that essentially the decision in *Anns* was a consumer protection decision, allowing the occupier of a defective building to recover his losses from the deepest pocket, which in the event of the insolvency of the builder means the local authority. It meant in effect that local authorities became insurers of buildings constructed in their area in the sense that they guaranteed that they were constructed in accordance with the Building Regulations. That doctrine was criticised by some commentators as being contrary to principle.[23] In *Murphy* the House of Lords clearly accepted that criticism and, as already stated, emphatically eschewed any consumer protection role for this area of law.

That leaves to be decided the question of what is the nature of the local authority's supervisory role in relation to building control. Is it simply to protect subsequent occupiers of a building from personal injury and damage to property other than the building itself? In appearing to overrule *Anns* in its entirety in *Murphy*, the House of Lords has implied that even that much may now be in doubt. The concluding words of the Lord Chancellor sound rather ominous in this respect:

> I should make it clear that I express no opinion on the question whether if personal injury were suffered by an oocupier of defective premises as a result of a latent defect in these premises, liability in respect of that personal injury would attach to a local authority which had been charged with the public law duty of supervising compliance with the relevant building by-laws or regulations in respect of a failure properly to carry out such duty.[24]

NOTES

1. See, generally, *Knight's Building Regulations* (Supplement No. 13) 1992.
2. [1978] AC 728.
3. *Ibid.*, n.2, p. 753.
4. *Ibid.*, n.2, p. 761.
5. [1990] 2 All ER 908.
6. *Ibid.*, n.5, pp. 942–43.
7. Holyoak, J.H. and Allen, D.K., *Civil Liability for Defective Premises*, Butterworths, 1982, p. 119.
8. See the Building Regulations (Inner London) Regulations 1985 and 1987 (SI 1985 No.1936 and SI 1987 No.798).
9. In addition to requirements imposed under the Building Act 1984, the provision of adequate means of escape from certain buildings is controlled by the Fire Precautions Act 1971. This requires designated buildings to have a fire certificate which, among other matters, certifies that the means of escape is adequate considering the use and occupancy of the building. See, further, Allen, D., Holyoak J. and Everton A., *Fire Safety and Law*, 2nd edn, Paramount Publishing, 1990, Ch.2.
10. This part was added by the 1991 Regulations.
11. The Building (Approved Inspectors) Regulations 1985, SI 1985 No. 1066. An approved inspector is a person approved by the Secretary of State under the provisions of section 49 of the Building Act 1984.
12. *Supra*, n.2, p. 759.
13. *Supra*, n.5, p. 943.
14. *Equitable Debenture Assets Corporation v. William Moss* (1984) 2 Con. LR 1.

15. *Lindenberg v. Canning* (1992) *Construction Law Digest* (May) p. 21. See also subclauses 6.1.2 and 6.1.5 of the JCT '80.
16. [1972] 1 QB 373.
17. *Supra*, n.2, p. 759.
18. See, in particular, the decision of the House of Lords in *Junior Books Ltd v. Veitchi Co. Ltd* [1983] 1 AC 520 (allowing a building owner's claim against a subcontractor for replacement of defective flooring and thereby opening the door to general recovery for economic loss in the tort of negligence).
19. Fleming has described Lord Wilberforce's speech in *Anns* as 'an affirmation of judicial sovereignty, a provocation to the partisans of judicial restraint': (1990) 106 LQR 525, p. 525.
20. [1984] 3 WLR 953.
21. [1986] 1 All ER 787.
22. [1990] 1 All ER 296
23. See especially Duncan Wallace (1991) 107 LQR 228.
24. *Supra*, n.5, p. 912.

5 Liability of Subcontractors

INTRODUCTION

Under the traditional form of contracting in the construction industry, initially one contractor, known as the main contractor, is engaged to construct the whole of the works. However, it is usual for the majority of the work on a substantial construction contract to be carried out by a large number of (specialist) subcontractors. The subject of this chapter is the duties and liabilities of these subcontractors and the liability of the main contractor for their work.

These duties and liabilities will be examined from three points of view:

(1) the relationships between the employer and each subcontractor;
(2) the relationships between the principal contractor and each subcontractor; and
(3) the liability of the main contractor for the work of the subcontractors.[1]

EMPLOYER AND SUBCONTRACTOR

Under the traditional JCT form of contract, a subcontractor is not a party to the contract between the contractor and the employer. In technical language, there is no privity of contract between employer and subcontractor. The employer, therefore, cannot sue a subcontractor in contract for deficiencies or delays in the contractual work.

The doctrine of privity of contract can be bypassed by the employer obtaining a direct warranty from a subcontractor, known as a collateral warranty. The JCT has produced a standard form of employer/nominated subcontractor agreement.[2] Under clause 2.1 of this form a contractor warrants that he has used reasonable care and skill in:

(1) the design of the subcontract works in so far as the subcontract works have been or will be designed by the subcontractor;

(2) the selection of materials and goods for the subcontract works in so far as such materials and goods have been or will be selected by the subcontractor; and
(3) the satisfaction of any performance specification or requirement in so far as such performance specification or requirement is included or referred to in the description of the subcontract works included in or annexed to the tender.

The essential point to note about such a warranty is that it adds nothing to the implied duties owed by the supplier in a contract for work and materials: it simply allows a third party (the employer) to take the benefit of those duties.

In the absence of any such direct warranty the only means by which the employer can sue a subcontractor is in the tort of negligence. In practice, any losses sustained by the employer as a result of the negligence of a subcontractor are likely to be economic and as we have seen in Chapter 2, this is a problematical area of law. Construction cases, including those involving the liability of subcontractors, have played a prominent part in the recent history of negligence and economic loss and it is, therefore, worth recounting that history.

Until the 1960s the law concerning negligence and economic loss seemed to be clear: where a negligent act or negligent words *forseeably* led to another person suffering economic (i.e. financial) loss, then the defendant was not liable for that loss. In the 1960s and 1970s there occurred a number of developments which, in effect, created exceptions to this rule.

(1) The House of Lords in *Hedley Byrne* v. *Heller*[3] said, *obiter*, that a person who suffers financial loss through relying on a false statement made negligently has, in certain circumstances, a claim in negligence against the maker of the statement.[4]
(2) In the so-called 'building cases' a builder's liability in tort for defective premises was extended to include what, in effect, was economic loss.[5]
(3) In *Spartan Steel & Alloys Ltd* v. *Martin & Co. (Contractors) Ltd*[6] the Court of Appeal held that economic loss resulting from a negligent act was recoverable where it was consequent upon damage to property.

These developments culminated in the decision of the House of Lords in *Junior Books Ltd* v. *Veitchi Co. Ltd*,[7] a Scottish case involving the liability of a subcontractor for negligence. A firm of builders was engaged to construct a factory for the building owner. The defendants were engaged as subcontractors to lay a composition floor. Because of their negligence the floor was defective and cracked up. There was no danger to health or safety or any other property of the building owner but the floor needed to be replaced. The building owner sought to recover the cost of replacement, including the loss of profits incurred while the floor was being relaid, from the subcontractors. There was no contract between the parties and the building owner therefore sued in the tort of negligence. The House of Lords treated the building owner's loss as economic and they held, by a majority, that his allegations disclosed a cause of action. The majority said that where the relationship between the parties was sufficiently close the scope of the duty of care extended to a duty to avoid causing economic loss consequent upon defects in the work and to avoid defects in the work itself.

The leading speech for the majority was given by Lord Roskill. He based his analysis on Lord Wilberforce's famous two-stage test for establishing a duty of care in *Anns.* Lord Wilberforce said that in order to establish that a duty of care arises in a particular situation, it is not necessary to bring the facts of that situation within those previous situations in which a duty of care has been held to exist. Rather the question has to be approached in two stages:

(1) Is there a sufficient relationship of proximity between the plaintiff and defendant for a duty to arise?
(2) If the first question is answered affirmatively, are there any considerations which ought to negative or limit the scope of the duty?[8]

In applying the first stage of Lord Wilberforce's test, Lord Roskill in his speech referred to two specific factors which gave rise to an adequate degree of proximity for the subcontractors to owe a duty of care to the pursuers. Firstly, the subcontractors had expert knowledge of the flooring trade and of the requirements of the factory owners and they relied on that expertise. Secondly, the relationship between the parties was all but contractual in character and it must have been clear to the subcontractors that bad workmanship on their part would result in increased expenditure by the factory owners. As to the second stage of Lord Wilberforce's test, Lord Roskill said that there were no policy factors which negatived or restricted the duty: in particular, there was no question of the subcontractors being liable to an indeterminate class.

In general terms, the decision in *Junior Books* seemed to open up the possibility of a general rule of recovery for economic loss in an action in negligence. In relation to defective buildings it was thought that the law might develop so that any owner of a building in disrepair because of negligence on the part of those constructing it would be able to recover the expense of repair, subject to satisfying the two parts of the *Anns* test and subject to the rules relating to the limitation of actions. Those hopes were soon dashed. Subsequent cases in this area have regarded *Junior Books* as a special case confined to its own facts, and the decision of the House of Lords there has been distinguished on all these occasions. Moreover, as we have seen in Chapter 2, the *Anns* line of cases was overruled in *Murphy* v. *Brentwood DC.*[9]

It is not even clear now as to whether *Junior Books* could be relied upon by an employer suing a subcontractor. In four cases involving claims in tortious negligence by employers against subcontractors the courts have distinguished *Junior Books.* In *South Water Authority* v. *Carey*[10] the predecessors of Southern Water Authority entered into a contract for the construction of a sewage works. The actual works were carried out by subcontractors. Under the *main* contract the main contractors were to be responsible for making good defects in the works arising within twelve months of completion as a result of defective materials, workmanship or design. The main contract also stated that the acceptance of this liability by the main contractor was to be *instead of* any condition or warranty implied by law as to quality and fitness for any particular purpose of the work. The work proved to be defective, with the result that the whole sewage scheme was a failure. The plaintiff sued the subcontractor for negligence in the design and supply of defective equipment and the installation of this equipment. The High Court held that the subcontractors could not be liable in tort because the main contract negatived the duty of care which would otherwise have been owed by the subcontractors. In other words, the wording of the main contract defined the area of risk which the plaintiff had chosen to accept and in doing this it had limited the scope of the subcontractor's liability.

In *Norwich City Council* v. *Paul Clarke Harvey & Briggs Amasco Ltd*[11] the plaintiff entered into a contract with Bush Builders Ltd to build an extension to a swimming pool complex. Bush entered into a subcontract for felt-roofing with Briggs Amasco Ltd. In the course of the felt roofing work an employee of Briggs Amasco set fire with a blowtorch to both the existing buildings and the new extension, causing extensive damage. The terms of the subcontract contained a provision which bound Briggs Amasco to the terms and conditions of the main contract. The main contract provided that as between the plaintiff and Bush the existing structures and works would be at the sole risk of the plaintiff as regards loss or damage by fire. The plaintiff therefore tried to recover their losses from the subcontractors in tort. The High Court held that the duty of care owed by the defendants to the plaintiff was qualified by the terms of the main contract. Accordingly, the subcontractors were not liable to the plaintiff.

In *Greater Nottingham Co-operative Society Ltd* v. *Cementation Piling and Foundations Ltd*[12] the plaintiff building owner entered into a contract with a contractor for the extension and alteration of his office premises.

Subcontractors were engaged to provide piles for the extension. The subcontractors entered into a collateral contract with the building owner which required them to exercise reasonable care and skill in the design of the piling works and in the selection of materials. That collateral contact was silent as to the manner in which the piling works were to be executed. In the event, the piling equipment was operated negligently by one of the subcontractors' employees and damage was caused to an adjoining building. Work was suspended while a revised piling scheme was worked out and the plaintiff sued the subcontractors in tort for his economic loss resulting from delayed completion of the building. The Court of Appeal held that the collateral contract entered into by the subcontractors defined the extent of their responsibility to the plaintiff building owner. As that collateral contract made no mention of liability for the execution of the piling work, the subcontractors were not responsible in tort for the building owner's economic loss.

In *Simaan General Contracting Co.* v. *Pilkington Glass Ltd (No. 2)*[13] the plaintiffs were the main contractors for the construction of a building in Abu Dhabi. The supply and erection of curtain walling was subcontracted to an Italian company. The terms of the subcontract required the subcontractors to obtain specified double-glazed units of green glass from Pilkingtons, the defendants. When erected, the glass was found to be not of a uniform colour and the building owner withheld part of the contract price from the main contractors. The main contractors sought to recover this loss from Pilkingtons by suing them in negligence. The Court of Appeal distinguished this case from *Junior Books* and held that the defendants were not liable for the plaintiffs' losses. There was not a sufficiently close relationship between the plaintiffs and Pilkingtons to give rise to a duty of care; there had been no technical discussions about the product between the plaintiffs and Pilkingtons, and the plaintiffs could not be said to have relied on Pilkingtons in this matter.

A number of factors can be identified in this retreat from *Junior Books*. Firstly, it is part of the general retreat of the law of negligence. The courts now see the function of the law of negligence as being to protect the plaintiff's interest in his person and his property but not his purely financial interests. Secondly, the giving of a warranty by the subcontractor will restrict the subcontractor's liability in tort towards the building owner. The warranty is seen as defining the extent of the subcontractor's liability to the building owner and the courts do not regard it as proper for the law of tort to add to that liability. Thirdly, the courts have laid great stress on the risk of a tort action disturbing the allocation of responsibilities down the chain of contracts. In particular, emphasis has been laid on the possibility that if the employer is allowed to sue a subcontractor directly in tort then this could outflank an exemption clause either in the main contract or in the contract between the main contractor and the subcontractor.[14] All of these factors can be reduced to the general point that the dominant trend in this area of law since *Junior Books* has been to emphasise the law of contract as the means for recovering economic loss.

The conclusion from this survey is therefore clear: as a general rule, an employer will not be able to successfully sue a subcontractor directly in tort for economic loss suffered as a consequence of the subcontractor's negligence. However, there may be two exceptions to this general rule. Firstly, the employer may be able to successfully sue a subcontractor in negligence if he can show that his relationship with the subcontractor can be brought within the scope of the reliance doctrine first laid down in *Hedley Byrne*. Secondly, an action in negligence against a subcontractor may succeed if the loss suffered can be brought within the scope of the complex structure theory.

The first of these exceptions is based on the interpretation of *Junior Books* by Lord Keith in *Murphy*.[15] He said there that *Junior Books* is an application of the *Hedley Byrne* principle: the subcontractors owed a duty to the building owner because the building owner relied on their expertise.

The second exception derives from the attempts of the Law Lords in *D & F Estates* v. *Church Commissioners for England*[16] to reconcile their decision in that case with *Anns*. They introduced a distinction between simple and complex structures and said that damage to one part of a structure caused by a defect in another part could be treated as damage to other property.[17] Not surprisingly, such a theory is fraught with problems and in *Murphy* it was considerably modified. Lord Bridge said there that it applied only to a distinct item incorporated in the structure (e.g. a central heating boiler which malfunctions so as to damage the structure) and not to the structure itself. Thus, where the foundations of a building were inadequate to support its superstructure, that was a defect of quality. Lord Jauncey said that the only context in which the complex structure theory could arise in the case of a building would be where one integral component of the building was built by a separate contractor and where a defect in that component caused damage to other parts of the structure. He gave an example of a steel frame erected by a specialist contractor which failed to support adequately the floors and walls. Lord Jauncey went on to say that defects in such ancillary equipment as central heating boilers or electrical equipment which caused damage to other parts of the building were subject to *Donoghue* v. *Stevenson* principles.

It seems that before a subcontractor can be sued by the employer under the complex structure theory it must be established that the subcontractor supplied a distinct component within the building but did not also supply the part damaged by a defect in this component. It is obviously difficult to determine what constitutes 'other property' for the purposes of this theory.

Why is damage caused by defective foundations regarded differently from damage caused by a defective steel structure? The law in this area can hardly be said to be crystal clear.

Finally in this section, one point needs to be underlined: *Junior Books* has *not* been overruled. Indeed, far from being overruled, the interpretation placed upon it in *Murphy* may give it a new lease of life!

PRINCIPAL CONTRACTOR AND SUBCONTRACTOR

The duties owed by the subcontractor to the main contractor in relation to the quality of the subworks are based on contract. These duties are of two kinds: express and implied.

Express duties

There will generally be a written agreement between the main contractor and each subcontractor and this agreement will contain the express obligations of the subcontractor. A standard form of agreement between main contractor and subcontractor is published by the JCT – Sub-Contract NSC/4.[18] This is the form most frequently used in the industry.

The subcontractor's obligations for the quality of the subcontract works under this form are contained in clause 4.1. They are as follows:

(1) The subcontractor must carry out and complete the subcontract works in compliance with the subcontract documents and in conformity with the directions and requirements of the main contractor.
(2) All materials and goods supplied by the subcontractor must be of the kinds and standards described in the subcontract documents. Where the architect has responsibility for approval of the quality of the materials and goods supplied they must be to his satisfaction.
(3) All workmanship must be of the standards described in the subcontract documents. If no such standards are specified, then the workmanship must be of a standard appropriate to the subcontract works. Where approval of workmanship is subject to the opinion of the architect, then such workmanship must be to his satisfaction.
(4) All work must be carried out in a proper and workmanlike manner.

More specifically, clause 11.1 states that the subcontractor must carry out and complete the subcontract works in accordance with the agreed programme details in the tender and in accordance with the progress of the main contract works. If the subcontractor is in default of this obligation, then under clause 29.1 the main contactor must inform the architect. If the architect so instructs, the main contractor must then issue a notice to the subcontractor specifying the default. If the subcontractor continues with such default for 14 days after the receipt of such notice the main contractor may terminate the employment of the subcontractor.

In substance these express obligations add little or nothing to the subcontractor's obligations under the general law.

Implied duties

A subcontract is, like the main contract, a contract for work and materials. As such, a subcontractor will be subject to the same implied obligations in relation to the work and materials as is the main contractor under the main contract. They are as follows:

(1) that the subcontractor carry out the works with reasonable care and skill; and
(2) that any materials supplied by the subcontractor be of good quality and fit for any particular purpose specified by the main contractor.

These duties are now contained in the Supply of Goods and Service Act 1982.[19] A detailed commentary on these implied duties is provided in Chapter 1, but two points are worth repeating here. Firstly, liability attaching to a breach of the duties relating to the materials supplied is strict, in contrast to liability attaching to defective workmanship which is negligence based. Secondly, if the main contractor does not rely on the expertise of the subcontractor in the selection of the materials, the implied duty of fitness for purpose is excluded; however, the subcontractor will still be responsible for the quality of the materials supplied.[20]

LIABILITY OF THE MAIN CONTRACTOR FOR THE WORK OF SUB-CONTRACTORS

The main contractor is entitled under the provisions of the JCT '80 to subcontract the work. Even if the main contract is not subject to the provisions of this standard form, the main contractor will almost certainly have implied powers to subcontract, since subcontracting is such an established custom in the construction industry.

When the main contractor subcontracts part of the work, he is not liable in tort to either the owner or the occupier of the building for the negligence of the subcontractor. The main contractor's only duty is to employ a competent subcontractor. This rule was explained by Lord Bridge in *D & F Estates* in the following terms:

> It is trite law that the employer of an independent contractor is, in general, not liable for the negligence or other torts committed by the contractor in the course of the execution of the work.[21]

Lord Bridge subsequently went on to say that if the fact of employing a contractor does not involve the assumption of any duty of care by the employer, then the contractor assumes no such liability when he employs an apparently competent subcontractor to carry out part of the work for him. This means that in the event of a subcontractor's negligence in the execution of the subcontract works the employer's only remedy lies against the subcontractor in the tort of negligence, and, as we have seen in the first part of this chapter, where the employer's loss is purely economic it will be very difficult for him to establish that the subcontractor owed him a duty of care.

Lord Bridge pointed to one exception to the above rule. If the main contractor exercises a degree of supervision over the subcontractor and in the course of that supervision discovers defects in the subcontractor's work, which he approves, then he will be potentially liable for the consequences jointly with the subcontractor. The result of this proviso is that the main contractor is under a duty to warn the employer of any defects in the work of a subcontractor which comes to his attention.

Where the employer relies on the skill and judgement of the main contractor for the selection of the materials to be used, then the main contractor will remain liable to the employer in the event of a subcontractor supplying materials which are not of good (or merchantable) quality. The main authority for this rule is the decision of the House of Lords in *Young & Marten Ltd* v. *McManus Childs*.[22] In that case, contractors were building dwelling-houses on their own land. They subcontracted the roofing and they specified that a particular type of tile, Somerset 13, was to be used for the roof. These tiles were made by only one manufacturer and in specifying these tiles the contractor's representative relied on his own skill and judgement. The supplying and laying of tiles was further subcontracted. The tiles had a latent defect, not apparent on inspection, which was the result of a fault in their manufacture. This defect became apparent after the tiles were fixed and exposed to the weather. The House of Lords held that in a contract for work and materials two warranties may be implied in respect of the materials supplied, a warranty of their reasonable fitness for the purpose and a warranty of their good quality – in particular, against latent defects. Where the materials are chosen by the party for whom the work is to be done, a warranty of their fitness is not implied but, unless excluded by the circumstances or by the contact, a warranty of quality will be implied. As the contractors' representative relied on his own skill and judgement in the selection of the tiles in question, the subcontractors were held not liable for breach of the warranty of fitness for purpose, but they were held liable in damages for breach of the implied warranty of quality. Strictly speaking, of course, this case concerns the liability of a subcontractor who then further subcontracted the work in question. The first subcontractor was held liable for the defective tiles which the sub-subcontractor obtained from the manufacturer and used. However, it seems virtually certain in these circumstances that had it been an employer suing the main contractor for the work of a subcontractor, the result would have been the same.

The rationale underlying this rule was discussed most fully in the speech of Lord Reid. He set out two reasons for implying a warranty of quality. The first of these reasons he expressed as follows:

> If the contractor's employer suffers loss by reason of the emergence of the latent defect, he will generally have no redress if he cannot recover damages from the contractor. If, however, he can recover damages the contractor will generally not have to bear the loss: he will have bought the defective materials from a seller who will be liable under section 14(2) of the Sale of Goods Act 1893, because the material was not of merchantable quality; and if that seller had in turn bought from someone else there will again be liability, so that there will be a chain of liability from the employer who suffers the damage back to the author of the defect.[23]

This chain may of course be broken because the contractor or an earlier buyer contracted subject to a clause excluding his supplier's liability under the Sale of Goods Act. Lord Reid said that should not deprive the employer of a remedy; in the event of such an exclusion clause the risk should lie with the party concerned if the goods proved defective.

What would be the position if the manufacturer was a monopolist and willing to sell only on terms which excluded or limited his liability? Lord Reid suggested that if this fact was known to the employer it would be unreasonable to impose liability for latent defects on the contractor. That, of course, was some time before the days of the Unfair Contract Terms Act 1977. Under the provisions of that Act the court may strike down a clause in a contract between a monopolistic supplier and a buyer without such market power excluding the supplier's liability under the Sale of Goods Act as unreasonable.[24] Imposing liability for latent defects on the contractor in these circumstances now, therefore, should not prevent such liability being passed on to the manufacturer.

Lord Reid's second reason for implying a warranty of quality in contracts of work and materials was to bring them into line in that respect with contacts for the sale of goods. Thus, if an employer bought a machine and installed it himself, that would be a contract of sale and the employer would have a warranty under section 14(2) of the Sale of Goods Act. If the seller agreed to install the machine that would be a contract for work and materials. Lord Reid said that it would be strange if installation by the seller made any difference.[25] Any doubt about this matter has of course been laid to rest by the Supply of Goods and Services Act 1982.[26]

The decision in *Young & Marten* must be considered alongside the decision of the House of Lords in *Gloucestershire County Council* v. *Richardson*.[27] In that case a contractor contracted with employers to build an extension to a technical college. The employers laid down that certain concrete columns were to be supplied by nominated suppliers at a quoted price. The contract between those suppliers and the contractors contained a clause limiting the supplier's liability for defective goods and excluding their liability for consequential loss or damage. The columns contained latent defects which became apparent when used in the building work. The House of Lords held that in view of these circumstances any warranty by the contractor of the quality or fitness of the columns supplied by the suppliers was excluded.

It must be emphasised that the decision in *Gloucestershire County Council* v. *Richardson* is generally considered to be an exception to the rule laid down in *Young & Marten*. Confirmation for this conclusion is provided by the following dictum of Lord Fraser in *IBA* v. *EMI Ltd and BICC Ltd*:

> ... in a building contract for work and materials a term is normally implied that the main contractor will accept responsibility to his employer for materials provided by a nominated subcontractor.[28]

A more interesting and unusual exception to the reasoning of *Young & Marten* occurred in *University of Warwick* v. *Sir Robert McAlpine and Others*.[29] Between about 1963 and 1968 the University erected a number of buildings. They had a uniform white ceramic tile cladding. In about 1969 the tiling began to fail. The contractors, McAlpine, carried out remedial works, but in 1973 it became apparent that they would be far more extensive than anticipated. An epoxy resin injection was considered as an alternative. The sole British licensee of this process was Cementation Chemicals Ltd (CCL). The University instructed McAlpine to employ CCL as subcontractors. McAlpine was not involved in the decision to use the CCL system. In fact, they had substantial reservations about the system and obtained an indemnity from CCL. The system failed and the University sued, *inter alios,* McAlpine for breach of an implied term to supply epoxy resin that was fit for its purpose. (The University accepted that the resin injection was of merchantable quality.) Garland J. held that a term that the resin be fit for its purpose could only be implied in the main contract if the University had relied on McAlpine. They had not done so and no such term could therefore be implied.

In the course of his judgement Garland J. distinguished *Young & Marten* and *Gloucestershire County Council.* He said that in *Young & Marten* fitness was never prima facie implied (the main contractor's representative selected the tiles) and in *Gloucestershire County Council* only quality was at issue because the columns had been chosen by the architect. Garland J. further pointed to the fact that the University could have obtained an express warranty of fitness from McAlpine, which they did not, as evidence of absence of reliance by the University on McAlpine.

Garland J.'s decision meant that the chain of contractual liability on which so much emphasis was placed in *Young & Marten* was broken at the first stage. In the view of the editor of the *Building Law Reports* the judge's analysis is faced with the difficulty that McAlpine obtained an indemnity from CCL. In his view this indicates that the parties wished to maintain the contractual chain of liability and that the judge was unduly restrictive in his interpretation of the concept of reliance.[30] In the author's view this argument is tenuous and Garland J.'s conclusion on this aspect of the case is to be preferred. McAlpine's reservations about the epoxy resin system were clear and they made those reservations known to the University. The University, far from relying on that advice, specifically ignored it. To the author, it seems that obtaining an indemnity from CCL indicates not a wish to preserve the usual contractual chain of liability, but caution on McAlpine's part in the event of their being successfully sued by the University; a form of litigation insurance, if you like.

NOTES

1. This structure is based on *Emden's Construction Law,* 8th edn, Butterworths, 1990 (Issue 28, February 1993), Binder 1, Chapter 6.
2. NSC/2. This form is published in *Emden's Construction Law,* Binder 4, Division M.
3. [1964] AC 465.
4. Their Lordships differed in their formulation of these circumstances, but they have subsequently been reformulated by the House of Lords in *Caparo v. Dickman* [1990] 1 A11 ER 568 and further refined by the

Court of Appeal in *James McNaughten Paper Group Ltd v. Hicks Anderson & Co.* [1991] 1 A11 ER 134 (per Neill L.J., pp. 144–45).

5. *Dutton v. Bognor Regis UDC* [1972] 1QB373; *Anns v. Merton LBC* [1978] AC 728; and *Batty v. Metropolitan Realisations* [1978] QB 554.
6. [1973] QB 27.
7. [1983] 1AC 520.
8. *Supra*, n.5, *Anns v. Merton LBC*, pp. 751–52.
9. [1990] 2 All ER 908.
10. [1985] 2 All ER 1077.
11. (1988) 4 Const. L.J. 217.
12. [1988] 2 All ER 971.
13. [1988] 1 All ER 791.
14. See, for example, the judgement of Bingham L.J. in *Simaan v. Pilkington, ibid.*, n.13, p. 804.
15. *Supra*, n.9, p. 919.
16. [1988] 2 All ER 992.
17. See, for example, the speech of Lord Bridge, *ibid.*, n.16, pp. 1006–7.
18. This is published in *Emden's Construction Law*, Binder 4, Division M.
19. See sections 2–5 and section 13.
20. See *Young & Marten v. McManus Childs Ltd* [1968] 2 All ER 1169; and section 4 of the Supply of Goods and Services Act 1982.
21. *Supra*, n.16, p. 1008.
22. *Supra*, n.20.
23. *Supra*, n.20, p. 1172.
24. See Schedule 2 of the Act and, in particular, guidelines (a) and (b).
25. *Supra*, n.20, p. 1172.
26. See section 4.
27. [1968] 2 All ER 1181.
28. (1986) 14 BLR 1, pp. 44–45.
29. (1988) 42 BLR 1.
30. See the commentary on the case, *ibid.*, n.29, p. 4.

6 Liability of Architects and Engineers

INTRODUCTION

This chapter is concerned with the liability in professional negligence of those professions who provide services in connection with building and engineering projects, especially large-scale ones. The most important of those professions are architecture and engineering. Essentially the services which they provide in relation to a construction project can be divided into two broad categories:

(i) the preparation of skilful and economic designs for the works; and
(ii) the supervision and administration of the works in the best interest of the employer.

The architect or the engineer is not a party to the main contract between the contractor and the employer. Nor is he a party to any subcontract, except in the case of a design and build contract.[1] In the traditional form of building contract there will be a contract between the employer and the contractor and another contract between the employer and the architect or engineer. Under this traditional form of building contract the architect or engineer both has a design function and will play a leading role in the administration of the building contract itself, i.e. the contract between the employer and the contractor.

The position in law of the architect or engineer will vary according to which of their functions they are performing. At the initial (design) stage of the project he will almost certainly be an independent contractor, but in the supervision of the building contract he will have a dual role: firstly, he will be the employer's agent acting on his behalf, and secondly, he will issue certificates, in which capacity he must act impartially as between the employer and the contractor. We can accordingly divide this chapter into three broad areas:

(1) liability to the employer;
(2) supervision of the building contract; and
(3) liability to third parties.

LIABILITY TO THE EMPLOYER

In contract

The primary basis of the duties of the architect or engineer is the contract under which he is engaged by the employer. Those are his *express* duties. Generally, those duties are set out in one of the standard form contracts used for the engagement of architects or engineers. Thus, architects are usually engaged subject to the RIBA standard form, *Architect's Appointment*,[2] and the most common form in use for engineers is the ACE Conditions of Engagement.[3] The express duties of the architect employed in a building project cover a range of tasks: surveying the site, producing drawings, advising on building regulations, selecting materials, supervising the works, issuing certificates, etc.[4] An engineer will perform a similar range of functions in relation to a civil engineering project.

The *implied* duty of the architect or engineer is to carry out his express duties with reasonable care and skill.[5] As a general rule there appears to be no stricter duty of guaranteeing that a particular result will be produced; an architect or engineer is contractually liable only if he has failed to exercise reasonable care and skill.[6] This is in direct contrast to the legal position of the builder. As we have seen in Chapter 1, a builder's contractual duties to his employer are strict duties in a number of respects: he guarantees the quality of the materials used and, if he is building a house, that it will be fit for habitation when completed.

The concept of reasonable care and skill in the context of professional duties means the standard required of the ordinary skilled and competent practitioner in the profession concerned. This is known as 'the Bolam standard', after McNair J's famous dictum in *Bolam v. Friern Barnet Hospital Management Committee:*

> The test is the standard of the ordinary skilled man exercising and professing to have that special skill .... A man need not possess the highest expert skill; it is well established law that it is sufficient if he exercises the ordinary skill of an ordinary competent man exercising that particular art.[7]

Thus, an architect or engineer must carry out his duties as would a reasonably competent member of his profession. Essentially the standard of a reasonably competent architect or engineer would be decided on the basis of evidence (if any) of accepted standards of conduct in the profession concerned.

The meaning of reasonable care and skill in the context of the particular duties carried out by architects and engineers must now be examined. Most of the case law involves architects, but the principles laid down apply also to engineers.

Design duties

What constitutes reasonable skill and care in the design of a building depends upon the circumstances of each case. The duty will normally be discharged by following established practice. Where there is no established practice, such as where a new construction technique is used, the duty of reasonable care and skill may be discharged by taking the best advice available and by warning the employer of any risks involved. In *Turner v. Garland and Christopher*[8] the employer instructed his architect to use a new patent concrete roofing which proved to be a failure. It was held that where an untried process was used, failure might still be consistent with reasonable skill.

Supervision

The architect or engineer has a duty to see that the works are carried out in accordance with the contract. This does not require him to be on site continuously but his supervision must be such as to allow him to certify honestly that the work has been done as the contract requires.

Liability for materials

The architect or engineer owes a duty of care to ensure that the materials which are to be used by the contractor are suitable for the purpose. No stricter duty is generally implied, i.e. the architect or engineer does not normally guarantee that the materials to be used are fit for the purpose. The key question for the architect is: what does he have to do in order to fulfil this duty? Such authority as there is on this point suggests that it is not sufficient for the architect to rely solely on the recommendations, if any, of the supplier or the manufacturer of the product. The architect appears to be obliged in law to conduct his own investigations into the suitability of the building materials that he recommends. In *Holland Hannen & Cubitts Ltd v. Welsh Health Technical Services Organisation*[9] the architects were held to be under a duty to ask probing questions of a subcontractor about the design of window assemblies used in the construction of a hospital. In *George Hawkins v. Chrysler (UK) Ltd and Burne Associates*[10] an engineer selected shower room tiles after careful investigation of RIBA product data sheets and trade brochures and after consulting a specialist flooring firm.

The tiles turned out to be slippery and an employee of the building owner sustained injuries in the shower room. The engineer was held on these facts not to have been negligent.

If the materials are selected by the employer without reference to the architect or engineer, then the only duty imposed upon the architect or engineer is a duty to warn of any defects in the materials known to him.

There is one exception to the rule of reasonable care and skill in these circumstances: where the architect or engineer supplies materials as well as services as part of his contract with the employer he will be strictly liable for the quality and fitness of those materials.[11]

Recommending a builder

If the architect selects a builder, then he must exercise reasonable care in that selection. In *Pratt v. George J. Hill Associates*[12] the plaintiff retained a firm of architects for the construction of a bungalow. They obtained tenders from builders, including two whom they described as 'very reliable'. The plaintiff accordingly entered into a contract with one of those builders, Swanmore Builders Ltd. Swanmore proved to be very unreliable and failed to complete the work. They subsequently became insolvent. The plaintiff commenced proceedings against the architects, claiming damages for negligence in recommending Swanmore. The Court of Appeal upheld her claim, stating that the architect was in breach of his duty to recommend a suitable reliable builder.

Compliance with the law

Architects and engineers have a duty to ensure that the works comply with the relevant statutory obligations. In particular, the architect is under a duty to ensure that the building complies with the Building Regulations.

An obligation of fitness for purpose

The design liability of the architect or engineer may be stricter than reasonable care and skill in two situations. Firstly, a strict duty may be imposed where the architect or engineer delegates part of the design work; as a general rule he will remain liable for the design unless the employer agrees to the delegation. Secondly, a stricter obligation than reasonable care and skill may be implied into the contract between the architect or engineer and the employer from the surrounding circumstances.[13]

The first exception is illustrated by *Moresk Cleaners v. Hicks.*[14] An architect was engaged to prepare plans and specifications for the extension of the plaintiff's laundry. He deiegated the design of the structure to the building contractor. Within two years of completion cracks appeared in the structure and the roof purlins sagged. Expert investigation showed that these defects were caused by faults in the design. The plaintiff sued the architect. In his defence the architect argued: (1) that it was an implied term of his contract of engagement that he should be entitled to delegate specified design tasks to qualified specialist subcontractors; and (2) that he had implied authority to employ the contractor to design the structure. These defences were rejected by the trial judge, Sir Walter Carter, Q.C., who said:

> ... if [the architect] takes upon himself the design of a building, he cannot in my view escape his liability for that design by delegating his duty to the contractor who is going to do the building.[15]

The architect will not be liable, however, if he reasonably relies on the manufacturer's expertise. In *London Borough of Merton v. Lowe* [16] the plaintiffs engaged the defendants, a firm of architects, to design and supervise the erection of a new indoor swimming pool. The design included the use of a proprietary plaster manufactured by Pyrok Ltd for the ceiling. After completion cracks appeared in the ceiling and the architects asked Pyrok Ltd to remedy them. This they did. The architects did nothing further and issued a final certificate. Later more cracks appeared in the ceiling, which expert examination revealed was unsafe. The trial judge, Judge Stabb, Q.C., held that the architects were not liable to the plaintiffs for accepting and approving Pyrok's specification for the ceiling. They were, however, held liable for failing to check the design and for failing to see that the defective design was replaced by an effective one. The judge further held that they were negligent in issuing the final certificate. In the course of his judgement Judge Stabb adopted the words of Sachs L.J. in *Brickfield Properties v. Newton*:

> The architect is under a continuing duty to check that his design will work in practice and to correct any errors which may emerge.[17]

The judgement of Judge Stabb was upheld by the Court of Appeal.

It is the second exception which has attracted the most attention. At the outset it needs to be stressed that the nature of the general duty owed by professionals involved in the design of construction projects has not always been entirely free from doubt. Indeed, for a time, it was thought that architects and engineers were subject to a general regime of strict liability. The authority most often quoted for this view is *Greaves & Co. (Contractors) Ltd v. Baynham Meikle*. In that case contractors agreed to design and construct a warehouse and office for a company who intended to use the warehouse as a store for oil drums. Those oil drums were to be kept on the first floor and moved into position by fork-lift trucks. The contractors engaged structural engineers to design the structure of the warehouse and the contractors told them the purpose for which it was required. The engineers in their design did not take into account the effect of the vibrations from the fork-lift trucks. The result was that the floor cracked under the weight of the oil drums and of the trucks. It was held that the defendants were in breach of an implied warranty that the floor would be fit for the purpose for which they knew it was required. Lord Denning said:

> ... the owners made known to the contractors the purpose for which the building was required, so as to show that they relied on the contractor's skill and judgement. It was therefore the duty of the contractors to see that the finished work was reasonably fit for the purpose for which the building was required. It was not merely an obligation to use reasonable care.[18]

However, the Court of Appeal was careful to emphasise that there was no such general implied term in contracts for the supply of services and that the decision depended upon the particular facts of the case. Thus, Lord Denning stated:

> The law does not usually imply a warranty that [a professional person] will achieve the desired result, but only a term that he will use reasonable care and skill. The surgeon does not warrant that he will cure the patient. Nor does a solicitor warrant that he will win the case. But, when a dentist agrees to make a set of false teeth for a patient, there is an implied warranty that they will fit his gums: see *Samuels v. Davis* [1943] 2 All ER 3.[19]

Geoffrey Lane L.J. said:

> No great issue of principle arises in this case .... The suggestion that by reason of this finding every professional man or every consultant engineer by implication of law would be guaranteeing a satisfactory result is unfounded.[20]

Even without these caveats *Greaves* would not be an entirely satisfactory case on which to base a general principle of professional liability in the construction industry, because the case involved a package deal or design and build contract instead of the usual JCT form of contract where the architect or engineer is employed directly by the building owner and has no contractual relationship with the contractor. Further, the leading judgement in the case, that of Lord Denning, was not entirely unequivocal on the question of professional liability in the construction industry. After his remarks on the standard of duty required of the professional person in general he went on to say of construction industry professionals:

> What then is the position when an architect or an engineer is employed to design a house or a bridge? Is he under an implied warranty that, if the work is carried out to his design, it will be reasonably fit for the purpose? Or is he only under a duty to use reasonable skill and care? This question may require to be answered some day as a matter of law. But, in the present case I do not think we need answer it.[21]

The door to the imposition of a general duty of strict liability on construction professionals was not, it seems, shut tight and in *Independent Broadcasting Authority v. EMI Ltd* and *BICC Ltd*, certain dicta of Roskill L.J. in the Court of Appeal and Lords Fraser and Scarman in the House of Lords seemed to push it open a little further. That case concerned a contract to erect a 1250 foot (380 metre) high TV mast for the IBA. EMI were the main contractors and BICC the subcontractors who were responsible for the design of the mast. In bad, though not exceptional, weather conditions the mast collapsed, after just over three years in service. The Court of Appeal held that there was an implied term in the contract for the construction of the mast that it should be fit for its intended purpose and there was nothing in the contractual documents to exclude that implied term. The contractors had promised to erect a mast, and it was implicit in that promise that the mast would achieve the desired object, in so far as it was within the power of the contractors to determine that. Roskill L.J., in referring to a builder employed to build a house, said:

> We see no good reason ... for not importing an obligation as to reasonable fitness for the purpose into these contracts or for importing a different obligation as to design from the obligation which plainly exists in relation to materials.[22]

The House of Lords upheld the Court of Appeal's decision, though on different grounds. The basis of their decision was that BICC had been negligent in the design of the mast and EMI were under a contractual responsibility to IBA for the design of the mast which included responsibility for a negligent design.

In effect, the House of Lords' decision amounted to an imposition of strict liability on the main contractor, though by a different route from the decision of the Court of Appeal. The main significance of their Lordships' decision for design professionals, however, was certain dicta of Lords Fraser and Scarman which appear to lend support to the Court of Appeal's importation of an implied term as to fitness for purpose in building contracts. Lord Fraser said:

> The principle that was applied in *Young v. Marten Ltd* in respect of materials, ought in my opinion to be applied here in respect of the complete structure, including its design. Although EMI had no specialist knowledge of mast design, and although IBA knew that and did not rely on their skill to any extent for the design, I see nothing unreasonable in holding that EMI are responsible to IBA for the design seeing that they can in turn recover from BICC who did the actual designing.[23]

Lord Scarman said:

> In the absence of any term (express or implied) negativing the obligation, one who contracts to design an article for a purpose made known to him undertakes that the design is reasonably fit for the purpose.[24]

Further support for the view that the law was moving towards an obligation of fitness for purpose on the part of design professionals seemed to be provided by the decision of Judge Davies, Q.C., in *Viking Grain Storage Ltd v. T.H. White Installations Ltd.*[25] The defendants entered into a design and build contract to construct a grain storage and drying installation on the plaintiffs' land. The plaintiffs alleged that: (i) some of the materials used by the defendant were defective; (ii) aspects of the construction work were inadequately performed; and (iii) the ground of the site was not adequately prepared. One of the preliminary issues in the case was whether the defendants' duty was one of reasonable care and skill or whether they were under a duty to produce a building which would be suitable for its contemplated purpose. The judge held that the defendants were liable if the installation fell below the standard of reasonable suitability for purpose and the exercise of reasonable care and skill would not amount to a defence.

The question of whether or not an architect or engineer is under an implied warranty that his design will be reasonably fit for the purpose was considered again by the Court of Appeal in *Hawkins v. Chrysler (UK) Ltd* and *Burne Associates.* The defendants (Chrysler) wished to have new showers installed in their foundry and they employed Burne, a firm of engineers, to prepare the design and specifications and to supervise the installation. After the work was completed the plaintiff, Hawkins, slipped on a puddle of water in the shower room after using the shower and sued Chrysler and Burne for his resulting injuries. He argued that (a) it was a term of the contract that Burne would use reasonable care and skill in selecting the material to be used for the floor, and (b) there was an implied warranty that the material used for the floor would be fit for use in a wet shower room. At first instance, the judge found that Burne was not negligent but was in breach of an implied warranty that they would provide as safe a floor as was practicable.

The Court of Appeal upheld the judge's finding on negligence but they were unanimous that there was nothing in the case to give rise to the implication of a warranty other than to take reasonable care and skill in preparing the design. Thus, Fox L.J. stated unequivocally:

> ... a professional man, in the exercise of his profession, is normally obliged only to use reasonable care and skill. That is reflected in the standard conditions of employment of architects in the RIBA Conditions, and in the standard conditions of engagement for design of engineering projects which is the ACE document – both of which stipulate for the use of reasonable care and skill.[26]

The decision in *Hawkins v. Chrysler* must remove much of the doubt that the ordinary duty of an architect or engineer is one of reasonable care and skill and that any higher duty will be the exception from this general rule. If confirmation for this conclusion is needed, then it is provided by a medical case, that of *Thake v. Maurice.*[27] The plaintiffs, who were husband and wife, contracted with the defendant surgeon for a vasectomy to be performed. The surgeon emphasised to the plaintiff the irreversible nature of the operation, but he failed to point out the risk of it not proving successful. In the event, the operation was not successful, as was evidenced when Mrs Thake became pregnant for the sixth time. The plaintiffs' action for breach of contract succeeded at first instance, Pain J. stating that the surgeon had contracted to produce a particular result, viz. rendering Mr Thake permanently sterile. However, his judgement on this point was reversed by a majority of the Court of Appeal, who said that the surgeon's statements did not amount to a guarantee.

These two latest decisions of the Court of Appeal on this subject must strengthen the view that there is *no* general duty of fitness for purpose imposed upon a supplier of professional services. Such a duty will, however, exist if the supplier expressly or implicitly agrees that the provision of his services will achieve a particular result – on reflection, a not dissimilar position from that obtaining in contracts for the sale of goods by virtue of section14(3) of the Sale of Goods Act 1979.

A continuing duty?

We have seen that there is a dictum of the Court of Appeal to the effect that a design professional has a duty to see that his design works in practice.[28]

This was referred to as a continuing duty, though in fact it is simply an aspect of the normal duty to use reasonable care and skill to produce an effective design. If, some years later, defects in the design are revealed, this is merely evidence that on completion of the design contract the design was defective.[29]

In *Eckersley v. Binnie*[30] the question of whether a professional person may continue to owe a duty to his client to advise him of professional developments after the terms of his engagement have been completed arose.

Between 1972 and 1979 a link was designed and built between the River Lune and the River Wyre at Abbeystead. The link was designed by the first defendants, Binnie & Partners (Binnie) between 1972 and 1978, constructed by the second defendants (Nuttalls), tunnelling contractors, and after 1979 operated by the third defendants, the *North West Water Authority*. In May 1984 a party of 38 people visited the pumping works at Abbeystead. While they were at the pumping works there was an explosion in the valve house, caused by an accumulation of methane in a void in the ground which was pumped into the valve house and probably ignited there by a match or cigarette lighter. All those in the valve house were injured and 16 died. The trial judge held all three defendants to be negligent and apportioned the losses between them. All three appealed. The Court of Appeal held:

(1) The first defendant's appeal failed because there was a risk of methane being present which should have been taken account of in the design. The presence of the methane would have been detected by adequate testing and the later activities of the third defendants did not break the chain of causation.
(2) Although the tunnelling contractors were in breach of their contractual duty to test for methane, that did not give rise to breach of any duty of care to the plaintiffs because the scope of that duty was restricted to ensuring that the tunnel was safe for those who used it in the construction process.
(3) There was no negligence on the part of the water authority because at the date of the accident they had no reason to suspect that the first defendants had negligently failed to supervise the construction of the link.

At first sight, this decision suggests that the design engineers had a duty to monitor developments in the tunnel after completion of the design stage of the project. Bingham L.J., while not ruling out entirely the existence of such a duty, struck a very cautious note about it, pointing out how novel and burdensome such an obligation would be. He said:

> What is plain is that if any such duty at all is to be imposed, the nature, scope and limits of such a duty require to be very carefully and cautiously defined. The development of the law on this point, if it ever occurs, will be gradual and analogical. But this is not a suitable case in which to launch or embark on the process of development, because no facts have been found to support a conclusion that ordinarily competent engineers in the position of the first defendants would, by May 1984, have been alerted to any risk of which they were reasonably unaware at the time of handover. There was, in my view, no evidence to support such a conclusion. That being so, I prefer to express no opinion on this potentially important legal question.[31]

In tort

It was assumed until the 1970s that where a professional practitioner had a contractual relationship with a person alleging negligence against him, any claim had to be a claim for breach of contract only, the contract defined the duty and there could be no liability in the tort of negligence. This approach was taken in *Groom v. Crocker,*[32] a case involving a claim against a firm of solicitors for damages for injured feelings and reputation. It was held that the claim had to be in contract, not in tort. Scott L.J. said:

> A solicitor, as a professional man, is employed by a client just as much as is a doctor, or an architect, or a stockbroker, and the mutual rights and duties of the two are regulated entirely by the contract of employment.[33]

In *Hedley Byrne v. Heller*[34] the House of Lords held that 'if someone possessed of a special skill undertakes, quite irrespective of contract, to apply that skill for the assistance of another person who relies on such skill, a duty of care will arise'.[35] The relationship of this principle with the rule in *Groom v. Crocker* was assessed by the Court of Appeal in *Esso Petroleum v. Mardon.*[36] The defendant entered into pre-contractual negotiations with the plaintiffs with a view to becoming tenant of a garage. During the negotiations the plaintiffs made estimates of annual throughput which were prepared negligently. In reliance on these estimates, the defendant entered into a contract with the plaintiff and suffered loss for which he counterclaimed when sued by them for the price of petrol supplied. The Court of Appeal found the plaintiff liable both in contract and in tort under the principle in *Hedley Byrne.* Lord Denning expressly disapproved *Groom v. Crocker* and said:

> ... in the case of a professional man, the duty to use reasonable care arises not only in contract, but is also imposed by the law apart from contract, and is therefore actionable in tort.[37]

That decision was followed in *Midland Bank Trust Co. Ltd v Hett Stubbs & Kemp*[38]. Oliver J. held that there was no rule of law which precluded a claim in tort for breach of a duty to use reasonable care and skill if there was a parallel contractual duty of care. He preferred the decision in *Esso* to that in *Groom*.

The effect of these decisions was clearly to establish that a professional person may face concurrent liability, i.e. liability in tort and in contract.

The development of concurrent liability is of importance for the liability of professional persons in two particular respects: (i) the rules relating to remoteness of damages in tort and contract; and (ii) the different limitation periods which may exist in contract and tort.

In relation to remoteness of damages, the ambit of liability is likely to be much wider in tort than in contract. In tort the defendant is liable for all the damage of any kind that is reasonably foreseeable. In contract the defendant is liable for such loss as he should have realised would be sufficiently likely to result from the breach.[39]

In relation to limitation periods, under the Limitation Act 1980 an action in tort or contract cannot be brought after the expiration of six years from the date on which the cause of action arose. In breach of contract cases the limitation period will begin to run from the date of the breach. In actions in negligence the limitation period does not begin until the damage takes place, which may be some years later. Thus, a plaintiff may be out of time in contract, but still in time in tort. In *Midland Bank v. Hett Stubbs & Kemp*, for example, a solicitor negligently failed to register an option as an estate contract, and when the grantor of the option later sold the land in question to a third party and defeated the option, the grantee sued the solicitor for tortious negligence. The solicitor argued that the cause of action lay in contract only and that since his failure to register the option had occurred more than six years before the commencement of the action against him, it fell outside the limitation period. However, the limitation period in tort began when the option was sold which was less than six years before the grantee commenced his action.

Doubt has been cast upon the whole question of alternative causes of action by certain dicta of Lord Scarman delivering the advice of the Privy Council in *Tai Hing Cotton Mill Ltd v. Liu Chong Hing Bank Ltd*:

> Their Lordships do not believe that there is anything to the advantage of the law's development in searching for a liability in tort where the parties are in a contractual relationship.[40]

Lord Scarman went on to say that it is correct in principle and necessary for the avoidance of confusion in the law to adhere to the contractual analysis.

If taken literally, this dictum would rule out any action for negligence between the parties to a contract. A more likely interpretation of it is that where a contract imposes a duty of care upon one party towards the other, the scope of that duty is governed exclusively by the contract, and will be no wider if the action is framed in tort. This is illustrated in particular by *Greater Nottingham Co-operative Society v. Cementation.*[41] The plaintiffs were building owners and the defendants were subcontractors for piling. The subcontractors entered into a collateral warranty agreement requiring them to exercise reasonable care and skill in the design of the works and the selection of materials. This contract was silent as to the manner in which the piling works were to be executed. As a result of the negligent operation of the piling equipment by one of subcontractors' employees, damage was caused to an adjoining building and work was suspended while a revised piling scheme was worked out. The defendants agreed that they were liable for the damage to the adjoining building, but the plaintiffs also claimed, *on the basis of tort,* damages for:

(i) the additional cost to them paid under the main contract as a result of executing the revised piling scheme (£68 606);
(ii) the additional sums which they paid to the main contractor as a result of the delay in putting in piles (£79 235) and;
(iii) their consequential loss resulting from delayed completion of the building (£282 697).

This was a claim for economic loss. The Court of Appeal said that as a matter of policy the circumstances in which such losses were recoverable in tort was limited to exceptional cases. Further, if there was a contract between the parties, it was to be assumed that they had defined in that contract on what basis, if any, one party was to be liable to the other for economic loss. On the facts, the parties had defined their relationship in the collateral contract. That contract did not provide for the defendants to be liable for the manner in which they executed the piling work or for them to be directly responsible to the plaintiffs for economic loss. The Court of Appeal said that, given the existence of that contract, the defendants had not assumed any responsibility beyond that expressly undertaken in it.

Three recent decisions of the Official Referee show that the boundaries of concurrent liability have yet to be drawn with certainty. In *Hiron and Hiron and Legal Assurance Society Ltd v. Pynford South Ltd*[42]. Judge Newey said that where there was a contract between two parties the only result of adding a tortious obligation would be to give the plaintiff a longer period in which to sue. He went on to say, with reference to the instant case, that if that had been the intention of the parties then they could have provided as such in the contract. In *Lancashire and Cheshire Association of Baptist Churches Inc. v. Howard Seddon Partnership*[43] Judge Michael Kershaw, Q.C., held that there could be a tortious duty of care where the parties were in a professional relationship. However, the implied as well as the express terms of the contract would limit the extent of that duty. The judge said that the existence of a duty in tort is not precluded by the existence of a contract. In laying down this principle the judge rejected the defendant's argument that there should not be a concurrent duty in tort because that would deprive him of his rights under the statute of limitations. The judge said that if limitation was relevant in this context, it showed that it was just and reasonable that there should be concurrent liability. It is important to note, however, that the judge held that the employer in this case could not recover purely financial loss, but only for personal injury and damage to property. In *Wessex Regional Health Authority v. HLM Design & Others,*[43a] Judge Fox-Andrews held that an architect and an engineer engaged under standard terms of appointment by an employer in the context of a JCT 80 building contract did owe to the employer concurrent duties in contract and tort to avoid or prevent financial loss. The judge based his decision on the reliance principle; he said that where a person enters into a contract with a professional person there is not only reliance on that professional person to exercise care in the performance of his skill, but also reliance that he will take care to avoid or prevent financial loss.

It seems that concurrent liability is not yet dead; indeed, such liability may be about to experience a further renaissance.[44]

SUPERVISION OF THE BUILDING CONTRACT

In supervising the building contract the architect (or, in the case of an engineering contract, the engineer) takes on two quite separate and distinct roles. In the first place, he becomes the agent of the employer to see that the works are executed in accordance with the design. Secondly, he has the task of issuing certificates authorising payment to the contractor when each stage of the project has been satisfactorily completed, up to and including the issue of the final certificate when the project has been completed. Each of these roles requires independent examination in this section of the chapter.

Duties as agent

Agency is a concept central to commercial law but it is possible in this work to deal with its application to the role of the architect or engineer in supervising the works in outline only.[45]

The most important concept in the law of agency is that of the agent's authority. A distinction is usually made between the express authority, the implied authority and the ostensible authority of an agent. The express authority of an agent is the authority which is conferred on him by agreement with the principal. The implied authority of an agent is the power which he has to do everything which is necessary to the carrying out of his express duties or which an agent of his type would usually be empowered to do. The ostensible authority of an agent is his authority as it appears to others.

The express powers of the architect or engineer are contained in the standard form building contracts.[46] These powers do not normally extend to entering into contracts on behalf of the employer. Essentially they amount to representing the interests of the employer during the course of the works. As a consequence the implied authority of the architect or engineer is very limited. He has an express duty to certify payments to the contractor and this will usually mean that he has implied authority to ensure that the work is carried out according to the terms of the contract. He has no implied authority to vary the terms of the contract or to order variations of the works.

Duties as certifier

In *Sutcliffe v. Thackrah* Lord Salmon expressed the architect's duty as certifier in the following terms.

> The building owner and the contractor make their contract on the understanding that in all such matters the architect will act in a fair and unbiased manner and it must therefore be implicit in the owner's contract with the architect that he shall not only exercise due care and skill but also reach such decisions fairly, holding the balance between his client and the contractor.[47]

The architect's duty of impartiality in acting as certifier has raised the question of whether he can be successfully sued if he performs this role negligently. For reasons of public policy,[48] judges and arbitrators have immunity from actions for negligence and it was once thought that this immunity extended to an architect in his role as certifier. The main authority for this point of view is *Chambers v. Goldthorpe*,[49] where the

Court of Appeal, by a majority, held that in issuing certificates the architect occupied the position of an arbitrator and so could not be sued for negligence in the exercise of those functions.

That view was overruled by the House of Lords in *Sutcliffe v. Thackrah.* In that case the plaintiff employed the defendants, a firm of architects, to design a house for him. Subsequently, he entered into a contract with a firm of builders to build the house. The defendants were appointed architects and quantity surveyors. During the carrying out of the works they issued interim certificates to the builders. Before the builders had completed the works the plaintiff turned them off the site, and another firm completed the works at higher cost. The original builders subsequently went into liquidation. The plaintiff brought an action against the defendants for damages for negligence and breach of duty in supervising the building of the house and in certifying for work not done or improperly done by the original builders. The House of Lords held that in issuing interim certificates an architect did not, apart from specific agreement, act as an arbitrator between the parties, and that he was under a duty to act fairly in making his valuation and was liable to an action in negligence at the suit of the building owner. The rationale of this decision was expressed with characteristic robustness by Lord Reid:

> There is nothing judicial about an architect's function in determining whether certain work is defective. There is no dispute. He is not jointly engaged by the parties. They do not submit evidence as contentious to him. He makes his own investigations and comes to a decision. It would be taking a very low view to suppose that without his being put in a special position his employer would wish him to act unfairly or that a professional man would be willing to depart from the ordinary honourable standard of professional conduct.[50]

LIABILITY TO THIRD PARTIES

Personal injury

The liability of the architect or engineer in negligence for personal injuries sustained by third parties has been laid down in a trilogy of cases reported in the Building Law Reports: *Clayton v. Woodman & Son (Builders) Ltd,*[51] *Clay v. A.J. Crump & (Contractors) Ltd and Others*[52] and *Oldschool v. Gleeson (Contractors) Ltd and Others.*[53]

In *Clayton v. Woodman* the plaintiff was a bricklayer employed by Woodman & Son, who were building contractors. They were engaged by the South Western Regional Hospital Board to install a lift in one of their hospitals. The lift was designed by a firm of architects. The design provided for the demolition of part of a roof adjacent to a gable wall. This work weakened the gable wall and the plaintiff tried (unsuccessfully) to persuade the architect to instruct that it should be demolished. When the plaintiff, during the course of construction work, removed part of the wall, the wall toppled and fell onto him, injuring him. The trial judge held that the contractors, the regional hospital board and the architects were liable. The architects appealed and the Court of Appeal held that they were not liable in these circumstances. They said that an architect does not undertake to advise a builder as to what safety precautions should be taken or as to how the building operations should be carried out. That is the function of the builder.

In *Clay v. Crump* an architect supervising some demolition work instructed the demolition contractor to leave temporarily standing a wall. He accepted the contractor's word that the wall was safe and did not check it himself. In fact, the wall was tottering unstably over a 6 foot (1.8 metre) trench and collapsed, injuring one of the contactor's men. The Court of Appeal held that the architect, together with the demolition contractor and the contractor, was liable because the plaintiff's injuries were a foreseeable consequence of his not inspecting the wall.

In *Oldschool v. Gleeson* the plaintiffs owned two houses. They employed the first defendants, the contractors, to redevelop them. The second defendants were the consulting engineers. The works required one of the houses to be demolished. When this was done the party wall between that house and the adjoining property collapsed. Under a party wall agreement the owners of that property were awarded damages of £16 788 against the plaintiffs. The first defendants admitted their liability to indemnify the plaintiffs, but sought to recover that indemnity from the consulting engineers. Judge Stabb dismissed their claim. He said that the duty of the consulting engineers to the contractors did not extend to the execution of the works. It was no more than a duty to warn the contractors to take the necessary precautions. This they had done.

In conclusion, it may be said that the architect or engineer visiting the site in a supervisory capacity does so in order to ascertain whether the works are being constructed in accordance with the design, and not in order to control the contractor's execution of the work. The architect or engineer may be liable for personal injuries which result from a defect inherent in the design or from his actual control of the works. However, he will not be liable if the plaintiff's injuries result from the contractor's negligently constructing the works.

Liability to the purchaser for defects in the building

As we saw in Chapter 2, the law of negligence in the area
not dangerous, buildings has been the subject of considerable change over the last two decades. In *Dutton v. Bognor Regis UDC*[54] and *Anns v. Merton LBC*[55] it was held that purchasers of properties, who were not party to any contract with the contractors or design professionals, could claim against them in negligence if the building was a danger to the health and safety of the occupants. Those decisions were overruled by the House of Lords in *Murphy v. Brentwood DC.*[56] Their Lordships in that case strongly emphasised that a dangerous defect in a building once it became apparent was a defect in quality and the building was therefore worth less than it was supposed to be. The cost of repairing such a building was a form of economic loss and the view of the House of Lords was that to permit the purchaser to recover such loss would lead to an unacceptably wide category of claims. The Law Lords laid great stress on the fact that they saw the existence of such a duty as leading to liability in negligence for defective, though not dangerous, products. It is now virtually impossible, therefore, for the purchaser or lessee of a building which is defective because of a negligent design to successfully sue the architect or engineer who produced that design. The only circumstances in which such purchaser or lessee may be able to succeed against the design professional is if he can show that he relied on the design.[57] In practice, such reliance will be very difficult to establish.

Liability to the contractor for economic loss

The principal question which arises in this context is the extent, if any, to which the architect/engineer can be held liable for economic loss to the contractor resulting from his negligence.

If the contractor's economic loss can be said to result from a negligent *act* of the architect/engineer, then it must be clear, following *Murphy*, that such loss will not be recoverable. If, however, the contractor's economic loss can be said to result from a negligent *statement* made by the architect/engineer, then the position is not so clear-cut.

In *Hedley Byrne v. Heller* the House of Lords limited the circumstances in which liability for loss resulting from a statement will be imposed to cases where there was a special relationship between the parties. Such a relationship may be said to arise where the defendant makes an undertaking, whether expressly or impliedly, that he will exercise care in giving information or advice and the person to whom he gives that information or advice, or to whom he can reasonably apprehend such information or advice will be passed on, places reliance on it, irrespective of whether there is a contract between the maker of the statement and its receiver.

The precise scope of this principle remains unclear and the extent to which architects or engineers are liable to third parties under it is still not certain. In *Arenson v. Cason Beckman Rutley & Co.* Lord Salmon stated:

> The architect owed a duty to his client, the building owner, arising out of the contract between them to use reasonable care in issuing his certificates. He also, however, owed a similar duty of care to the contractor arising out of their proximity.[58]

That was in the heady days of *Dutton* and *Anns* and the expansionist phase of the tort of negligence. Since then the courts have been less willing to create new tortious duties and have re-emphasised the network of contractual relationships as the means of recovering losses. The architect's duty to the contractor to prevent his occurring economic loss must be looked at in the light of this new orthodoxy.

In *Michael Salliss & Co. Ltd v. Calil and William F. Newman & Associates*[59] the architect was alleged by the contractors wrongfully to have granted an extension of 12 weeks instead of the 29 claimed. Judge James Fox-Andrews held that the contractor could have a right of action against an architect who failed to exercise reasonable care and skill in certification. However, the judge went on to say that in many respects the architect owes no duty to the contractor.

> He owes no duty of care to contractors in respect of the preparation of plans and specifications or in deciding matters such as whether or not he should cause a survey to be carried out. He owes no duty of care to a contractor whether or not he should order a variation.[60]

In *Pacific Associates v. Baxter*[61] the plaintiffs were contractors who had tendered 'for dredging and reclamation' work on the basis, *inter alia*, of reports prepared by the defendant engineer. The contractor claimed that the dredging process was rendered more expensive and more difficult due to the presence in the creek to be dredged of a high percentage of hard material which necessitated the use of more powerful machinery. He contended that the information given by the engineer in his reports at the tender stage was inaccurate in that it failed to indicate the extent of the presence of the hard rock. The plaintiffs argued that the relationship between themselves and the engineer was so close that the engineer would be aware that any negligence by him would lead to loss on the part of the contractor and that the engineer must be taken to have assumed responsibility for any such foreseeable losses. This argument was rejected by the Court of Appeal because under the terms of the contract between the engineer and the contractor the engineer was not to be liable for any such losses incurred by the contractor. The main judgement was that of Purchas L.J., and the key passage in his judgement is as follows:

> I have come to the conclusion ... that no liability can be established in tort under which the engineer owed a direct duty to the contractor in the circumstances disclosed in this case. I emphasise, however, in coming to this conclusion it does depend on the particular circumstances of the case, not the least of which were the contractual provisions in the contract which afforded an avenue enabling the contractor to recover from the employer.[62]

The decision in *Pacific Associates* has been followed by the High Court of Hong Kong[63] and by the Supreme Court of Canada.[64] However, because the circumstances of the case are rather special, the decision cannot be said to be conclusive of the issue under consideration. Moreover, the liability of the architect or engineer for the negligent infliction of economic loss on the contractor must now be considered afresh in the light of the decision of the House of Lords in *Caparo v. Dickman.*[65] In that case their Lordships proposed a new and specific test for the duty of care concerning the recovery of economic loss caused by negligent misstatement. Under this test liability for negligent misstatement is established if:

(1) the defendant knew that his statement would be communicated to the plaintiff, either as an individual or as a member of an identifiable class;
(2) he knew it would be communicated specifically in connection with a particular transaction or transactions of a particular kind;
(3) the plaintiff would be very likely to rely on it for the purpose of deciding whether or not to enter upon that transaction or upon a transaction of that kind; and
(4) the plaintiff did in fact rely on it.[66]

The question for present purposes is whether, following the *Caparo* test, an architect/engineer will owe a duty of care to a contractor for economic loss caused by, say, a negligent design or the negligent issue of a certificate. All four limbs of this test appear to be satisfied in circumstances of that kind. Firstly, the architect/engineer must know that his certificate or design will be communicated to the contractor. Secondly, he clearly knows that such documents are communicated specifically in connection with a particular transaction, i.e. the construction contract. The third limb, reliance, is more problematical. The issue in this respect is whether the contractor relied on the architect/engineer to produce an accurate design and to make fair and accurate statements in his certificates. In *Caparo* the House of Lords said that there will be reliance where there are 'such close and direct relations' between the parties as to amount to a relationship of proximity. Arguably, under the usual JCT and ICE contracts, where the architect or engineer is given considerable powers of supervision, the relationship of contractor and architect/engineer is close enough to satisfy the third limb of the *Caparo* test. Fourthly, the contractor clearly does in fact place reliance on the architect or engineer's design and certificates. It cannot be long before this issue is put before the appellate courts.

The Defective Premises Act 1972

Section 1 of the Defective Premises Act 1972 creates a general duty on all persons taking on work for or in connection with the provision of dwellings to see that the work is done in a workmanlike or professional manner, with proper materials and so that the dwelling will be fit for habitation. The duty applies to professional persons such as architects or engineers as well as to builders and developers. It may be enforced independently of any contract which may exist, by any person acquiring an interest in the dwelling.

In a number of ways, the duty imposed by this statutory provision is narrow. Firstly, it applies only to dwellings; there is no liability under the provision for defective work on factories, offices and warehouses. Secondly, section 2 excludes actions for breach of the duty created by section 1 in respect of losses covered by an 'approved scheme'. The scheme principally envisaged by this section was the NHBC scheme, but the last NHBC scheme to be approved was their 1979 scheme. The 1985 and 1992 schemes are not approved, and owners of houses covered by these schemes can claim against builders and construction professionals under section 1.

Until recently the 1972 Act was not relied upon by owners of defective homes because the contractual and tortious duties imposed upon builders and construction professionals provided more effective remedies. However, the retreat of the law of negligence may well mean that owners of defective dwellings will seek to use its provisions as a means of obtaining a remedy. As we saw in Chapter 3, the key question for determination is the meaning of 'fitness for habitation' and, thereby, the extent of the loss recoverable under the Act.

NOTES

1. See *Greaves v. Co. (Contractors) Ltd v. Baynham Meikle & Partners* [1975] 3 All ER 99; and *Independent Broadcasting Authority v. EMI Electronics and BICC Construction* (1980) 14 BLR 1.
2. This form was issued in 1982 and superseded the RIBA Conditions of Engagement. It was amended in 1988. It is reprinted in *Emden's Construction Law*, 8th edn, Butterworths, 1990 (Issue 28, February 1993), Binder 4, Division F.
3. The latest edition of this form was issued in 1984 and amended in 1988. It is also reprinted in *Emden's Construction Law*, Binder 4, Division F.
4. For a full list of these duties see *Hudson's Building and Engineering Contracts*, 10th edn, 1970, pp. 103–4.
5. This duty is now contained in section 13 of the Supply of Goods and Services Act 1982.
6. But see later for a discussion on the question of whether an obligation of fitness for purpose can be imposed on an architect or engineer.
7. [1957] 2 All ER 118, p. 121.
8. (1853) cited in *Hudson's Building and Engineering Contracts* 10th edn, p. 127 and in *Jackson & Powell on Professional Negligence*, 3rd edn, 1992, p. 129 and p. 143, n.98. Cf. the approach to a novel design in *IBA v. EMI and BICC*, op.cit.
9. (1981) 18 BLR 80.
10. (1986) 38 BLR 36.
11. Section 4 of the Supply of Goods and Services Act 1982; see also *Young and Marten v. McManus Childs* [1969] 1 AC 454.
12. (1987) 38 BLR 25.
13. Section 16(3) of the Supply of Goods and Services Act 1982 expressly permits a duty stricter than that contained in section 13 to be imposed on the supplier of a service.
14. (1966) 14 BLR 50.
15. *Ibid.*, n.14, p. 55.
16. (1981) 18 BLR 130.
17. [1971] 1 WLR 862, p. 873.
18. *Ibid.*, n.1, p. 103.
19. *Ibid.*, n.1, p. 103.
20. *Ibid.*, n.1, p. 106.
21. *Ibid.*, n.1, p. 104.
22. (1979) 11 BLR 29, p. 52.
23. *Ibid.*, n.1. p. 45
24. *Ibid.*, n.1, (1980) 14 BLR 1, p. 48.
25. (1985) 33 BLR 103.

26. Supra, n.10, p. 51.
27. [1986] QB 644.
28. See n.17.
29. Similarly, in a contract for the sale of goods, where defects in the goods appear some time after the contract was made, that may be evidence that the seller was in breach of his statutory duty to supply goods under the contract of merchantable quality. There is no question, under the present law, of the seller being under a duty to sell goods which are durable (though see the proposals of the Law Commission in Law Com. No. 160 (1987)).
30. (1988) 18 Con. LR 1.
31. *Ibid.*, n.30, p. 147.
32. [1939] 1KB 194.
33. *Ibid.*, n.32, p. 222.
34. [1964] AC 465.
35. *Ibid.*, n.34 pp. 502–503.
36. [1976] QB 801.
37. *Ibid.*, n.36, p. 819.
38. [1978] 3 All ER 571.
39. *Koufos v. Czarnikow, The Heron* II [1969] 1 AC 350.
40. [1986] AC 80, p. 107.
41. [1988] 2 All ER 971.
42. Reported in (1992) *Chartered Surveyor Weekly* (6 February) 82.
43. [1993] 3 All ER 467.

43a. Reported in *Building*, 18 March 1994, p. 30.

44. For a more detailed analysis of concurrent liability see Holyoak (1990) 6 PN 113.
45. For a more detailed discussion of this subject see *Keating on Building Contracts*, 5th edn, 1991, pp. 305–12.
46. See, in particular, JCT '80, subclauses 13.2 and 13.3; and RIBA Architect's Appointment, subclauses 3(2), (3) and (4).
47. [1974] AC 727, p. 737.
48. See *Rondel v. Worsley* [1969] 1 AC 191.
49. [1901] 1 KB 624.
50. Supra, n.47, pp. 737–38.
51. (1977) 4 BLR 65 (judgement given on 9 March 1962).
52. (1977) 4 BLR 80 (judgement given on 30 July 1963).
53. (1977) 4 BLR 103.
54. [1972] 1 QB 373.
55. [1978] AC 728.
56. [1990] 2 All ER 908.
57. See the dicta of Lord Keith and Lord Oliver in Murphy, *ibid.*, n.56, p. 919 and p. 930, respectively.

58. [1977] AC 405, p. 438.
59. (1987) 13 Con. LR 68.
60. *Ibid.*, n.59, p. 79.
61. [1989] 2 All ER 159.
62. *Ibid.*, n.61, pp. 179–80.
63. *Lean Engineering and Construction Co. Ltd v. KA Duk Investment Co. Ltd* (1989) 47 BLR 139.
64. *Edgeworth Construction Ltd v. N.D. Lea & Associates* (1991) 54 BLR 11.
65. [1990] 1 All ER 568.
66. Per Lord Bridge, *ibid.*, n.65, p. 576, and Lord Oliver, *ibid.*, n.65, p. 589.

7 Liability of Surveyors

INTRODUCTION

We have seen in Chapters 2 and 6 that in the absence of a contract it is extremely difficult now for the purchaser of a defective building to bring a successful action against either the builder or the designer of the building. The reason for this is that the loss in such circumstances is likely to be economic and such loss is irrecoverable in the tort of negligence except where the relationship between the plaintiff and defendant can be brought within the scope of the principle in *Hedley Byrne v. Heller.*[1] This has had vital implications for surveyors because, following the decisions of the House of Lords in *Murphy v. Brentwood District Council*[2] and *Department of the Environment v. Bates,*[3] the only means by which a purchaser of a defective building may be able to recover his losses is to sue his surveyor. The liability of surveyors has, therefore, assumed a unique, and, for surveyors, an ominous, importance in Construction Law.

In order to grasp fully this particular subject it is necessary to make clear at the outset that a surveyor may be employed to carry out one of three different types of survey:

(i) a structural survey, which is a report on the structural soundness of the property concerned;
(ii) the RICS House Buyer's Report and Valuation (HBRV), which is a standard survey and report following a limited inspection of the property and which contains an indication of the value of the property; and
(iii) a mortgage valuation survey carried out under section 13 of the Building Societies Act 1986[4] in order to indicate whether the property is adequate security for the loan.

In the case of the first two types of survey the surveyor's client is usually the purchaser of the property concerned and any liability on the part of the surveyor will be contractual. In the case of a mortgage valuation survey, however, the client is the mortgagee and any liability owed by the surveyor to the purchaser will be tortious. It is in the case of mortgage valuation surveys that the most controversial developments in surveyors' liability have occurred, controversial in that they raise the vexed question of the true extent of a professional person's liability to third parties.

This chapter is divided into the following components of liability: the duty of care, the standard of care, damages recoverable for breach of the duty of care, and exclusion of liability. These are, of course, the components of the tort of negligence. Surveyors' liability has been at the forefront of recent developments in this tort but it must not be forgotten that a surveyor's principal obligation is contractual.

THE DUTY OF CARE

To the client

In considering the duty which is owed by a surveyor the most obvious starting point is to consider the duty which he owes to his client, with whom he will have a contract. The contract will normally be set out in writing and the written terms will determine the extent of the surveyor's obligations. Such a contract is known as a contract for services and the common law implies a term into this category of contract which requires the supplier of the service to carry out his duties under the contract with reasonable care and with the skill and competence of an ordinarily competent member of his profession or calling.[5]

A contract for services does not normally contain a term that the supplier will achieve a particular result and there is no term implied by law to that effect. However, the law does not prevent the supplier from taking on an obligation stricter than that of reasonable care and skill,[6] and there may be circumstances where such a term can be implied as a matter of fact.[7] The important point for the surveyor to remember is that in giving oral answers to questions from his client he must take great care to stress the limitations of his survey and avoid making statements which could amount to the giving of a guarantee and to the imposition of strict liability.

Following developments in the law of professional negligence in the 1970s it seems that a surveyor also owes a duty in tort (under the principle of *Hedley Byrne v. Heller*) to his client.[8] These developments must, however, be read subject to the dicta of the Privy Council in *Tai Hing Cotton Mill v. Lin Chong Hing Bank Ltd*[9] that where the parties are in a contractual relationship, there is nothing to the law's advantage or the law's development in searching for a liability in tort.[10]

To third parties

The most controversial development in the law of professional negligence has concerned the question of whether or not a professional person should owe a duty of care to a third party with whom he has no contract. In relation to surveyors this question has arisen in a case concerning a vendor's survey, *Shankie-Williams v. Heavey,*[11] and in three cases involving mortgage valuation surveys: *Yianni v. Edwin Evans & Sons,*[12] and *Smith v. Bush* and *Harris v. Wyre Forest District Council.*[13]

Vendors' surveys

In *Shankie-Williams v. Heavey* the owners of a house which had been converted into flats entered into negotiations for the sale of the ground floor flat. The prospective purchasers and plaintiffs, Mr and Mrs Shankie-Williams, suspected that the flat had dry rot. To reassure them the owners called in a dry rot specialist who reported that the flat contained no evidence of dry rot, though as a precaution he sprayed the timbers and gave a 30 year guarantee against reinfestation. As a result of these assurances the purchase went ahead. Meanwhile, the surveyor's report had been passed on to a prospective purchaser of the first floor flat, who took it as an indication that the whole house was free from dry rot and so he too went ahead with his purchase. Two years later substantial infestation of dry rot was discovered in both flats. The Court of Appeal held that the surveyor owed the ground floor purchasers a duty of care because he knew that his report would be passed on to them (that was the whole purpose of the survey). In legal terms, there was sufficient proximity between the parties to give rise to a duty of care. In the case of the purchaser of the first floor flat, the Court of Appeal held that the surveyor owed no duty to him because there was insufficient nexus or proximity between the parties.

Mortgage valuation surveys

Mortgage valuation surveys are the most controversial of all the situations involving the liability of a surveyor to a third party. In *Yianni,* the plaintiff, who wished to buy a house at a price of £15 000, applied to the Halifax Building Society for a mortgage. The Halifax engaged the defendants, a firm of valuers and surveyors, to value the property. The plaintiff had to pay for their report. They valued the property at £15 000 and assessed it as suitable for maximum lending. The Halifax offered the plaintiff a loan of £12 000 which he accepted and he purchased the house. After he moved in, cracks caused by subsidence were discovered and two years later the cost of repairing the property was estimated to be £18 000. The defendants admitted that they had been negligent in preparing the valuation report but they argued that they did not owe a duty of care to the plaintiff because his loss was the result of his own negligence in failing to commission an independent survey. This argument was dismissed by Park J., who found for the plaintiff. The judge held that a surveyor who carries out a mortgage valuation survey of a property for a building society which is contemplating advancing a loan to a prospective purchaser of that property owes a duty of care in tort to that purchaser.

The facts of *Smith v. Bush* are similar to those of *Yianni.* Mrs Smith bought a home, valued at £16 500, for £18 000 with the aid of a £3500 mortgage from the Abbey National Building Society. The building society, in pursuance of its statutory duty under section 13 of the Building Societies Act 1986, instructed Eric S. Bush, a firm of surveyors and valuers, to report on the value of the house. Mrs Smith paid a fee to the building society in respect of that report and she was sent a copy of it. The report contained a disclaimer of liability for the accuracy of the report covering both the building society and the surveyor. It also stated that it was not a structural survey and advised Mrs Smith to obtain independent professional advice. None the less, she relied on it and purchased the house without an independent survey. The building society's surveyor negligently failed to check the chimney supports, which were defective, and later a flue collapsed, causing substantial damage to the property. The surveyor conceded that he owed a duty of care to Mrs Smith and relied as a defence on the disclaimer in his report. The House of Lords approved the rule in *Yianni,* held that the disclaimer of liability was caught by the Unfair Contract Terms Act 1977, and ruled that it did not satisfy the reasonableness test in that Act.

The existence of the valuer's duty in tort to the mortgagor was unequivocally recognised by Lord Templeman in the following terms:

> ... in the absence of a disclaimer of liability the valuer who values a house for the purpose of a mortgage, knowing that the mortgagee will rely and the mortgagor will probably rely on the valuation, knowing that the purchaser mortgagor has in effect paid for the valuation, is under a duty to exercise reasonable care and skill and that duty is owed to both parties to the mortgage for which the valuation is made.[14]

It must be noted, however, that Lords Griffiths and Jauncey said that this duty applied essentially to valuations of dwelling-houses of modest value. They hinted strongly that the duty would be much more difficult to establish in the cases of valuations of industrial property and very expensive houses, where it would seem reasonable for the purchaser to obtain his own structural survey.[15]

In *Harris v. Wyre Forest* Mr and Mrs Harris purchased a small terraced house for £9000 with the aid of a 95 per cent mortgage from the defendant council. They completed and signed the council's standard mortgage application form and paid the inspection fee. The form stated that the valuation was confidential and intended solely for the benefit of the council and that no responsibility was accepted by the council for the value or condition of the property by reason of such inspection and report. It also advised the mortgagors to instruct their own surveyors, though it was found that neither Mr nor Mrs Harris read those words. The council's valuation surveyor valued the house at £9450 and recommended a mortgage subject to certain repairs. He noticed various signs of settlement but concluded that all the symptoms were referable to movement which had long since ceased. The purchasers were not shown the report but they were subsequently offered, and accepted, a mortgage by the council. Three years later they attempted to sell the house, but a survey revealed that structural repairs amounting to £13 000 were required. The house was regarded as uninhabitable and thus unsaleable.

This case differed from *Smith v. Bush* in that the valuation was carried out by an in-house valuer. Essentially this raised the issue of whether or not a mortgagee owes a duty of care to a mortgagor in respect of a valuation report on the property to be negotiated. In *Odder v. Westbourne Park Building Society*[16] Harman J. held that a building society owed no duty of care to purchasers in respect of a valuation report for mortgage purposes prepared by the chairman of the society. Their Lordships in Harris overruled that decision and concluded that the valuer owed a duty of care to the purchasers and that the local authority, as his employers, were vicariously liable for breach of that duty.[17] In coming to this conclusion the view of the Court of Appeal of Northern Ireland in *Curran v. Northern Ireland Co-ownership Housing Association Ltd*,[18] that a mortgagee who accepts a fee to obtain a valuation of a small house owes no duty of care to the mortgagor in the selection of the valuer to whom he entrusts the work, was disapproved.[19]

The theoretical basis of the valuer's duty in tort

Although the existence of the duty owed by a valuer to a mortgagor can now be stated with a reasonable degree of certainty the same cannot be said of its conceptual basis. There has in fact been considerable criticism of this duty, judicial as well as professional, and in *Smith v. Bush*, etc., there were differences of emphasis in the speeches of their Lordships on this point. Lords Templeman and Jauncey traced in detail the historical development of the valuer's tortious duty of care and if the difficulties in defining the rationale of that duty are to be fully appreciated, then it is necessary to recount this history.

In *Cann v. Willson*[20] a valuer instructed by a mortgagor sent his report to the mortgagee, who made an advance in reliance on the valuation. The valuer was held liable in the tort of negligence to the mortgagee for failing to carry out the valuation with reasonable care and skill on the ground that he knew that the valuation was for the purpose of a mortgage and would be relied on by the mortgagee. In *Le Lievre v. Gould*,[21] however, the Court of Appeal declared that decision to be wrong on the ground that it was inconsistent with, and overruled by, *Derry v. Peek*,[22] where the House of Lords held that the maker of a statement could only be liable in the tort of deceit when the statement was made with knowledge of its falsity or recklessly. In other words, there could be no liability where the maker of a statement possessed an honest belief in its truth, i.e. where the statement was made negligently or innocently.

This remained the law for another 70 years and various attempts to argue that the law had changed following the decision of the House of Lords in *Donoghue v. Stevenson*[23] failed. The one exception was the famous dissenting judgement of Denning L.J. in *Candler v. Crane, Christmas and Co.*[24] In that case the accountants of a company were asked by the company to prepare their accounts expressly for the purpose of being shown to a potential investor in the company. Denning L.J. said that the accountants owed a duty to the investor to exercise reasonable care and skill in preparing the draft accounts. In considering the question of whom accountants owe a duty to, he said:

> They owe a duty, of course, to their employer or client, and also, I think, to any third person to whom they themselves show the accounts, or to whom they know their employer is going to show the accounts so as to induce him to invest money or take some other action on them. I do not think, however, the duty can be extended still further so as to include strangers of whom they have heard nothing and to whom their employer without their knowledge may choose to show their accounts.[25]

The most significant development in the relationship of professional persons to third parties occurred in *Hedley Byrne v. Heller*. Since that decision, it has been clear that the absence of a contractual relationship is no longer a bar to a successful claim for economic loss resulting from a negligent misstatement. A duty of care will exist in such circumstances if there is a special relationship between the parties, such that it may fairly be said that the defendant has expressly or impliedly undertaken to exercise reasonable care and skill in giving information or advice. However, the precise circumstances which give rise to a special relationship were not laid down by their Lordships and they were far from unanimous in their ideas as to what the underlying basis of that relationship was. Thus, Lord Morris, with whom Lord Hodson agreed, said that a special relationship arises whenever it is reasonable for the plaintiff to rely on the defendant's words.[26] Lord Devlin, however, appeared to base the special relationship on the concept of a voluntary undertaking of responsibility.[27]

The implications of the decision in *Hedley Byrne* for the disclosure by a building society to a house buyer of a mortgage valuation report have been the subject of much debate. The decision of Park J. in *Yianni v. Evans* was a landmark in that debate. His judgement is interesting on two counts. Firstly, he applied Lord Wilberforce's well-known two-stage test to the facts and held that there was a sufficient degree of proximity between the surveyor and the mortgagor for a duty of care to arise. Secondly, he seemed to greatly extend the scope of the concept of reasonable reliance by stating that there was a sufficient degree of proximity between the surveyor and the mortgagor for a duty of care to arise, principally because evidence showed that most mortgagors did not arrange to have their own independent survey carried out and therefore the surveyor knew, or ought to have known, that the mortgagor would rely on his report to the building society.

That reasoning was subsequently criticised on the grounds that Park J.'s view of reasonable reliance was overgenerous; the mortgagor had not asked the building society for advice and the purpose of the survey was to assess the value of the security offered for the loan. In *Harris v. Wyre Forest* Kerr L.J. referred to the 'inherent jurisprudential weakness' of the reasoning in *Yianni* and subjected it to intensive scrutiny.[28] Significantly, however, he went on to say that the particular circumstances of purchasers of houses with the assistance of loans from building societies or local authorities are capable of leading to a different analysis and conclusion. In these circumstances it is now the practice of the lending institutions to show their valuer's report to the intending purchaser. Thus, in *Roberts v. Hampson & Co.* [29] Ian Kennedy J. said that the valuer knew, from the fact that a building society survey was being undertaken, that it was very unlikely that the intending purchaser was relying on an independent survey of the property. In *Davies v. Parry*[30] McNeill J. concluded that a sufficiently proximate relationship existed between the valuer and the purchaser in that case because the valuer had known that his report would be made available to the purchaser and there was only a one in four chance that he would arrange for a structural survey to be carried out.

In *Smith v. Bush* Lord Templeman said that the relationship between the valuer and the purchaser is 'akin to contract' in the sense that the valuer assumes responsibility to both mortgagee and purchaser, because he knows that the valuation fee has been paid for by the purchaser and the purchaser will probably rely on the valuation in deciding whether or not to purchase the house. Lord Griffiths doubted whether the voluntary assumption of responsibility was likely to be a helpful or realistic test in most cases.[31] He went on to say that a duty of care for advice was owed where three conditions were satisfied: (1) it must be foreseeable that if the advice is negligent the recipient is likely to suffer damage; (2) there must be a sufficiently proximate relationship between the parties; and (3) it must be just and reasonable to impose the liability.[32] Lord Griffiths said that in the case of a surveyor valuing a small house for a building society or local authority the application of all three criteria led to the imposition of a duty of care. The requirement of foreseeability was satisfied because, if the valuation was negligent and relied upon, the purchaser would obviously suffer economic loss. The necessary proximity arose from the fact that the surveyor must know that the overwhelming probability is that the purchaser will rely on the valuation. It was just and reasonable for a duty of care to be imposed because the advice was given in a professional, as opposed to a social, context and there was no danger of creating liability in an indeterminate amount to an indefinite class. Lord Jauncey drew attention to the difference between the cases of *Cann v. Willson, Candler v. Crane, Christmas & Co.* and *Hedley Byrne v. Heller*, and *Smith v. Bush.*[33] In each of the three former cases there was direct contact between the provider of the advice on the one hand and the plaintiff or his agent on the other hand; in *Smith v. Bush*, however, there was no direct contact between Mrs Smith and the valuer. Lord Jauncey thought that the relationship between valuer and purchaser was not 'equivalent to contract' in the sense used by Lord Devlin in *Hedley Byrne v. Heller*, but there was sufficient proximity between the parties for the valuer to be deemed to have assumed responsibility towards her; the valuer knew that Mrs Smith would be likely to rely on his valuation without obtaining independent advice and she had paid the valuation fee.

Given the lack of agreement on a test for determining when a duty of care for words arose, it is hardly surprising that *Smith v. Bush* has proved of little significance in the development of the tort of negligent misstatement as a whole. Of more significance in that respect was the decision of the House of Lords in *Caparo Industries plc v. Dickman*,[34] where it was held that auditors owe no duty of care either to members of the public or to existing shareholders who buy shares in a company in reliance on its audited accounts. Their Lordships restated the test for the existence of a duty of care for statements in the following terms:

(i) the person making the statement must be fully aware of the nature of the transaction which the plaintiff had in mind;

(ii) he must know that the statement would be communicated to the plaintiff either directly or indirectly;
(iii) he must know that it is very likely that the plaintiff would rely on that statement; and
(iv) it is so relied on by the plaintiff to his detriment.[35]

In relation to the duty of care of a mortgage valuation surveyor their Lordships emphasised that the crucial feature of *Smith v. Bush*, etc., was that the existence and scope of that duty were limited to the very person and the very transaction which were in the contemplation of the valuer at the time of the valuation, i.e. the mortgagor and the purchase of the property. In other words, the facts of the *Smith v. Bush* situation met the criteria laid down by the *Caparo* test.

It must be pointed out that the status of the *Caparo* test is still uncertain. In *Beaumont v. Humberts*,[36] where the defendant valuer was instructed by the mortgagee bank to carry out a valuation for insurance reinstatement purposes as well as a mortgage valuation, the question of whether the valuer owed a duty of care to the mortgagors was decided without reference to the test laid down by the House of Lords in *Caparo*. Instead the duty issue was approached on the basis of the three-stage test first put forward by the Court of Appeal in *Caparo*, i.e.:

(i) it must be foreseeable that if the advice is negligent the recipient is likely to suffer damage;
(ii) there must be a sufficiently proximate relationship between the parties; and
(iii) it must be just and reasonable to impose the liability.[37]

The overall result of these decisions is that the scope of surveyors' liability is now much wider than that of other professional advisers – in particular, accountants. The reasons for this disparity in treatment seem to rest largely on policy factors – in particular, the fact that the typical mortgagor is more likely to be in need of protection from the law than the takeover bidder and the fact that the damages awarded against a negligent mortgage valuation surveyor are more easily insurable than the damages awarded against a negligent auditor.[38]

THE STANDARD OF CARE

In circumstances where a duty of care is owed the key question is: what must a surveyor do to meet that duty? The essential principle governing this aspect of surveyors' liability is that a surveyor or valuer must carry out his duties with the care and skill of an ordinarily competent member of his profession. This is often referred to as the *Bolam* standard, after the dictum of McNair J. in *Bolam v. Friern Barnet Hospital Management Committee*:

> The test is the standard of the ordinary skilled man exercising and professing to have that special skill. A man need not possess the highest expert skill at the risk of being found negligent ... it is sufficient if he exercises the ordinary skill of an ordinary competent man exercising that particular art.[39]

This test of professional negligence has been approved by the House of Lords in a number of cases involving medical negligence.[40] However, it is of general application.[41]

The *Bolam* standard seems to imply that the courts are prepared to accept that professional negligence is a question to be determined by evidence from other practitioners. It is generally accepted, however, that the courts have the power to set the standard required of a profession. This means that a practitioner may still be liable in negligence even though he has complied with the collectively adopted standards in his profession. In practice, a court will rely heavily on expert evidence and any codified standards adopted by a profession.[42]

One thing is clear – a mere error of professional judgement will not amount to negligence unless 'it is so glaringly below proper standards as to make a finding of negligence inevitable'.[43] That principle has been applied on several occasions to valuations which have proved inaccurate.[44]

Three points need to be emphasised about the *Bolam* standard in the context of surveyors. Firstly, it is the standard which the surveyor must meet whether his duty is owed in contract to his client or in tort to a third party. Secondly, it is a negligence standard and, as such, this aspect of surveyors' liability is an application of the ordinary principles of negligence. Thirdly, in those circumstances where a surveyor owes a duty of care to a third party the scope of that duty is governed by the terms of the contract which he has made with his client.

The surveyor's contract

The first point of reference in determining whether or not a surveyor has been negligent is the contract which he has entered into. The basic obligation which the law imposes upon a surveyor is that he must carry out his instructions with reasonable care and skill. In other words, in determining whether or not a surveyor is guilty of negligence, it is first necessary to know what he was employed to do. If he was employed to carry out a valuation survey, then his duty is to conduct that kind of survey with the standard of care and skill which would be expected of an ordinary competent surveyor who performs valuation surveys. This point is illustrated by *Sutcliffe v. Sayer*.[45] In that case the plaintiffs, realising that the house which they wished to buy was priced rather lower than other apparently comparable properties, asked the defendant, a local estate agent who was experienced but unqualified, to report on its price and any defects which might affect its value. The defendant identified various defects but none the less recommended a purchase at about the asking price. The plaintiffs went ahead with the purchase at this price, but three years later when they put the property on the market they found that it was unsaleable because it was built on a substratum of peat (a factor which the defendant had not mentioned). The Court of Appeal held that the defendant was not negligent; the evidence established that his valuation of the property was accurate and he had not been asked to do anything more, such as investigating structural factors affecting resaleability.

The essentials of the negligence standard

The problem with the concept of reasonable care and skill is that it is difficult to determine in advance what must be done in a given situation to meet that requirement. Each case will turn on its own facts and in that sense the question of whether a surveyor has been negligent is one of fact rather than law. However, the law does lay down general guidelines to aid the courts in determining whether or not the standard of reasonable care and skill has been met in a particular situation, and in that respect the standard is a legal standard. A detailed treatment of these guidelines can be found in any text on the law of tort and it is necessary here only to outline them. They are:

(i) unforeseeable harm;
(ii) the magnitude of the risk;
(iii) the social utility of the defendant's conduct; and
(iv) the practicability of precautions.

Firstly, if the danger could not reasonably have been foreseen, then the defendant has not acted negligently.[46] Secondly, if the damage is foreseeable, then the defendant is only negligent if he fails to exercise a degree of care which is commensurate with the risk attaching to the activity concerned; the greater the risk of harm the greater the precautions that need to be taken.[47] Thirdly, the social utility of the defendant's activity may justify taking greater risks than would otherwise be the case.[48] Fourthly, reasonableness involves striking a balance between the risks involved and the expenditure required to eliminate, or at any rate reduce, that risk.[49]

It now remains to examine how the courts have applied these general principles to the various surveys undertaken by surveyors.

The HBRV

As already stated, this is a modified form of structural survey. The question of the difference between the two kinds of survey was discussed in *Cross v. David Martin & Mortimer.*[50] In that case the plaintiffs, a husband and wife, employed the defendant surveyor to conduct an HBRV on a house that they were considering purchasing. He reported that there was no evidence of structural fault or significant disrepair and they went ahead with the purchase. After moving in, the plaintiffs discovered that the lounge floor was irregular and that the hall had a noticeable 'hump'. Independent advice revealed subsidence, misalignments of doors on the first floor and problems with the loft conversion. Phillips J. found that the defendant was negligent on all three of the above counts, although he added that the survey was not slapdash and was not a reflection on his general competence. In general terms, the significance of the case is that in coming to this decision the judge noted the view of an RICS Working Party on the HBRV form that the same level of expertise was expected from a surveyor carrying out an HBRV as for a structural survey. This seems a surprising piece of evidence, given that an HBRV is less comprehensive than a structural survey and consequently carried out for a lower fee. The decision seems contrary to the general principles outlined above.

Mortgage valuations

It is the standard required in preparing a reasonably competent mortgage valuation which has caused the most concern in recent years.

Following the decision in *Yianni*, it was feared by surveyors that a mortgage valuation would have to become in effect a structural survey. These fears were increased by Kennedy J.'s (infamous) description of a competent mortgage valuation in *Roberts v. J. Hampson & Co.*[51] After stating the general principle that a mortgage valuation was an appraisal by a professional man and that his basic duty was to take reasonable care in providing a valuation, the judge went on to say:

> The second aspect of the problem concerns moving furniture and lifting carpets. Here again, as it seems to me, the position the law adopts is simple. If a surveyor misses a defect because its signs are hidden, that is a risk that his client must accept. But if there is specific ground for suspicion and the

> trail of suspicion leads behind furniture or under carpets, the surveyor must take reasonable steps *to follow the trail* [author's italics] until he has all the information which is reasonable for him to have before making his valuation.[52]

That dictum was quoted with approval by Lord Templeman in *Smith v. Bush*. However, Lord Griffiths defined the valuer's duty in more moderate terms:

> ... the inspection carried out is a visual one designed to reveal any obvious defects in the property which must be taken into account when comparing the value of the property with other similar properties in the neighbourhood. .... It is only defects which are observable by a careful visual examination that have to be taken into account.[53]

Recent decisions show that it is the more moderate approach which is prevailing in the courts. In *Whalley v. Roberts & Roberts*[54] the plaintiff mortgagors purchased a detached bungalow, built in 1978, with the aid of a mortgage from the Royal Bank of Scotland. The valuation for the mortgage was made by the defendant firm of surveyors. The mortgage valuation report stated that its purpose was to provide a valuation for a mortgage and was not a structural survey. It reported the standard of construction and the condition of the main structure to be satisfactory. On the day that the plaintiffs moved in they noticed that the floor of the bungalow sloped, though they had not noticed this on visits before moving in. The valuer's report made no mention of this defect and he said in evidence that it was not something for which he would have checked unless there was evidence of movement. In fact the fall from right to left, looking at the bungalow, was 3½ inches (88 mm) over a total width of 23 ft 6 in (7.16 m). There were no signs of subsidence but there was evidence of steps taken to camouflage the existence of the slope. Auld J., after referring to Lord Griffiths's dictum in *Smith v. Bush*, held that the valuer had not been negligent. In essence, this judgement illustrates the principle that a mortgage valuer is not negligent if the risk of harm suffered by the plaintiff was not reasonably foreseeable.

In *Lloyd v. Butler*[55] the plaintiff purchased a filthy and dilapidated property for £37 500 with the aid of a mortgage of £20 000 from the Alliance Building Society. The society instructed the defendant surveyor to carry out a mortgage valuation of the property. He reported that although it was a poorly maintained house of very basic quality, it provided the basis for a comfortable home and was acceptable as a security in its present condition. In a box on the report form headed 'Essential Repairs' he wrote 'None'. The plaintiff, relying on this, completed the purchase, but when, with the aid of a builder, she started to repair and improve the house, she discovered a number of serious defects – in particular, that it was heavily infested with woodworm, many of the roof tiles needed replacing, the bay window was in a state of collapse, and the wiring and central heating pipes needed to be replaced. Henry J. in his judgement set out his view of the nature and scope of a mortgage valuation. He said:

> It is clearly not a structural survey; it is a valuation. It is taken on the basis of the inspection which on average should not take longer than 20–30 minutes. It is effectively a walking inspection by someone with a knowledgeable eye, experienced in practice, who knows where to look ... to detect either trouble or the potential form of trouble. *He does not necessarily have to follow up every trail* [author's italics] to discover whether there is trouble or the extent of any such trouble. But where such an inspection can reasonably show a potential trouble or the risk of potential trouble, it seems to me that it is necessary ... to alert the purchaser to that risk, because the purchaser will be relying on [the valuation report] ....[56]

He held that the valuer had been negligent for failing to warn of the defects in the property.

The decisions in *Whalley* and *Lloyd* provide evidence that the courts are applying the basic principles of negligence to the question of the standard of care required of a mortgage valuer. In both cases the judges seemed well aware that a mortgage valuation was only a limited survey carried out for a limited price and did not amount to a structural survey. In practical terms the significance of the decisions can be stated as follows:

(i) if there are visible defects in the property or defects are discovered, the valuer's duty is to warn the mortgagee and the mortgagor of those defects, rather than investigate fully as in a structural survey; and
(ii) there is no duty on the valuer to discover unusual defects in the property, i.e. to guard against unusual risks.

On a more general note, the question of interest for mortgagors is whether the duty laid down in *Yianni*, and confirmed in *Smith v. Bush*, will lead to a rise in professional standards among valuers. This is a difficult question to determine, but those decisions have led to a change in the format of the mortgage valuation in that the RICS and the ISVA have drawn up joint guidelines for mortgage valuations.[57] Whether compliance with these guidelines will be sufficient to satisfy the duty imposed upon valuers has yet to be determined by the courts, but in *PK Finans International (UK) Ltd v. Andrew Downs & Co. Ltd* the judge passed the following comment upon them:

> These ... are not to be regarded as a statute. I suspect that they are as much for the protection of surveyors as anything else, in that they set out various recommendations which, if followed, it is hoped will protect the surveyor from the unpleasantness of being sued. *In any event, mere failure to comply with the guidance notes does not necessarily constitute negligence* [author's italics].[58]

Insurance valuations

In *Beaument v. Humberts* the Court of Appeal had to decide the meaning of valuation for insurance reinstatement purposes of a Grade II listed building. The appeal judges said that three meanings could be given to 'reinstatement':

(i) an exact copy;
(ii) a replacement which was as near as practicable to an exact copy; or
(iii) a sensible reconstruction in the same style but redesigned in parts to make it more liveable and more convenient.

The valuer adopted the third of these approaches and the majority of the Court of Appeal held that this was not negligent. In their view, the issue turned on the instructions given to the valuer, which were to provide the valuation for insurance re-instatement purposes; that did not mean an estimate for an exact copy. Dillon L.J., in his minority judgement, favoured the second of the above approaches. In the author's view, the minority view is to be preferred; if a house is burnt down completely, then surely the owner is entitled to have it rebuilt as nearly as possible to its original specification and not just a reconstruction in the same shape and style. However, the wider principle of the case – that the duty owed by a valuer cannot be divorced from the instructions given to him by his client – is sound.

DAMAGES

There are three issues which arise in relation to the question of damages awarded against a surveyor for a negligent survey:

(i) the appropriate measure of damages;
(ii) the scope for awarding compensation for distress to the purchaser and the basis on which it should be calculated; and
(iii) the measure of damages for a mortgagee relying on a negligent survey.

The measure of damages

There are two possible methods of assessing the general damages to be awarded for a negligent survey. Firstly, they can be assessed on the basis of the difference between the price paid for the property and what it was really worth at the time of purchase. Secondly, the damages can be assessed on the basis of the cost of repairing the defects in the property.

The question of which of these two measures is the correct one came before the Court of Appeal in *Phillips v. Ward*.[59] There, the plaintiff instructed the defendant surveyor to carry out a structural survey of a property which he was considering for purchase. The surveyor noted various minor defects in his report and valued the property at between £25 000 and £27 000. In reliance upon this report the plaintiff purchased the property for £25 000. It was subsequently discovered that the timbers in the property were badly affected by death-watch beetle and the cost of remedying that defect was estimated to be £7800. The official referee awarded damages of £4000, representing the difference between the surveyor's valuation (£25 000) and its value in its actual condition (£21 000). The Court of Appeal unanimously upheld that award.

The principles underlying their decision were stated in the judgement of Denning L.J. (as he then was). He said that the correct measure of damages was the amount of money which will put the plaintiff into as good a position as if the survey had been properly conducted. This was the difference between the value of the property in its assumed good condition and the value in the bad condition which should have been reported. As to whether the cost of the repairs was the correct measure, Denning L.J. said:

> ... if the plaintiff were to recover from the surveyor £7000, it would mean that the plaintiff would get for £18 000 (£25 000 paid less £7000 received) a house and land which were worth £21 000. That cannot be right.[60]

The reasoning of *Phillips v. Ward* was unanimously followed by the Court of Appeal in *Perry v. Sidney Phillips & Son*.[61]

The difference in value formula for measuring damages has not gone unchallenged, and it has been argued that it needs to be qualified in certain situations:

(i) where there is no market for the property in its defective state of repair; and
(ii) where it is not reasonable to expect the purchaser to place the property on the market once he has bought.

An example of the first of these situations was provided by *Steward v. Rapley*.[62] There, the Court of Appeal held that where the defects in the property are such that the ordinary purchaser would not buy without further investigation, then the repair costs were the basis for calculating the difference in value. The plaintiff had purchased a house for £58 500, slightly below the defendant surveyor's valuation of £60 000. Shortly after purchase, dry rot was discovered and there was evidence that an open market valuation of the house immediately after that discovery would have been £50 000. The final cost of repairing the house, once the true extent of the rot was discovered, turned out to be £26 800. The Court of Appeal said that diminution in value was the rule to be applied but refused to accept that £50 000 could be taken as the market value and £8500 (the difference between the alleged market value and purchase price) as the damages payable. The market value for the speculative buyer might have been £50 000, but for the ordinary purchaser the house had no market value until the full cost of repair had been calculated. Hence, the true market value was the original valuation of £60 000 minus the cost of repair, £26 800, producing a valuation of £33 200. The difference in value measure was then £58 500 (purchase price) minus £33 200 (market value calculated in accordance with the cost of repair). The result was an award of £25 300.

In a number of recent first instance decisions the cost of repair method has been held to be the proper basis for calculating damages.[63] Those decisions raised the question of whether the difference in value method was still the general rule. However, in *Watts v. Morrow*,[64] the Court of Appeal robustly defended the difference in value method and unanimously reaffirmed the principle laid down in *Phillips v. Ward*.

In *Watts*, the plaintiffs, a professional couple, purchased an old farmhouse in Dorset as a second home. They instructed the defendant to carry out a full structural survey. He produced a 27 page report and advised that the valuation was fair. Although the report listed a number of defects and recommended repairs, the defendant said that none of these would be very expensive. Subsequently, it was discovered that the defendant had overlooked a number of defects – in particular, the state of the roof – and that it would cost some £33 000 to put them right. The difference in value between the property in the condition the surveyor described and its actual condition in need of repair was £15 000. At first instance, Judge Bowsher awarded damages on the basis of the cost of repair (i.e. £33 961). His award was unanimously set aside by the Court of Appeal, who substituted damages of £15 000. In so doing they reaffirmed the rule in *Phillips*. Ralph Gibson L.J. said that the decision in *Phillips* is based on the principle that it is the task of the Court to award that sum of money which would, as far as possible, put the purchasers of the house in as good a position as if the contract for the survey had been properly fulfilled. He went on to say that the cost of repairs to put right defects negligently not reported may be relevant to proving the market value of the house in its true condition. But if the cost of repairs exceeds the diminution in value, then the ruling in *Phillips* prohibits recovery of the excess because it would put the purchasers in the position of recovering damages for breach of warranty that the condition of the house was correctly described by the surveyor, and in the ordinary case no such warranty was given. Bingham L.J. agreed, and added that if on learning of defects which should have been, but were not, reported a purchaser decides not to sell the house, then it was doubtful whether his losses could be laid at the door of the contract-breaker.

Finally, in this particular section, it should be noted that the cases have involved assessing damages for the clients of negligent surveyors. Actions by third parties, such as mortgagors, against surveyors have not raised the question of assessing damages. It has been argued that in circumstances where the mortgage valuer's report is not shown to the buyer the true measure of damages is the difference (if any) between the actual value of the property and the mortgage loan.[65]

Damages for distress and inconvenience

It seems now to be an accepted principle that damages can be awarded under this heading, but the crucial question is: On what basis are they made?

In *Perry v. Sydney Phillips* Lord Denning justified the award of a small sum for distress resulting from the purchase of a defective property on the ground that 'if a man buys a house for his own occupation on the surveyor's advice that it is sound and then finds out that it is in a deplorable condition, it is reasonably foreseeable that he will be most upset'. Kerr L.J. justified damages for distress in narrower terms, viz. that physical consequences to the purchasers were foreseeable as a result of the negligence.

In *Hayes v. Dodd*[66] Staughton L.J. stated that distress awards should be made only where the object of the contract was comfort, pleasure or the relief of discomfort. In *Watts* Judge Bowsher sought to award damages for distress on the basis of that principle. He stated:

> A prospective buyer of a house goes to a surveyor not just to be advised on the financial advisability of one of the most important transactions of his life but also to receive reassurance that when he buys the house he will have 'peace of mind and freedom from distress'.

The Court of Appeal in *Watts* stated the grounds on which damages for distress and inconvenience could be awarded much more narrowly. They said that such damages were only recoverable for distress caused by physical discomfort resulting from a breach of contract. There was no express or implied promise on the part of the surveyor for the provision of peace of mind or freedom from distress.

Damages for a mortgagee's losses

If a mortgagor defaults on the loan, then it is the mortgagee who stands to lose if the valuer has negligently overvalued the property. The principles on which these losses should be assessed were discussed by the House of Lords in *Swingcastle v. Gibson.*[67]

As the law stood before the House of Lords' ruling in *Swingcastle*, the lender who advanced money on the strength of a negligent overvaluation was treated differently from a purchaser who bought the property. The principle underlying the lender's position was stated by the Court of Appeal in *Baxter v. F.W. Gapp & Co. Ltd* as follows:

> The measure of damages ... is that which the plaintiff has lost by being led into a disastrous investment.[68]

In *Baxter* the mortgagees were unable to recover part of the money due to them under the mortgage, and the valuers were liable to restore this shortfall and, in addition, the unpaid interest owed by the borrower at the date when the security was realised.

In *Swingcastle* the plaintiff finance company lent £10 000 secured on a property which the defendant valuer said was worth £18 000. The loan was regarded by the plaintiffs as a high-risk loan and the interest charged was 36.5 per cent, rising to 45.6 per cent on everything outstanding if the borrowers fell into arrears. They did fall into arrears, and the plaintiffs took possession of the house and sold it a year later for £12 000. They sued the valuer for, among other things, the interest accrued under the mortgage contract, i.e. they calculated how much *should* have been repaid by the time that the property was resold. In the House of Lords, Lord Lowry, with whom their other Lordships agreed, said that *Baxter v. Gapp* was 'not an attractive precedent' because its approach seemed contrary to principle. Lord Lowry said that the principle on which damages should be assessed in this case was as follows:

> The aggrieved party was entitled to be placed in the same position as if the wrong had not occurred, and not to receive from the wrongdoer

compensation for lost interest at the rate which the borrower had contracted to observe.[69]

In other words, the lender is due for compensation on the basis of the rate of interest which the money could have earned if it had not been lent to the mortgagors, and *not* on the basis of the (high-risk) rate of interest under the terms of the mortgage. To assess damages on this latter basis would make the valuer, in effect, the guarantor of the mortgagors' creditworthiness.

EXCLUSION OF LIABILITY

The expansion of surveyors' liability in tort to third parties shifted the emphasis from whether such duties existed to whether liability for such duties could be excluded. As we have seen, it is standard practice for surveyors who conduct mortgage valuation surveys to include a clause in their report disclaiming responsibility for the report in the event of their negligence and advising mortgagors to commission their own independent survey. Clauses which attempt to exclude a restrict liability for negligence are controlled by the Unfair Contract Terms Act 1977 (UCTA). But before discussing the effect of that Act, it must first be asked whether its provisions do in fact apply to the clause in question.

The nature of disclaimers

There are two approaches to contractual clauses and notices which disclaim liability for negligence. Firstly, they can be regarded as defining primary obligations in contract or as preventing a tortious duty from arising. The second approach to such disclaimers involves the courts in determining whether or not there has been a breach of contract or whether a tortious duty arises and then seeing whether liability for such breach or duty has been effectively excluded.

Since the coming into effect of UCTA, generally the courts have adopted the second approach. However, in *Harris v. Wyre Forest DC* the Court of Appeal adopted the first approach. They said that although the local authority's valuation of the plaintiffs' house was negligent and although the plaintiffs as purchasers had relied on that valuation, the local authority owed no duty of care to the plaintiffs because the disclaimer in the mortgage application form prevented a duty of care from arising. The appeal court judges relied on the approach taken to such disclaimers by the House of Lords in *Hedley Byrne v. Heller*, where Lord Devlin stated:

> A man cannot be said voluntarily to be undertaking a responsibility if at the very moment when he is said to be accepting it he declares that in fact he is not.[70]

The Court of Appeal's approach in *Harris* was widely criticised. To begin with, it took no account of section 13(1) of UCTA, which prevents the exclusion or restriction of any liability by reference to terms and notices which exclude or restrict the relevant obligation or duty. The House of Lords in *Harris* were not slow to point out this and they went on to say that the Court of Appeal's approach would seriously undermine UCTA.

The effect of UCTA

The provisions governing exclusion of liability for negligence are found in section 2 of the Act. Occasionally a surveyor's negligence may result in personal injury or even death. By section 2(1) any attempt to exclude or limit liability for these losses is void. Generally, however, a surveyor's negligence will result in financial loss. By section 2(2) any attempt to exclude or restrict liability for loss or damage other than death or personal injury resulting from negligence is subject to the requirement of reasonableness contained in the Act. The Act is not very helpful in defining reasonableness in this context, despite the fact that this concept is central to its strategy. Such guidance as there is is contained in section 11. This section distinguishes between contractual terms and non-contractual notices. A term will satisfy the requirements of reasonableness if it was a fair and reasonable one to be included in the contract having regard to the circumstances which were, or ought reasonably to have been, known to or in the contemplation of the parties to the contract at the time the contract was made. In relation to a notice, the requirement of reasonableness under the Act is that it should be fair and reasonable to allow reliance on it having regard to all the circumstances obtaining when the liability arose or (but for the notice) would have arisen.

Beyond these (limited) provisions it has been left to the courts to work out the exact meaning of reasonableness in the context of excluding liability for negligence. In *Smith v. Bush*, etc., the House of Lords had the opportunity to take a comprehensive view of the matter and Lord Griffiths in his speech laid down a number of guidelines for assessing reasonableness. Strictly speaking, these guidelines are concerned with the reasonableness or otherwise of disclaimers in mortgage valuation reports, but there seems to be no reason whey they are not capable of a wider application. The guidelines are as follows:

(a) the relative bargaining strength of the parties;
(b) the availability of alternative sources of advice;
(c) the difficulty of the professional task involved; and
(d) the practical consequences of the decision – in particular the effect on insurance.

Lord Griffiths made it plain that in the case of mortgage valuations of *low and moderately priced dwellings* these guidelines pointed to a disclaimer being unreasonable.

The decisions of the House of Lords in *Smith v. Bush*, etc., point to the conclusion that it is very difficult for a surveyor to exclude his liability for negligence if his client or the third party concerned is acting as a private individual or consumer. In one case where a disclaimer in a mortgage valuation report was found to be reasonable the mortgagor was an (unqualified) estate agent![71]

One final point needs to be made in this section. If a surveyor should seek simply to limit his liability, then section 11(4) of UCTA provides that in assessing the reasonableness of such limitation regard must be had, in particular, to:

(a) the resources which he could expect to be available to him for the purpose of meeting the liability should it arise; and
(b) how far it was open to him to cover himself by insurance.

The purpose of this provision is to protect small firms (including small professional firms) with limited financial resources who are able to obtain only limited insurance cover. Thus, a clause limiting a firm's liability to its insurance cover is likely to satisfy the requirements of section 11(4).[72]

NOTES

1. [1964] AC 465. See Chapter 6 for the principle of this case.
2. [1990] 2 All ER 908. See Chapter 2.
3. [1990] 2 All ER 943. See Chapter 2.
4. This section, which was originally section 25 of the Building Societies Act 1962, imposes a duty on every director of a building society to satisfy himself that arrangements are made for an independent assessment of the adequacy of the security to be taken in respect of advances made by the society for the purposes of purchasing land.

5. This implied term is now contained in section 13 of the Supply of Goods and Services Act 1982.
6. Thus, section 16(3)(a) of the Supply of Goods and Services Act 1982 provides that a duty stricter than one of reasonable care and skill may be imposed on the supplier.
7. See *Thake v. Maurice* [1986] QB 644.
8. See *Midland Bank Trust Co. Ltd v. Hett, Stubbs and Kemp* [1978] 3 All ER 571 and *Batty v. Metropolitan Property Realisations Ltd* [1978] 2 All ER 445. For an analysis of the significance of these developments see Chapter 6.
9. [1985] 2 All ER 947, p. 957.
10. See also *Nottingham Co-operative Society Ltd v. Cementation Piling & Foundation Ltd* [1988] 2 All ER 971.
11. [1986] 2 EGLR 139.
12. [1982] QB 438.
13. [1989] 2 All ER 514. These cases were heard as consolidated appeals by the House of Lords.
14. *Supra*, n.13, p. 523.
15. *Supra*, n.13, pp. 532 and 541–42.
16. (1955) 165 EG 261.
17. See, in particular, the speech of Lord Griffiths.
18. (1986) 8 NILR 1.
19. The question of a possible duty owed by the mortgagee to the mortgagor is discussed further, though not conclusively, in *Berrisforde v. Chesterfield District Council* [1989] 39 EG 176. See also *Beaton v. Nationwide Building Society, The Times*, October 8, 1990, and *Halifax Building Society v. Edell* [1992] 3 All ER 389.
20. (1888) Ch.D 39. This decision was approved by the House of Lords in *Hedley Byrne v. Heller, supra*, n.1.
21. [1893] 1 QB 491.
22. [1889] 14 App. Cas. 337.
23. [1932] AC 562. See Chapter 2.
24. [1951] 2 KB 164.
25. *Ibid.*, p. 179. Denning L.J.'s judgement was approved by the House of Lords in *Hedley Byrne v. Heller, supra*, n.1.
26. *Supra*, n.1. pp. 502–3, 514.
27. *Supra*, n.1. pp. 528–29.
28. [1988] 1 All ER 691, p. 701.
29. (1988) NLJ 166.
30. [1988] 20 EG 92.
31. *Supra*, n.13, p. 534.
32. This is the same test as that used by the Court of Appeal in *Caparo Industries plc v. Dickman* [1989] 1 All ER 798.

33. *Supra*, n.13, pp. 540–41.
34. [1990] 1 All ER 568.
35. See, in particular, the speeches of Lords Bridge and Oliver. In laying down this formula for the special relationship, the House of Lords specifically endorsed the conditions for the creation of a duty of care for statements suggested by Denning L.J. (as he then was) in *Candler v. Crane, Christmas & Co.*
36. [1990] 49 EG 46.
37. [1989] 1 All ER 798.
38. See the judgement of Hoffman J. in *Morgan Crucible Co. plc v. Hill Samuel Bank Ltd* [1990] 3 All ER 330, p. 335.
39. [1957] 2 All ER 118, p. 121.
40. *Whitehouse v. Jordan* [1981] 1 All ER 267; *Maynard v. West Midlands Regional Health Authority* [1985] 1 All ER 635; and *Sidaway v. Bethlem Royal Hospital Governors* [1985] 1 All ER 643.
41. [1989] EGCS 175.
42. Note, in particular, the RICS/ISVA guidance notes for mortgage valuations. The latest edition of these guidance notes was published on 1 June 1992. This edition, together with background commentary, is reprinted in RICS, *Manual of Valuation*, as VGN 2A.
43. *Whitehouse v. Jordan* [1981] 1 All ER 267, p. 276 (per Lord Edmund-Davies).
44. See, in particular, the judgement of Watkin J. in *Singer and Friedlander Limited v. John D. Wood & Co.* (1977) 243 EG 212, p. 213.
45. [1987] 1 EGLR 155.
46. See *Roe v. Minister of Health* [1954] 2 QB 66.
47. See *Bolton v. Stone* [1951] AC 850.
48. See *Watt v. Hertfordshire County Council* [1954] 1WLR 855.
49. See *Latimer v. A.E.C Ltd* [1953] AC 643 and *The Wagon Mound (No. 2)* [1967] 1 AC 617.
50. [1989] 1 EGLR 154.
51. [1988] 2 EGLR 181.
52. *Ibid.*, n.49, p. 185.
53. *Supra*, n.13, p. 528.
54. [1990] 06 EG 104.
55. [1990] 47 EG 56.
56. *Ibid.*, n.55, p. 64.
57. *Supra*, n.42.
58. [1992] 24 EG 138, p. 140.
59. [1956] 1 All ER 874.
60. *Ibid.*, n.59, p. 876.
61. [1982] 3 All ER 705.
62. [1989] 1 EG 159.

63. See, in particular, *Syrett v. Carr and Neave* [1990] 48 EG 118; and *Watts v. Morrow* (1991) 7 PN 54.
64. [1991] 4 All ER 937.
65. [1988] 07 EG 83.
66. [1990] 2 All ER 815.
67. [1991] 2 All ER 353. For a critique of this case see Dugdale (1991) 7 PN 84 and (1992) 8 PN 152; and Hughes (1992) 8 PN 103.
68. [1934] 2 KB 271, p. 274 (per Mackinnon L.J.).
69. *Supra*, n.67, p. 363.
70. *Supra*, n.1, p. 533.
71. *Stevenson v. Nationwide Building Society* (1984) 272 EG 633.
72. Since 1 January 1986, the RICS has required its members to take out professional indemnity insurance.

8 Collateral Warranties and Alternative Solutions[1]

INTRODUCTION

As we have seen in Chapter 2, the role of the tort of negligence as a means of compensation for defective design and building work has diminished greatly following the decision of the House of Lords in *Murphy v. Brentwood District Council.*[2] That decision was the culmination of a trend in the law of negligence which began in the mid-1980s. Three features of this decline in the tort of negligence need to be emphasised. Firstly, where a right of action in contract exists, any parallel action in tort will depend upon the terms of that contract. It may well be the case that those terms preclude altogether an action in tort. Secondly, tortious claims for economic loss are now unlikely to succeed unless they can be brought within the scope of the reliance doctrine first laid down in *Hedley Byrne v. Heller*[3] and redefined in *Caparo v. Dickman.*[4] Thirdly, the House of Lords in *Murphy* enlarged the concept of economic loss to include the loss suffered as a result of defects in the product itself.

Three parties in the construction process have been particularly affected by these legal trends:

(1) the tenant;
(2) the subsequent purchaser; and
(3) the funding institution.

None of these parties is likely to have privity of contract with the contractor or designer of the building concerned. Further, the decision in *Murphy* means that none of these parties is likely to succeed in any claim in negligence brought against the contractor or designer.

The tenant

A commercial lease will normally contain a repairing covenant imposing an obligation on the tenant to repair the premises. The nature and extent of that obligation depend on the precise wording of the repairing covenant. The important question for the tenant is whether such a covenant requires him to remedy latent defects in the premises. The law does not provide a very precise answer to this question. The general principle governing such covenants was laid down by Forbes J. in *Ravenseft Properties Ltd v. Davstone Holdings Ltd*:

> The true test is, as the cases show, that it is always a question of degree whether that which the tenant is asked to do can properly be described as a repair, or whether on the contrary it would involve giving back to the landlord a wholly different thing from that which he demised.[5]

In any particular case it may not be clear whether a latent defect is within the scope of a repairing covenant. The essential point for a tenant is that it *may* fall within such a covenant and therefore it is important for him to seek a means to protect himself from liability for repairing such defects.

The subsequent purchaser

A contract for the sale of land and buildings contains nothing akin to the implied terms of quality and fitness which are imposed on a seller or supplier of goods. It is subject to the doctrine of *caveat emptor*, which means that the onus to discover any latent defects in building will be on the purchaser. If the purchaser is a subsequent purchaser, or purchases from a developer, then he will not have a contract with the builder or designer of the premises and therefore will not receive the benefit of the implied obligations imposed upon the supplier in a contract for work and materials or a contract for services. It is therefore common for a purchaser to survey the property before purchase, but such surveys cannot always be relied upon to reveal a latent defect. Purchasers of dwellings will generally have the benefit of the warranties in the NHBC scheme. That scheme does not extend to commercial buildings and the purchasers of these buildings will therefore frequently require collateral warranties from the builder and the design team.

The funding institution

Many developments are funded by banks, pension funds, etc. If the developer runs into financial difficulties, then frequently the funding institution will want to take over the project itself. In other words, it will want to stand in the shoes of the developer and enforce his contracts with the contractor and the designer. Such an arrangement is known as a novation.

It is the purpose of this chapter to examine in detail the alternatives to an action in negligence which the above parties now frequently seek following the decision in *Murphy*. It must be emphasised at this point that these alternatives are sought largely, if not wholly, by commercial parties, though the decision in *Murphy* also has important implications for the consumer.[6] These alternative solutions are as follows:

(1) collateral warranties;
(2) first party buildings insurance; and
(3) assignment of legal rights.

COLLATERAL WARRANTIES

A collateral warranty is a contract which stands alongside the main contract. The existence of such contracts has long been recognised by the common law. The best and most well-known description of this concept is that of Lord Moulton's in *Heilbut Symons & Co. v. Buckleton*:

> It is evident, both on principle and on authority, that there may be a contract the consideration for which is the making of some other contract. If you will make such and such a contract I will give you £100 is in every sense of the word a complete legal contract. It is collateral to the main contract but each has an independent existence and they do not differ in respect of their possessing to the full the character and status of a contract.[7]

Collateral warranties are of two kinds: (a) implied and (b) express.

Implied collateral warranties[8]

The courts have in a number of circumstances implied a contractual warranty. In this sense, a collateral warranty is a device used by the courts to get round what they see as an unnecessarily harsh rule of common law. Thus, the collateral warranty has been used to mitigate the harshness of the parol evidence rule, that if the contract is reduced to writing then only that writing can be used as evidence of the terms of the contract. If a preliminary statement or assurance is not included in the written contract, the courts may be prepared to treat such statement or assurance as a contractual warranty collateral to the principal agreement.[9] More commonly, the implied collateral warranty has been employed where the person giving, or the person receiving, the assurance is not a party to the main contract.[10]

One overriding principle governs implied collateral warranties: on the totality of evidence the parties must have intended that there should be contractual liability in respect of the accuracy of the statement.[11]

Express collateral warranties

An express collateral warranty is one agreed upon by the parties themselves, rather than implied by the courts. It is this form of collateral warranty which is now so important a feature of legal relationships in the construction industry. At the risk of repetition it is worth highlighting the reasons for this development. The fundamental reason is the doctrine of privity of contract, which is a basic rule of the English law of contract. This doctrine states that as a general rule only a party to a contract can take the benefits of that contract or is subject to its burdens or obligations. Thus, only the first purchaser of a building can taken the benefits of the implied obligations of quality, fitness, etc., which the law imposes on a vendor/builder. A subsequent purchaser or tenant does not take the benefit of these implied obligations, because he is not a party to the contract with the vendor/builder. For a time the tort of negligence filled this gap in the law of contract but the effect of the decision in *Murphy* is to remove this cause of action. Collateral warranties are seen as a means of overcoming the effects of the doctrine of privity of contract and the restrictive view of negligence which the courts now take.

The terms of express collateral warranties

There are no standard forms of warranty agreement which are universally accepted throughout the construction industry. However, the following terms are commonly contained in warranty agreements used in the industry.

Duty of care Virtually all express contractual warranties are duty of care warranties. The giver of the warranty rarely, if ever, guarantees to the recipient that he will achieve a particular result. In other words, there is generally no question of a collateral warranty creating strict liability. There are three principal reasons for this provision. In the first place, the purpose of a collateral warranty is to create a contractual relationship in circumstances where there are no duties in tort owed by one party to the other. As tortious duties are generally based on the concept of reasonable care and skill, it is hardly surprising that this concept should provide the essential basis for a device used to plug gaps left by the law of tort. Secondly, collateral warranties in the construction industry essentially transfer obligations in the main contract to a party who is not privy to that contract. Generally, the main contract imposes an obligation of reasonable care and skill, rather than strict liability. For example, under clause 3.1 of the RIBA standard form, Architect's Appointment, the architect's duty in relation to design is expressed as follows:

> The Architect will exercise reasonable care and skill in conformity with the normal standards of the Architect's profession.

This duty is of course owed to the architect's employer, the building owner. If the building is leased and the tenant demands a collateral warranty from the architect in relation to design, then in all probability such design warranty will simply repeat the provisions of the above clause. Thirdly, a collateral warranty is only as good as the insurance which backs it up; few, if any, insurance companies are prepared to insure a warranty which provides a guarantee.

Insurance It is common for collateral warranties provided by an architect or engineer to provide a term that professional indemnity insurance (PII) is in force at the date of the warranty. The reason for the inclusion of such a provision is that most design professionals operate in partnerships, a form of business organisation which does not enjoy limited liability. As a result, they may be held personally liable for any contractual obligations they undertake. If their personal assets do not extend to meeting these obligations, then the only way in which they can be met is through PII.

PII, however, contains a number of problems whose effect may be to render the collateral warranty worthless.[12] Firstly, the liability of an architect or engineer under a collateral warranty will arise only when damage to the building concerned actually occurs. It is not uncommon for defects in buildings to manifest themselves many years after they have been completed – by this time any PII taken out by the design team may either be inadequate or have lapsed. Secondly, professional persons frequently change their PII to different insurers. If they fail to inform the new insurer of the existence of a collateral warranty, then it will not be covered by the new policy. Thirdly, PII is only for the benefit of the insured. The insured may compromise any claim against his insurers without taking into account the liability owed to the third party. For example, if a professional faced with a claim for, say, £1m settles with his insurers for £100 000, there is nothing that the third party can do about it. Winward Fearon in *Collateral Warranties*[13] cite a further problem with any PII provision. That problem revolves around the remedy available to the beneficiary of the warranty if the designer fails to honour his obligation to insure. Clearly the designer is in breach of contract under the warranty and would thereby be liable in damages for the amount of the PII premiums to the beneficiary. But it is highly unlikely that the beneficiary would be able to take out PII on behalf of the designer.

Deleterious materials Many collateral warranties contain a provision for proscribing certain materials for use in the construction of the building. Arguably such a list is unnecessary, as use of the most commonly proscribed materials would be a breach of the duty to exercise reasonable care and skill. If a list is to be included, then it must be made clear that it is not an exhaustive list and that it is not intended to be a substitute for the duty of reasonable care and skill.

Assignment

A warranty will frequently contain a term allowing the benefit of it to be passed on, i.e. assigned, to subsequent tenants or purchasers.[14] Assignment is a complex subject and these complexities are beyond the scope of this work.[15] All that can be done here is to outline the essential principles governing this topic.

The benefits arising under a contract, including a collateral warranty, is a chose in action, i.e. a personal right of property which can only be claimed or enforced by action, and not by taking physical possession.[16] It is not necessary for a contract to contain an express term granting a right of assignment in order for the benefit of the contract to be assigned. Assignment is a right which arises either by statute or in equity. The right to make a legal assignment is governed by section 136(1) of the Law of Property Act 1925. This provides that:

> Any absolute assignment by writing under the hand of the assignor (not purporting to be by way of charge only) of any debt or other legal thing in action, of which express notice in writing has been given to the debtor, trustee or other person from whom the assignor would have been entitled to claim such debt or thing in action, is effectual in law (subject to equities having priority over the right of the assignee) to pass and transfer from the date of such notice:
>
> (a) the legal right to such debt or thing in action;
> (b) all legal and other remedies for the same; and
> (c) the power to give a good discharge for the same without the concurrence of the assignor.

This provision means that certain formalities must be complied with if an assignment is to be an effective legal assignment:

(1) there must be an absolute assignment in writing signed by the assignor;
(2) there must be a debt or other legal thing in action; and
(3) there must be an express notice in writing to the debtor.

If these formalities are not complied with, then there may still be an equitable assignment. The essential principle governing an equitable assignment is that it may be in writing or oral, provided that there is a clear and unequivocal intention to assign.[17] If a collateral warranty expressly prohibits assignment, then that is likely to be effective at law and any attempt to assign in such a case would be invalid.[18]

Novation

This is a transaction by which, with the consent of all the parties concerned, a new contract is substituted for one that has already been made. A novation provision in a collateral warranty will be for the benefit of the purchaser or funding institution. It gives such parties the right to step into the shoes of the developer or building employer if either of those parties becomes bankrupt or goes into liquidation. In this way the main contract and the design contract can then be completed.

The essential difference between novation and assignment is that assignment does not require the consent of the giver of the warranty, whereas novation does.

The BPF warranty

The British Property Federation (BFP) has drawn up a standard form of collateral warranty for use by funding institutions.[19] This standard form was drawn up in collaboration with the ACE, RIBA and RICS. The essential features of this form are as follows:

(1) Like most, if not all, collateral warranties used in the construction industry, it is a duty of care warranty. By clause 1 the firm warrants that it has exercised reasonable care and skill in the performance of its duties to the client. This confirms that the obligation to the third party will be no greater than the obligations owed to the client.

(2) Under the provisions of clause 2 certain materials are proscribed:

(a) high alumina cement in structural elements;
(b) wood wool slabs in permanent formwork to concrete;
(c) calcium chloride in admixtures for use in reinforced concrete;
(d) asbestos products;
(e) naturally occurring aggregates for use in reinforced concrete which do not comply with British Standard 882.

This is a very limited clause; no attempt is made to include substances which do not comply with the relevant British Standards and Codes of Practice.

(3) By clause 9 the firm must maintain PII provided that such insurance is available at commercially reasonable rates. This clause does not specify the risks against which PII is to be maintained and it does not state where such insurance is to be obtained.

(4) By clause 11 the benefits of the warranty may be assigned to another company providing finance or refinance in connection with the development project without the consent of the client or the firm being required.

Warranties backed by guarantees

This is a form of strict liability, in that such warranties would impose liability for specific defects and damage on the providers irrespective of negligence. In France, for example, architects and builders are required by the Napoleonic *Code Civil* to repair any defects in building structures or ground movement for a period of ten years. This warranty is backed up by *Dommage Ouvrage* insurance.

The NEDC in their BUILD report[20] identified four potential problems with such guarantees:

(1) If applied to a whole building, strict liability could be a very onerous imposition on the construction industry; contractors could well resist, and even refuse, the imposition of such warranties.
(2) It may be difficult, or even impossible, to obtain the necessary insurance backing at reasonable premiums.
(3) If such a guarantee were to be given by a contractor who, in the event, failed to honour it, the success of any claim by a client would then depend upon the insurance policy taken out by the contractor.

(4) Should a client have a valid claim on a contractor's policy, litigation may be needed to recover damages, and a client may have to join a queue of debtors.

The BUILD report concludes that while building warranties with insurance-backed guarantees meet some of the objectives, they fail fully to meet the major requirement of providing clients with a secure route to redress.[21]

FIRST PARTY BUILDINGS INSURANCE

First party buildings insurance is a form of insurance whereby payment is made to the insured when certain specified kinds of damage appear in the building concerned. Such insurance is rare in the case of dwellings because they are usually covered by the provisions of the NHBC scheme during the first ten years of their lives. However, as we have seen in Chapter 3, the NHBC scheme does not extend to commercial buildings and in order to fill this gap a form of first party insurance has been recommended by the NEDC in their BUILD report.

The BUILD report was prepared by the Construction Industry Sector Group of the NEDC. In 1984 it appointed the Insurance Feasibility Steering Committee (IFSC) to investigate the desirability and feasibility of latent defects protection insurance for new commercial, industrial and other non-housing building. The IFSC recommended a form of first party material damage insurance, *Building Users and Insurance against Latent Defects* (BUILD).

The NEDC in their BUILD report pointed to a number of reasons why such insurance is important. Fault-free buildings cannot be guaranteed, and latent defects – defects which cannot reasonably be discovered at the stage of a building's practical completion or during the period of contractual liability for defects – are a common feature of buildings. The report suggests a number of reasons for the occurrence of these defects. They can be summarised as follows. Firstly, they may arise from what the report refers to as poor visualisation, i.e. the failure of the client or the builder to envisage how a building will actually perform when in use. Secondly, they may be caused by inadequate design, inappropriate specifications, the use of inadequate materials or lack of care in workmanship. Thirdly, defects may arise through technological change. Presumably, the report had in mind in this respect the use of new building materials and experimental designs.[22]

It should be noted that this report was published in 1988 and to these factors the effects of the decision in *Murphy* must be added.

The essential provisions of a BUILD policy

The most important provisions of a BUILD policy are as follows:

(1) It would be negotiated by the developer or building owner at the preliminary design stage. During its currency, the policy would be transferable to successive owners and whole-building tenants.
(2) It provides non-cancellable material damage insurance against specified latent defects and damage for a period of ten years from the date of practical completion.
(3) The cover is initially limited to structure (including foundations), the weathershield envelope and optionally loss of rent.

There are a number of exceptions from a BUILD policy:

- minor elements (e.g. stairs, partitions and suspended ceilings),
- engineering services, and
- consequential economic loss, i.e. disruption of the occupier's activities resulting from the carrying out of remedial works.[23]

The report states that minor elements are excluded because to include them would be administratively cumbersome. Engineering services are excluded because the risks associated with them are difficult to define and because much depends on their efficient operation and maintenance. The risks of consequential economic loss will differ greatly from one occupier to another and the report states that this form of loss is best insured by the insurer.

The advantages and disadvantages of BUILD[24]

The BUILD report sees BUILD policies as having a number of advantages for clients, producers and insurers. In the first place, all these parties would benefit from the avoidance of the cost, delay and uncertainty of litigation that would normally follow the discovery of defects covered by a BUILD policy. Clients would have the advantage of the cost of repairing the defects speedily and without the need for proof of fault. For designers there should be an easing of the burden of PII because some of the major risks will be removed. Contractors will be protected against currently uninsurable risks. For insurers, BUILD will create a new class of business. Professional indemnity insurers will be relieved of the consequences of many of the more costly defects.

The BUILD report identifies a number of disadvantages of BUILD policies. The cost of BUILD premiums will have to be met, in practice calls on deductibles are unlikely to differ much from PII deductibles and, initially at least, insurers will find the risks difficult to assess. The report also considers the argument that BUILD policies may lead to a decline in the quality of buildings by encouraging poor design and careless workmanship. To counteract any possibility of this occurring the report recommends, *inter alia*, that BUILD policies should contain a provision that the contractor discharge his responsibilities under the contract for correcting defects reported during the defects liability period and that they impose a deductible, i.e. the first amount of the claim (say £5000) would not be covered.

The IFSC concluded that the advantages of BUILD far outweigh its disadvantages and strongly recommended that the construction industry's clients should use BUILD policies as a feature of good management.

ASSIGNMENT OF LEGAL RIGHTS

This section is concerned with the question of whether or not it is possible for the original owner of a building to assign his legal rights to successive owners. It is important to note from the outset that we are here concerned not just with the assignment of contractual rights but also with the assignment of rights in tort. These matters arose for consideration in *Linden Gardens Trust Ltd v. Linesta Sludge Disposals Ltd* and *St. Martin's Corporation Ltd v. Sir Robert McAlpine & Sons Ltd.*[25]

Linden Gardens concerned a lease of four floors of a building. The leaseholders, Stock Conversion, employed contractors to carry out substantial refurbishment work, including the removal of all asbestos from the building. The contract was the JCT form, clause 17 of which prohibits assignment of the contract by the employer without the written consent of the contractor. The contract was completed in 1980. In 1985 more asbestos was found in the building and new contractors were employed for its removal. At the same time Stock Conversion commenced proceedings against the first contractors. The second contract was completed in August 1985. In December 1986 Stock Conversion sold their lease to new owners at its full market value and formally assigned their claim for damages against the first contractors. The new owners took over the legal action from Stock Conversion and, when even more asbestos was discovered, joined the second contractors as defendants. The main issue in this case was whether the clause prohibiting assignment bars any claim by the plaintiffs against the first and second contractors.

In the *St Martin's* case during the course of construction of a building its owners, a property company, transferred its ownership to the group's investment property subsidiary at the full market price, together with an assignment to the investment subsidiary of the benefit of the building contract. As in *Linden Gardens*, clause 17 of the JCT form prohibited assignment without the contractor's consent (which was not obtained). After completion, the podium deck of the main building was found to be leaking, and the new owners carried out the necessary repairs. There are two important differences between this case and *Linden Gardens*. Firstly, it was conceded that at the time of the assignment no relevant breach of the building contract had as yet occurred, in contrast to *Linden Gardens*, where breaches already existed at the time of assignment. Secondly, both the assignor and assignee sued as co-plaintiffs.

The House of Lords held that clause 17 of the JCT form prohibited the assignment of any benefit of the contract, including not only the assignment of the right to future performance but also the assignment of accrued rights of action. Accordingly, the plaintiffs' claim in *Linden Gardens* and the assignee's claim in the *St. Martin's* case failed.[26] The rationale for this was explained by Lord Browne-Wilkinson in his speech. He said that the prohibition on the assignment of accrued rights of action was not void as being contrary to public policy, since a party to a building contract may have a genuine commercial interest in seeking to ensure that he was in contractual relations only with the other party to the contract.

The House of Lords further held that the assignor in the *St Martin's* case was entitled to damages from the defendant contractor. These parties were to be regarded as having entered into a contract on the basis that the assignor would be entitled to enforce contractual rights for the benefit of the assignee. In coming to this conclusion the House of Lords relied on a very old exception to the general rule that a party cannot recover damages for breach of contract unless he himself has suffered loss. This exception was laid down in *Dunlop v. Lambert*,[27] where it was held that a consigner of goods who had parted with the property in the goods before the date of breach could even so recover substantial damages for the failure to deliver the goods. The rationale of that rule was explained by Lord Diplock in *The Albazero.* He said that:

> ... in a commercial contract concerning goods where it is in the contemplation of the parties that the proprietary interest in the goods may be transferred from one owner to another after the contract has been entered into and before the breach which causes loss or damage to the goods, an original party to the contract, if such be the intention of them both, is to be treated in law as having entered into the contract for the benefit of all persons who have or may acquire an interest in the goods before they are

> lost or damaged, and is entitled to recover by way of damages for breach of contract the actual loss sustained by those for whose benefit the contract is entered into.[28]

Applying this principle to the *St. Martin's* case, the House of Lords said that both the contractor and the assignor knew that the property was going to be occupied by a third party. It was therefore foreseeable that damage caused by a breach of contract by the contractor would cause loss to a subsequent owner.

The more interesting, and controversial, of these decisions is the one in the *St. Martin's* case. Very simply it means that a contractor cannot avoid liability for the cost of rectifying defective work because the employer has sold the building before the defects come to light. If the standard form building contracts are amended to prevent this result, then attention will surely turn to the question of what rights in tort, if any, the original building owner can assign to subsequent owners. This matter was considered at first instance by the Official Referee, Judge Lloyd, QC, who said that a prohibition on contractual rights did not preclude the assignment of any rights of action in tort.[29]

Damage to a building itself is now regarded as pure economic loss and such loss is only recoverable if it can be brought within the reliance principle. This principle depends on there being a highly proximate relationship between the parties, and while it may be possible for the original building owner to satisfy this requirement, it will prove very difficult, if not impossible, for a subsequent building owner to satisfy. In *Murphy* Lord Bridge said:

> There may, of course, be situations where, even in the absence of contract, there is a special relationship of proximity between builder and building owner which is sufficiently akin to contract to introduce the element of reliance so that the scope of the duty of care owed by the builder to the owner is wide enough to embrace purely economic loss. The decision in *Junior Books* can, I believe, only be understood on this basis.[30]

Arguably, therefore, the original building owner may have a tortious right of action which is not on conventional principles available to a subsequent owner. If that right of action can be assigned, then a significant inroad into the *Murphy* doctrine may be established.

CONCLUSION

A number of points need to be emphasised by way of a conclusion to this chapter. In the first place, a collateral warranty cannot create a tortious duty, i.e. it cannot be a mechanism for restoring the *Anns* duty of care between two parties. It can only create contractual rights and obligations between two parties who otherwise would not be in a contractual relationship. Secondly, the existence of a collateral warranty may well have the effect of defining in full the extent of the parties' relationship. In other words, the existence of a collateral warranty may well preclude the courts from finding a duty of care in tort.

Collateral warranties and the other substitutes for a tortious duty of care discussed in this chapter cannot be said to be adequate replacements for the *Anns* duty. We have seen the drawbacks to collateral warranties – inadequate or non-existent PII, the fact that there may be a bar to their assignment or, if there is no such bar, they may not in the event be assigned, etc. Added to this, it must be remembered that even if a third party does receive, and is able to enforce, a collateral warranty, that still does not put him in the position that he would have been under *Anns*. Contractual warranties give rise to contractual rights and as such they suffer from the same drawbacks *vis-à-vis* tortious rights as any other contractual right: in particular, a shorter limitation period and a different, and to the plaintiff a possibly less advantageous, approach to the calculation of damages.[31] First party buildings insurance may not cover the kind of damage suffered in *Murphy* and there may be deductibles which in effect exclude cover for more minor, though still serious, defects. The assignment of tortious rights is an unexplored subject.

NOTES

1. See, generally, Winward Fearon, *Collateral Warranties*, Blackwell Scientific, 1990.
2. [1990] 2 All ER 908.
3. [1964] AC 465.
4. [1990] 1 All ER 568.
5. [1980] QB 12, p. 21.
6. See National Consumer Council, *Murphy's Law*, 1991.
7. [1913] AC 30, p. 47.
8. What follows is an outline of this subject. For a full discussion of the principles and case law governing implied collateral warranties, see any of the established texts on contract law.
9. See, for example, *De Lassalle v. Guildford* [1901] 2 KB 215.
10. See, for example, *Shanklin Pier Ltd v. Detal Products Ltd* [1951] 2 KB 854; and *Andrews v. Hopkinson* [1957] 1 QB 299.
11. *Heilbut Symons & Co. v. Buckleton, supra*, n.7.
12. See Bates [1990] EG 57.

13. *Supra*, n.1, p. 139.
14. Cp. Ch. 3 of the NHBC scheme.
15. See Furmston M.P, *Cheshire, Fifoot v. Furmston's Law of Contract*, 12th edn, Butterworths, 1991, Ch. 16.
16. *Torkington v. Magee* [1902] 2 KB 427, p. 430 (per Channell J.).
17. *William Brandt's Sons & Co. v. Dunlop Rubber Co.* [1905] AC 454.
18. *Helston Securities Ltd v. Hertfordshire County Council* [1978] 3 All ER 262.
19. Form of Agreement for Collateral Warranty for funding institutions, Co WA/F.
20. *Building Users Insurance Against Latent Defects*, NEDO, 1988, para. 6.12.
21. *Ibid.*, n.20, para. 6.13.
22. For a full list of the suggested causes of defects in buildings, see section 9 of the BUILD report.
23. See section 10 of the BUILD report.
24. See section 11 of the BUILD report.
25. [1993] 3 All ER 417.
26. *Ibid.*, n.25, p. 430.
27. (1839) 6 Cl & F 600, 7 ER 824.
28. [1976] 3 All ER 129, p. 137.
29. See *Chartered Surveyor Weekly*, 24 January 1991.
30. *Supra*, n.2, p. 930.
31. See Chapter 6.

9 Limitation

INTRODUCTION

The subject of limitation deals with the time periods within which a plaintiff must commence his action. A plaintiff who fails to initiate proceedings within the applicable period will be barred from obtaining any remedy. The basis of the current law on limitation is to be found in the Limitation Act 1980, as amended by the Latent Damage Act 1986.

The fundamental principle underlying a statute of limitation is that it is a statute of peace. This principle was expressed in the following terms by Lord Simon in *The Amphthill Peerage*.

> There is a fundamental principle of English law [going back to Coke's Commentary on Littleton (Co.Litt) (1809) p. 303] generally expressed by a Latin maxim [*interest reipublicae ut sit finis litium*] which can be translated: 'It is in the interest of society that there should be an end to litigation'.[1]

The basis of this principle is that the law must strike a balance between allowing a plaintiff sufficient time to bring an action and yet not disadvantaging a defendant by allowing claims to be brought against him in respect of misconduct which occurred many years previously.

The issue of limitation periods is of particular importance in the area of Construction Law. Many defects in buildings are latent, i.e. they are not immediately apparent or discoverable and may not manifest themselves until many years after the buildings have been completed. The classic example is a building with foundations that are too shallow and therefore defective. The foundations are covered up at an early stage in the construction process and thereafter there is no means by which the defect can be discovered. Only when the obvious signs, such as cracking in the walls, appear does such a defect become patent. This may be many years after the building is completed. In such a case too short a limitation period would seriously disadvantage the plaintiff, but if the limitation period were to extend for too long a period, then it would cause hardship to the defendant builder, designer or local authority, who may not be able to obtain PII cover in respect of the building beyond a certain time-span.

Striking a balance between plaintiff and defendant in this area of law is clearly problematical. It is a balance which has shifted between plaintiff and defendant over the last twenty years or so and equilibrium has still not been achieved, despite recent legislative reform in the form of the Latent Damage Act 1986, which restored the balance in favour of the plaintiff. There has recently been a proposal for further reform in this area of law to shift the balance in favour of the defendant.[2] The effect of the decision of the House of Lords in *Murphy v. Brentwood District Council*[3] on the law of limitation is clearly to favour the defendant.

This chapter examines this subject from three standpoints:

(1) limitation in contract;
(2) limitation in negligence in respect of personal injury or death; and
(3) limitation in negligence in respect of latent damage to buildings.

LIMITATION IN CONTRACT

Under the provisions of section 5 of the Limitation Act 1980 an action for breach of a simple contract cannot be brought after the expiration of six years from the date on which the cause of action accrued. Section 8(1) provides that in the case of a contract made under seal an action cannot be brought after the expiration of twelve years from the date on which the cause of action occurred. In each case time begins to run from the moment when the breach of contract occurs, not when actual damage is suffered.

Where the plaintiff fails to discover the existence of his cause of action because of the defendant's fraud or because the defendant deliberately conceals his breach of contract, then under the provisions of section 32 of the 1980 Act the limitation period does not begin to run until the plaintiff has discovered the fraud or concealment or could with reasonable diligence have discovered it. Section 32 is plainly of great relevance to cases of defective buildings where the defect is often covered up during the construction process. The operation of this provision is illustrated by *Applegate v. Moss*,[4] a case involving defective foundations. By a contract made in February 1957 the defendant agreed to build two houses for the plaintiffs and to support them on a raft foundation reinforced with a specified steel network. The houses were completed towards the end of 1957. In 1965 wide cracks appeared beneath the houses, and the plaintiffs discovered that the foundations had been defectively laid: there was no raft and the reinforcement was grossly inferior to that specified. The plaintiffs claimed damages for breach. The Court of Appeal held that although their action was brought more than six years after the breach of contract, they were not time-barred, because there had been concealment within the meaning of what is now section 32 of the 1980 Act.

LIMITATION IN NEGLIGENCE: DEATH OR PERSONAL INJURY

Under section 2 of the 1980 Act actions in tort must be brought within six years from the date on which the cause of action accrued. In the case of personal injuries, however, section 11 of the 1980 Act provides that the limitation period is three years from the date on which the cause of action accrued, or the date (if later) of the plaintiff's knowledge of his injuries. A person has knowledge for the purposes of section 11 if he knows:

(a) that the injury in question was significant;
(b) that the injury was attributable in whole or in part to the defendant's misconduct; and
(c) the identity of the defendant or the person alleged to have committed the misconduct.

If the claim is under the Fatal Accidents Act 1976 in respect of death caused by the defendant's tort, then under the provisions of section 12 of the 1980 Act the defendant must bring the action within three years of the date of death or the date of the defendant's knowledge, whichever is the later.

Under the provisions of section 33 of the 1980 Act the court has power to override these statutory limits if it appears to them to be equitable to do so, having regard to the degree to which the primary limitation rules prejudice the plaintiff and whether or not any exercise of the power would prejudice the defendant. The court is directed to have regard to all the circumstances of the case and, in particular, to:

(a) the length of, and the reasons for, the delay on the part of the plaintiff;
(b) the effect of the delay upon the evidence in the case;
(c) the conduct of the defendant after the cause of action arose, including his response to the plaintiff's reasonable request for information;
(d) the duration of any disability of the plaintiff arising from the accrual of the cause of action;
(e) the extent to which the plaintiff acted promptly and reasonably once he knew he might have an action for damage; and
(f) the steps, if any, taken by the plaintiff to obtain medical, legal or other expert advice and the nature of any such advice as he may have received.

LATENT DAMAGE

Latent damage may be defined as damage which does not manifest itself until some time after the act or omission which 'causes' it. This kind of damage clearly poses considerable problems to plaintiffs and defendants. A plaintiff may be held time-barred because of the considerable length of time before the damage manifests itself. A defendant may find himself being sued long after a contract is completed and possibly when his PII cover in respect of such a contract has expired. To a plaintiff, therefore, the law of limitation offers the prospect of being a hapless victim without a remedy; to a defendant, especially an architect or an engineer who operates in a professional partnership, on the other hand, it offers the prospect of personal liability, and possible bankruptcy, long after a project has been completed. Reconciling these opposing interests has been a perennial problem for this area of law. The following review of the relevant case law and statutory intervention in this area shows that a satisfactory reconciliation has yet to be achieved.

The expansionist years

Developments in the law of limitation played a critical role in the expansionist phase of the tort of negligence. The origin of the modern law on limitation and latent damage is laid down in the decision of the House of Lords in *Cartledge v. E. Jopling & Sons Ltd.*[5] In that case the plaintiff had been exposed to dust, which damaged his lungs, and he contracted pneumoconiosis. This condition did not manifest itself until some years later. The House of Lords held that a cause of action in negligence accrues when the injury is suffered and not when it is discovered, *even when that injury is unknown to and cannot be discovered by the sufferer.* Thus, in this case the plaintiff's right of action was barred before he knew he had the disease.

The principle laid down in *Cartledge* is, of course, a very harsh one for plaintiffs. The Law Lords recognised the injustice of the rule that they laid down but they felt bound by the provisions of section 26 of the Limitation Act 1939. The Limitation Act 1963 was passed to remedy the unjust result produced by this decision. That Act extended the time limit for commencing claims for damages where material facts of a decisive character were outside the knowledge of the plaintiff until after the action would normally have been time-barred. That provision applied only to actions for damages relating to personal injuries. It said nothing about latent damage to buildings. That was left to the courts to determine. They have developed the law in this area first to the advantage of the plaintiff but subsequently to the advantage of the defendant.

In *Dutton v. Bognor Regis UDC* Lord Denning said that in the case of a defective dwelling caused by inadequate foundations the damage was done when the foundations were badly constructed and the period of limitation of six years began at that time.[6]

In *Sparham–Souter v. Town & Country Developments (Essex) Ltd*[7] Lord Denning withdrew that dictum and held that the cause of action in such a case accrues, not at the time of the negligent laying or passing of the foundations, nor at the time when the latest owner bought the house, but at the time when the house begins to sink and the cracks appear. Where a local authority negligently approves defective foundations and other work in progress which is then covered up, the limitation period begins to run only when the damage manifests itself and the person who then has an interest in the property discovers the defects, or should, with reasonable diligence, have discovered them. He justified this change of opinion in the following terms:

> That was the first time that any damage was sustained. None of the previous owners had sustained any damage. Each had bought and sold the house at a full price in the belief that the foundations were sound. The only person to sustain the damage was the man who owned the house at the time when the house sank and the cracks appeared. It is only at that time that he can reasonably be expected to know that he may have a cause of action. It would be most unfair that time should run against him before he knows – or has any possibility of knowing – that he has a cause of action.[8]

That view was supported by the other two members of the Court of Appeal, Roskill and Geoffrey Lane, L.J.J.

In *Anns v. Merton LBC*[9] Lord Wilberforce, with whom the other Law Lords agreed, said that the Court of Appeal was right when, in *Sparham-Souter,* it abjured the view that the cause of action arose immediately upon conveyance of the defective house. He went on to say that it can only arise when the state of the building is such that there is present or imminent danger to the health or safety of persons occupying it.[10] The defects to the maisonettes in question first appeared in 1970 and, since the writs were first issued in 1972, the actions were not time-barred.

The decision of the House of Lords in *Anns* clearly favoured plaintiffs. But it left a number of points on the law of limitation in relation to negligence unclear. Firstly, Lord Wilberforce did not give any indication of the meaning of 'present or imminent danger to health or safety'. Secondly, it was not clear whether the reasonable discoverability test laid down by the Court of Appeal in *Sparham-Souter* had been approved. Thirdly, it was not clear whether the test laid down by the House of Lords applied only to local authorities or whether it applied also to builders, developers and design professionals.

The meaning of 'present or imminent danger to health or safety' was considered by the Court of Appeal in *Percival v. Walsall Metropolitan Borough Council.*[11] In that case the plaintiff was the owner of a house built on inadequate foundations. He sued the local authority for negligence in carrying out its duties under the Building Regulations. The problems that arose included cracking of brickwork, ceilings and internal walls; tilting of the house; differential settlement of the exterior; cracking of the garage floor; sticking of doors, draughts; leaking; a risk to services, especially to drains; and a certainty of future deterioration because underpinning was not possible. The Court of Appeal held, *inter alia,* that these problems did not constitute a present or imminent danger to the health or safety of the occupiers.

The second and third of the above questions were considered by Judge Fay, Q.C., in *Eames London Estates Ltd v. North Hertfordshire District Council.*[12] That case concerned liability in negligence of a developer, a builder, an architect and a local authority, for defective premises. The judge held that the limitation period began to run upon the occurrence of either the date the plaintiff first acquired an interest in the property or the date upon which he first learned of the damage, whichever was the later.

Another factor which moved the law of limitation in favour of plaintiffs was the development of concurrent liability. This meant that in a contract involving a duty of care owed by one party to the other there could be liability in the tort of negligence to the other contracting party alongside liability in contract for breach of that duty. The particular significance of this development for limitation periods lies in the fact that a cause of action in contract accrues on the date of the breach, whereas the starting point for the limitation period in tort may be many years later. Thus, a plaintiff who is time-barred in contract may still be in time in tort. In *Esso Petroleum Co. Ltd v. Mardon*[13] the plaintiff entered into the tenancy of a petrol-filling station owned by the defendants, Esso Petroleum Co. Ltd, on the strength of estimates of throughput supplied by a representative of Esso. The estimates proved grossly inaccurate. The Court of Appeal held that the defendants were liable for breach of contractual warranty and for negligent misstatement under the principle laid down in *Hedley Byrne & Co. Ltd v. Heller & Partners Ltd*[14]. In *Batty v. Metropolitan Realisations Ltd*[15] the Court of Appeal held that a developer and a builder who built a house on a hill subject to landslips were liable both in contract and in tort to the plaintiff building owners. In *Midland Bank Trust Co. Ltd v. Hett, Stubbs & Kemp*[16] a solicitor negligently failed to register an option to purchase a farm as a land charge, with the result that it did not bind a third party who bought the land. Oliver J. held that the solicitor was liable to his client in tort, independently of any liability in contract. The option was granted in 1961, the sale to the third party took place in 1967 and the writ against the solicitor was issued in 1972. The cause of action in contract accrued in 1961, when the breach of contract occurred, and the plaintiffs were therefore time-barred in contract. However, the cause of action in tort accrued in 1967 when the damage occurred and the plaintiffs were therefore not time-barred in tort.

The decision in *Pirelli*

In *Pirelli General Cable Works Ltd v. Oscar Faber & Partners*[17] the House of Lords restored the balance of the law of limitation firmly in favour of the defendants. In March 1969 the plaintiffs engaged the defendants, a firm of consulting engineers, to design an addition to their factory premises, including the provision of a chimney. The chimney was built in June and July 1969. The material used in its construction was unsuitable and cracks developed not later than April 1970. The plaintiffs discovered the damage in November 1977. It was found that they could not with reasonable diligence have discovered it before October 1972. In October 1978 the plaintiffs issued a writ claiming damages for negligence by the defendants.

The House of Lords held that the date of accrual of a cause of action in tort for damage caused by the negligent design or construction of a building was the date when the damage came into existence, and not the date when the damage was discovered or should with reasonable diligence have been discovered. The plaintiffs' cause of action accrued not later than April 1970. Since that date was more than six years before the issue of the writ, the claim was statute-barred.

The leading speech was delivered by Lord Fraser. He reviewed the law of limitation and latent damage and rejected the distinction made in this area of law between personal injuries and damage to property. The key passage in his speech is as follows:

> Unless the defect is very gross it may never lead to any damage at all to the building. It would be analogous to a predisposition or natural weakness in the human body which may never develop into disease or injury .... The plaintiff's cause of action will not accrue until *damage* occurs, which will commonly consist of cracks coming into existence as a result of the defect even though the cracks or the defect may be undiscovered or undiscoverable. There may perhaps be cases where the defect is so gross that the building is doomed from the start, and where the owner's cause of action will accrue as soon as it is built, but it seems unlikely that such a

> defect would not be discovered within the limitation period. Such cases, if they exist, would be exceptional.[18]

This passage, and, in particular, the concept of 'doomed from the start', proved to be problematical and the decision in *Pirelli* certainly did not produce equilibrium in this area of law. The concept of a building being doomed from the start was considered in *Kettman v. Hansel Properties Ltd.*[19] In that case the plaintiffs bought houses from the first defendants, the builders. The foundations were laid between 1973 and 1975 in accordance with the design of the architects and they were approved by the local authority. They were faulty and in 1976 cracks appeared in the walls. In 1980 the plaintiffs issued a writ against the builders claiming damages for negligence and in 1982 they joined in the architect and the local authority. The Court of Appeal held that the plaintiffs' claims against the architects and the local authority were not statute-barred on the ground that the houses were doomed from the start; the plaintiffs' cause of action accrued when the physical damage to their houses occurred, i.e. when the cracks appeared in the walls in 1976. The Court of Appeal said that it was only in exceptional cases that a building could be 'doomed from the start'.

Like the decision in *Anns* in relation to limitation, the scope of the decision in *Pirelli* is not clear, and in subsequent cases it was not applied to the liability of local authorities or the liability of professional persons. In *Jones v. Stroud District Council*[20] the plaintiff in 1975 purchased a house built in 1964. In 1976, following a drought, cracks appeared as a result of subsidence caused by defective foundations. In 1981 the plaintiff issued a writ claiming damages against the local authority for negligence in failing to inspect the foundations. The Court of Appeal held that until the condition of the house gave rise to danger the authority was not in breach of a duty; the cause of action did not arise, therefore, until some time after the drought of 1976 and was not statute-barred.

In *Forster v. Outred & Co.*[21] the plaintiff, at her solicitor's office in February 1973, executed a mortgage deed charging her freehold property to a company as security for her son's liabilities to the company. The son went bankrupt owing money to the company. The company threatened to foreclose on the mortgage unless the plaintiff paid the amount of her son's liabilities. In March 1980 the plaintiff issued a writ against her solicitor alleging negligence in that he did not explain the full import of the mortgage deed. (She had thought that the mortgage was security for a bridging loan.) The Court of Appeal held that where a plaintiff alleged that he had suffered economic loss as a result of a solicitor's negligent advice, actual damage occurred and the plaintiff's cause of action arose when, in reliance on the solicitor's negligent advice, he acted to his detriment. Accordingly, the plaintiff suffered actual damage and her cause of action was complete when she executed the mortgage deed in February 1973. The writ which she issued in March 1980 was therefore issued too late to come within the statutory limitation period.

In *Secretary of State for the Environment v. Essex Goodman & Suggitt*[22] the defendants were surveyors who in February 1975 surveyed a recently erected building on behalf of the plaintiffs who were prospective lessees of the building. In July 1975, in reliance on the surveyors' report, the plaintiffs entered into a 25 year lease of the premises. In February 1976 defects appeared in the building and in January 1982 the plaintiffs issued a writ against the surveyors claiming damages for negligence. The Official Referee, Judge Lewis Hawser, Q.C., held that the duty of care owed by the surveyors to the plaintiffs was different from the duty owed by the designers or builders of the building. The surveyors had been employed to find out whether there were any defects in existence at the date of the survey and their duty was to report to the plaintiffs any such defects. The judge went on to say that if the damage occurred subsequently, or if it could not have been discovered by the exercise of reasonable care and skill, the surveyors would not have been liable since they would have complied with their duty. Accordingly, the plaintiffs' cause of action arose when they acted on the report, i.e. July 1975, and it was time-barred.

The Latent Damage Act 1986

Prior to this Act the law on limitation and latent damage could be summed up as follows:

(1) In an action alleging negligence in the design or construction of a building, the cause of action accrued when damage occurred to the building.
(2) If the defendant was a local authority, the cause of action accrued when there was a present or imminent threat to the health or safety of the occupants.
(3) If the defendant was a professional person providing advice, time began to run when the plaintiff acted to his detriment on reliance on the negligent advice.

In all these cases it was the occurrence of damage that was relevant, rather than discoverability of the existence of damage.

The 1986 Act is based upon the recommendations of the 24th Report of the Law Reform Committee, *Latent Damage*.[23] In this report the Committee identified three principles as being of critical importance in this area of law:

(1) that plaintiffs must have a fair and sufficient opportunity of pursuing their remedy;
(2) that defendants are entitled to be protected against stale claims; and
(3) that uncertainty in the law is to be avoided wherever possible.

The Committee's recommendations attempt to give effect to these principles by striking a balance between the hardship of the *Sparharm-Souter* test to defendants and their insurers, on the one hand, and the problems posed to plaintiffs by the *Pirelli* test, on the other hand.

Section 1 of the 1986 Act inserts a new section 14A and section 14B into the Limitation Act 1980. Section 14A provides that an action for damage not involving personal injuries cannot be brought after the expiration of either

(a) six years from the date on which the cause of action accrued; or
(b) three years from the starting date, if that period expires later than the period in (a) above.

Section 14A goes on to state that the starting date for reckoning the period of limitation is the earliest date on which the plaintiff had the knowledge required for bringing an action for damages in respect of the relevant damage. Section 14B introduces an overriding time limit, known as a long-stop, for negligence actions not involving personal injuries. It provides that an action for damages for negligence cannot be brought after the expiration of fifteen years from the date on which any act or omission alleged to constitute negligence occurred.

The result of these provisions is that there are now *three* limitation periods in actions for negligence which do not involve personal injury:

(1) a *primary* limitation period of six years starting from the date on which the cause of action accrued;
(2) a *secondary* limitation period of three years starting from the date when the damage was discovered or should have been discovered; and
(3) a long-stop of fifteen years starting from the date on which the act or omission alleged to constitute the negligence occurred.

These periods operate as follows. Where no latent damage is present time will run, as before, for six years from the date on which the cause of action accrued. This will also be the case where the three-year secondary period expires before the six-year primary period. If, however, damage occurs in, say, year one, and becomes discoverable in say, year five, then the primary period is overridden by the secondary period, i.e. time will run out eight years after the date on which the cause of action accrued. This is subject to the fifteen-year long-stop; in other words, in an action for damages for negligence not involving personal injuries time does not run out until fifteen years from the date on which the cause of action accrued.

Subsequent developments

The Latent Damage Act certainly moved the law of limitation once again in favour of plaintiffs. But two developments have occurred since the passing of the Act to favour defendants. Firstly, doubt has been cast on concurrent liability by Lord Scarman in delivering the decision of the Privy Council in *Tai Hing Cotton Mill Ltd v. Lin Chong Hing Bank Ltd*, when he said:

> Their Lordships do not believe that there is anything to the advantage of the law's development in searching for a liability in tort where the parties are in a contractual relationship; indeed it is correct in principle and necessary for the avoidance of confusion in the law to adhere to the contractual analysis.[24]

The implications of this dictum are still being worked out, but it has subsequently been held that where the parties define their relationship in a contract any duty in tort will be no wider under than any duty owed under the contract.[25] Thus, a contract may well deprive a plaintiff of an action in tort and therefore of the more generous tortious limitation period.

The second development was the decision of the House of Lords in *Murphy* and its effect on the rule in *Pirelli*. *Murphy*, it will be remembered, defined economic loss comprehensively to include damage to the product or the premises itself. On the basis of this definition, *Pirelli* is essentially a case about economic loss – the relevant damage was to the chimney itself. The House of Lords in *Murphy*, however, did not overrule *Pirelli*; rather they sought to explain it in terms of the reliance principle laid down in *Hedley Byrne v. Heller*. Thus, Lord Keith said:

> It would seem that in a case such as the *Pirelli General Cable Works* case, where the tortious liability arose out of a contractual relationship with professional people, the duty extended to take reasonable care not to cause economic loss to the client by the advice given. The plaintiffs built the chimney as they did in reliance on that advice. The case would accordingly fall within the principle of *Hedley Byrne & Co. Ltd v. Heller & Partners Ltd.*[26]

The problem with classifying *Pirelli* as a reliance case is that on this basis the cause of action accrued not when the physical damage occurred in 1970, but when the plaintiffs relied on the defendant's advice, which was in 1969 when the chimney was built. If Lord Keith's dictum in *Murphy* is taken to this conclusion, then the implications for plaintiffs are potentially serious. It will surely emaciate any revival of the law of negligence and economic loss on the basis of the reliance principle because the limitation period for a plaintiff in these circumstances would be no longer than the contractual limitation period. *Murphy* may therefore be a double blow for plaintiffs: under its general rule owners of defective premises are deprived of a cause of action in negligence and the possible exception to that rule may well turn out to be of very limited practical worth.

The law relating to negligence and economic loss and limitation has been reviewed in two recent decisions of the Official Referee: *Hiron and Hiron and Legal Assurance Society Ltd v. Pynford South Ltd & Others.*[27] Mr and Mrs Hiron were owner-occupiers of a house in Middlesex. The house was situated on a slope and in 1976 damage appeared in it. Mr and Mrs Hiron made a claim against their insurers, Legal and General Assurance Society Ltd, who employed a firm of structural engineers to advise them. In 1980 the Hirons employed a group of specialist construction companies, Pynford South Ltd and Pynford Services Ltd, to carry out a site investigation. Following this investigation they entered into a contract with Pynford South to carry out remedial works. Pynford guaranteed these works for a period of twenty years. In May 1985 further damage developed in this house, with the result that it became structurally unstable. The Hirons' building surveyor informed Pynford South that underpinning and antiheave precautions were required. In May 1989 the Hirons decided to sue the construction companies and their building surveyor and, further, the Legal and General issued a writ against their structural engineers.

One of the issues to which these facts gave rise was whether these causes of action arose more than six years before the issue of the writs. The loss suffered was economic and Judge Newey said that a cause of action in tort for economic loss arose when the damage was suffered, which was well before May 1985, and not when the damage was discovered. Therefore, the plaintiffs' claims were all statute-barred.

In *Nitrigen Eireann Teoranta v. Inco Alloys Ltd,*[28] Nitrigen were an Irish firm of chemical manufacturers who owned and operated a plant in Ireland. They contracted with Inco in 1981 for the supply of replacement tubes for their plant. One of these tubes cracked in July 1983. It was repaired but in June 1984 cracked again, causing damage to the structure of the plant. Nitrigen accepted that any claim in contract was statute-barred and they sued in tort. The main issue, therefore, was when the cause of action in tort arose, 1983 or 1984? If 1983 then that cause of action too was statute-barred.

May J. held that the cause of action in negligence arose in 1984. The cracking of the pipe in 1983 was damage to the thing itself, constituting a defect in quality resulting in economic loss, and was therefore irrecoverable in negligence. In 1984 physical damage to other property had occurred and the judge held that this did establish a cause of action. The plaintiffs were therefore not statute-barred. In coming to this conclusion the judge reviewed the law of negligence and economic loss and its relationship to the limitation of actions. He distinguished this case from *Pirelli* by applying Lord Keith's dictum in *Murphy* that *Pirelli* fell within the reliance principle. The defendants in *Pirelli* were a firm of consulting engineers; Inco, however, although specialist manufacturers, were not engaged in any professional capacity and the judge said that the relationship between Inco and Nitrigen did not come within the scope of the reliance principle.

These last two decisions clearly show that there are still unresolved problems in this area of law.

NOTES

1. [1977] AC 547, p. 575 and quoted in Derek Morgan, *Limitation Act 1980*, Current Law Statutes Annotated, Vol. 2, Ch. 58, Sweet & Maxwell, 1980.
2. DTI/DoE, *Professional Liability – Report of the Study Teams*, HMSO, 1989.
3. [1990] 2 All ER 908.
4. [1971] 2 All ER 747.
5. [1963] AC 758.
6. [1972] 1 QB 373, p. 396.
7. [1976] QB 858.
8. *Ibid.*, n.7, p. 868.
9. [1978] AC 728.
10. *Ibid.*, n.9, p. 760.
11. [1986] CLY 210; (1986) 279 EG 218.
12. (1980) 259 EG 491.
13. [1976] QB 801.
14. [1964] AC 465.
15. [1978] QB 554.
16. [1979] Cl.384.
17. [1983] 2 AC 1.
18. *Ibid.*, n.17 p. 16.
19. [1985] 1 All ER 352.
20. [1986] 1 WLR 1141.
21. [1982] 2 All ER 753.
22. [1986] 2 All ER 69.

23. Cmnd 9390, 1984.
24. [1985] 2 All ER 947, p. 957.
25. See *Greater Nottingham Co-operative Society v. Cementation* [1988] 2 All ER 971.
26. *Supra*, n.3, p. 919.
27. Reported in *Chartered Surveyor Weekly*, 6 February 1992, p. 82.
28. [1992] 1 All ER 854.

Part II

European Law

10 Introduction to the European Community

One of the principal aims of the European Community (the EC) is the creation of a single market, with an unrestricted flow of goods, persons, services and capital between the Member States. This is expressed in Article 2 of the Treaty of Rome 1957:

> The Community shall have as its task, by establishing a common market ... to promote throughout the Community a harmonious development of economic activities, a continuous and balanced expansion, an increase in stability, an accelerated raising of the standard of living and closer relations between the States belonging to it.

In order to create a single market, it is necessary that all the suppliers of goods and services in the EC operate in what is referred to as a 'level playing field'. If this is not the case, then some producers will operate at an advantage over other producers in the EC and competition will become distorted. The most effective way of achieving a single market in the EC would be for the Member States to adopt the *same* laws in those areas which affects costs of production. Politically this is not practicable and instead the EC has pursued a policy of harmonising the laws of the Member States. Thus, Article 3(a) of the Treaty of Rome states that one of the aims of the community is:

> ... the approximation of the laws of Member States to the extent required for the proper functioning of the common market.

At first, progress towards the creation of a single market was slow, and in order to speed up the process of achieving this goal the Commission of the EC in June 1985 presented to the European Council a White Paper, *Completing the Internal Market*. This proposed 31 December 1992 as the deadline for the coming into effect of a single market. In addition, the White Paper put forward two substantive proposals:

(i) the removal of non-tariff barriers between the Member States which prevented the completion of a single market; and
(ii) measures to increase the degree of protection provided to consumers in the EC.

These proposals were adopted in the Single European Act 1986, which came into force on 1 July 1987. The Act made a number of significant amendments to the Treaty of Rome. Article 13 introduced a new Article 8A into the Treaty of Rome, setting 31 December 1992 as the date for completing the internal market, and stating:

> The internal market shall comprise an area without frontiers in which the free movement of goods, persons, services and capital is ensured in accordance with the provisions of this Treaty.

Article 18 introduced a new Article 100A into the Treaty of Rome which provided for the adoption by 'qualified majority' of 'Directives for the approximation of such provisions laid down by law, regulation or administrative action in Member States as directly affect the establishment or functioning of the Common Market'.

The result of the Single European Act has been the adoption of the 'New Approach' directives removing legal, technical and fiscal barriers to the single market and also introducing a range of consumer protection measures. The following measures, in particular, impinge on Construction Law:

(i) the Product Liability Directive;[1]
(ii) the General Product Safety Directive;[2]
(iii) the Construction Products Directive;[3]
(iv) the proposed Directive on the Liability of Suppliers of Services;[4] and
(v) the Directive on Unfair Terms in Consumer Contracts.[5]

They are discussed in Chapters 11 and 12.

The process of harmonising the laws of the Member States in order to enable the establishment and functioning of the internal market and the provision of a high level of consumer protection in the community are continued by the Maastricht Treaty 1992.[6] However, the future extent of this process depends very much on the interpretation and application of one of the most important provisions of that Treaty, the subsidiarity principle. This principle is set out in Article 3b:

> In areas which do not fall within its exclusive competence the Community shall take action, in accordance with the principle of subsidiarity, only if and in so far as the objectives of the proposed action cannot be sufficiently achieved by the Member States and can, therefore, by reason of the scale or effects of the proposed action, be better achieved by the Community.

The precise effect of this principle on the process of harmonisation of the laws of the Member States is a matter which is yet to be determined. It is a question which affects in particular the harmonisation of laws relating to general liability for services and the liability of the participants in the construction process. A Commission staff discussion paper[7] has suggested that before the Community could be justified in taking action on these matters the following questions would need to be answered in the affirmative:

- Would Community action come under the removal of barriers to the free movement of goods, persons, services and capital?
- Would Community action be essential to the achievement of free movement?
- Would action by the Member States be insufficient, given the aims pursued?
- Would Community action enhance the action liable to be taken by the Member States?

It is not going to be easy to apply these guidelines to individual proposals for future harmonisation directives. But one thing does seem to be clear: the tide of harmonisation has reached its high water mark and is now ebbing.

NOTES

1. 85/374/EEC, OJ No. L210/29.
2. 92/59/EEC, OJ No. L228/24.
3. 89/106/EEC, OJ No. L40/12.
4. OJ 1991 C12/8.
5. 93/13/EEC, OJ No. L95/29.
6. Articles 100–2 and Article 129a. The Maastricht Treaty is not an entity in its own right but is a series of amendments and additions to the previous European Treaties. It has now been ratified by all the Member States and all the European Treaties have been officially consolidated into a *Treaty on European Union.*

7. Commission of the European Communities, *Commission staff discussion paper concerning possible community action with regard to liabilities and guarantees in the construction sector* (1993).

11 Construction Products Liability

INTRODUCTION

There are three measures of the EC which affect liability for construction products:

(1) the Product Liability Directive 1985,[1] which has been implemented into United Kingdom law by Part I of the Consumer Protection Act 1987;[2]
(2) the Construction Products Directive 1988,[3] which has been implemented into United Kingdom law by the Construction Product Regulations 1991;[4] and
(3) the General Product Safety Directive 1992,[5] which is due to be implemented by the Member States by June 1994.

These measures have two purposes. Their principal purpose is to harmonise the laws of the Members States in relation to product safety and thereby remove distortions in competition within the EC. They are part of the Commission's programme for the completion of a Single European Market. Their secondary purpose is the provision of consumer protection, i.e. to ensure that every consumer within the EC has the same high degree of protection in relation to injury or damage caused by defective products. In this second respect, they form part of a comprehensive Community code governing the obligations of producers and suppliers in respect of the safety of the goods and services which they sell.

THE PRODUCT LIABILITY DIRECTIVE

The purpose of this section is to outline the provisions of this Directive and to examine how they have been implemented by Part I of the Consumer Protection Act 1987 (CPA). A detailed critique of this legislation is beyond the scope of this work, though particular attention is paid to those provisions which are of particular relevance to liabilities in the construction industry.[6]

The basic principle

The basic principle on which the Directive is based is contained in Article 1, which states:

> The producer shall be liable for damage caused by a defect in his product.

This provision is implemented by section 2(1) of the CPA, which states:

> Subject to the following provisions of this Part, where any damage is caused wholly or partly by a defect in a product, every person to whom subsection (2) below applies shall be liable for the damage.

There are two important features of these provisions to be noted. In the first place, their significance lies in what they do *not* state. They do not state that there is any need to establish fault, and from this it can be deduced that the basis of liability under section 2(1) is strict. The second important feature of section 2(1) is that a claim under it does not depend upon the victim of a defective product having a contract with the producer of that product. In other words, the problem of privity of contract is avoided.

Until the implementation of this Directive the legal position of a person injured by a defective product varied under the legal systems of the Member States. Some systems required the victim to establish negligence on the part of the producer, while other systems imposed strict liability on the producer. In a system of strict liability for defective products the damage suffered by the victim is more likely to be passed on to the producer and to form part of the general cost of production than in a negligence system of product liability, where the victim often has difficulty in proving that the producer is at fault. Thus, costs of production are generally higher in a strict liability system of product liability than in a negligence system of product liability. Such differences in costs would distort competition between the Member States and prevent the completion of the Single Market. The implementation of a strict liability system throughout the Community removes these distortions and at the same time provides consumers in the EC with the same degree of protection.

Two points need highlighting in this context. In the first place, the implementation of the Directive does not replace the pre-existing product liability laws of the Member States; rather it is in addition to those laws. Thus, in the UK Part I of the CPA does not replace the pre-existing fault-based system of liability originating from *Donoghue v. Stevenson.*[7] Secondly, the new law is not free of difficulties for the victim: the burden of proof is still on him to show that he suffered damage, that the product was defective and that the defect caused the damage. These requirements may prove stumbling blocks in controversial areas such as defective drugs.

What is a product?

A product is defined in Article 2 of the Directive to include:

> ... all movables, with the exception of primary agricultural products and game, even though incorporated into another movable or into an immovable. 'Primary agricultural products' means the products of the soil, of stock-farming and of fisheries, excluding products which have undergone initial processing. 'Product' includes electricity.

It will be noted, for the purposes of Construction Law, that this definition extends to a movable which has been 'incorporated into an immovable'. The definition of product extends therefore to building components, but not to the building itself.

The definition of 'product' contained in the CPA is based on that contained in the Directive. By section 1(2) a product is defined as:

> ... any goods or electricity and ... includes a product which is comprised in another product, whether by virtue of being a component part or raw material or otherwise.

'Goods' are defined widely in section 45 to include substances, growing crops and things comprised in land by virtue of being attached to it, and any ship, aircraft or vehicle.

In the case of buildings and building components the relevant sections of the CPA are 46(3) and (4). Section 46(3) provides that:

> ... subject to subsection (4) below, the performance of any contract by the erection of any building or structure on any land or by the carrying out of any other building works shall be treated for the purposes of this Act as a supply of goods in so far as, but only in so far as, it involves the provision of any goods to any person by means of their incorporation into the building, structure or works.

Section 46(4) provides, so far as is material, that:

> ... references in this Act to supplying goods shall not include references to supplying goods comprised in land where the supply is effected by the creation or disposal of an interest in the land.

The cumulative effect of these provisions is that if a builder is employed to erect a building on land owned by the employer, the employer will have the protection of the CPA in respect of defective products supplied or produced by the builder and incorporated into the building.[8] Thus, if a builder installs a defective piece of electrical equipment in a building which causes personal injury, then liability will attach to the builder as supplier of that equipment. The builder in this case will not be liable under the provisions of the CPA if the building itself is defective.[9] In the case of a builder who erects a building on his own land and then disposes of that building by way of a contract for the sale or lease of the land, he will not be liable under the provisions of the CPA in respect of any defective products incorporated into the building. It is not clear whether, in this second case, the builder may be liable as producer under the provisions of the CPA in the event of the completed building being defective.[10]

Who is liable?

Under the provisions of Article 3 of the Directive, which are implemented by section 2(2) of the CPA, liability is imposed upon:

(a) the producer of the product;
(b) any person who, by putting his name on the product or by using a trade mark or other distinguishing mark in relation to the product, has held himself out to be the producer of the product;
(c) any person who has imported the product into a Member State from a place outside the Member States in order, in the course of any business of his, to supply it to another.

A producer in relation to a product is defined widely by section 1(2) of the CPA to include:

(a) the person who manufactured it;
(b) in the case of a substance which has not been manufactured but has been won or abstracted, the person who won or abstracted it;
(c) in the case of a product which has not been manufactured, won or abstracted but essential characteristics of which are attributable to an individual or other process having been carried out (for example, in

relation to agricultural produce), the person who carried out that process.

Beyond the above three groups, section 2(3) of the CPA provides that any other supplier may be liable, regardless of whether or not he produced the product or the constituent components giving rise to the damage. He must have been asked by a person who has suffered damage wholly or partly as a result of a defect in the product to identify one or more persons who fall within any of the above groups. The request must have been made within a reasonable time after the damage occurred and at a time when it was not reasonably practicable for the person making the request to identify all the persons in these groups. A supplier who fails to give information in response to such a request becomes liable and appears to remain liable even though the information is later discovered by some other means. Clearly, a builder will be liable under the CPA if he supplies defective building materials and cannot identify the person who supplied him with those materials. Further, he will be liable as a 'producer' if he has carried out an industrial process on the materials supplied, e.g. mixing concrete or cement.

What is a defect?

The cornerstone of both the Directive and Part I of the CPA is, of course, the concept of defectiveness. Under the provisions of Article 6 of the Directive and section 3(1) of the CPA, a product is defective when it does not provide the safety which persons generally are entitled to expect, taking into account all the circumstances. A great deal has been written about this concept,[11] and only a few brief comments will be offered here on it. In the first place, it should be noted that defectiveness is limited to the safety of the product. Products which are unmerchantable or unfit for their purpose, but otherwise safe, fall outside the scope of this definition. Secondly, the test of safety is based on consumer expectations. Thus, products which are inherently dangerous or which become dangerous if misused are not necessarily defective.

Section 3(2) of the CPA, implementing and expanding upon the provisions of Article 6 of the Directive, states that in assessing defectiveness all the circumstances must be taken into account, including:

(a) the manner in which, and purposes for which, the product has been marketed, its get-up, the use of any mark in relation to the product and any instructions for, or warnings with respect to, doing or refraining from doing anything with or in relation to the product;

(b) what might reasonably be expected to be done with or in relation to the product; and
(c) the time when the product was supplied by its producer to another.

Paragraph (a) makes it clear that a product may be 'defective', even though it fulfils its design function in precisely the manner in which the manufacturer intends, if hazards associated with its use are not sufficiently brought to the consumer's attention. Paragraph (b) requires the producer to be able to foresee predictable misuse and eliminate any hazards. If this is not possible or feasible, then adequate warnings or instructions must be provided. Under the provisions of paragraph (c) a product will not be considered defective simply because a safer product is subsequently put into circulation. A car with a rigid steering column and no seat belts would be considered defective if so designed today, but fifty years ago such features were acceptable. Section 3(2) of the CPA provides for this by adding:

> ... and nothing in this section shall require a defect to be inferred from the fact alone that the safety of a product which is supplied after that time is greater than the safety of the product in question.

Without this provision, producers would constantly have to recall or modify older products every time they introduced a safety improvement.

What damages are recoverable?

Under the provisions of Article 9 of the Directive, 'damage' means:

(a) damage caused by death or by personal injuries;
(b) damage to, or destruction of, any item of property other than the defective product itself, with a lower threshold of 500 ECU provided that the item of property:
    (i) is of a type ordinarily intended for private use or consumption, and
    (ii) was used by the injured person mainly for his own private use or consumption.

These provisions are implemented by section 5 of the CPA, where subsection (4) puts the lower threshold at £275.

A number of further points need to be noted in relation to these provisions. Firstly, there is no liability for damage to the product itself. This is, of course, the same as the position under the common law of negligence. The manufacturer of a defective, though not dangerous, building will thus not be liable, either in negligence or under the CPA. In each case, a claim is regarded as one for pure economic loss because it involves putting onto the market a product or building of less value than it was supposed to be under the contract.[12] The only possible exception to this rule would be if the plaintiff could show that the damage was caused by 'other property'. In relation to buildings this concept has been given a narrow interpretation following the decision of the House of Lords in *Murphy v. Brentwood DC.*[13] Thus, a defect in an integral part of the structure of a building which causes damage to the rest of the building will not be recoverable. On the other hand, a distinct item, such as a central heating boiler, which is incorporated into the building and which is defective, thereby causing damage to the building itself, may well give rise to a claim for damages. Secondly, there is no liability for damage to business property.[14] Thus, if a defective central heating boiler damages a private house, then that will give rise to a claim for damages, but not if the boiler were to cause damage to, say, an office block.

What defences are available?

The Directive and Part I of the CPA provide for a number of defences. The most important of these defences is the development risks defence, which is expressed in the Act in the following terms:

> ... that the state of scientific and technical knowledge at the relevant time was not such that a producer of products of the same description as the product in question might be expected to have discovered the defect if it had existed in his products while they were under his control.[15]

This version of the defence differs significantly from the form which it takes in the Directive:

> ... that the state of scientific and technical knowledge at the time when he put the product into circulation was not such as to enable the existence of the defect to be discovered.[16]

Thus, the test under Part I of the Act is whether a producer of similar products might have been expected to have discovered the defect; under the Directive the test is whether the knowledge existed to discover the defect.

The limitation period

Under the provisions of Articles 10 and 11 of the Directive, which are implemented by Schedule 1 of the CPA, there is a limitation period of three years for the recovery of damages. This period commences on the date that the plaintiff knew of the damage, the defect and the producer's identity. There is a ten year 'long stop' limitation period from the date that the producer put the product into circulation.

Summary

It is difficult thus far to attempt an overall assessment of this legislation for the construction industry, or any other industry, for that matter. The Act has yet to come before the courts and so the full extent of liability under its provisions cannot be accurately gauged. In essence, liability may attach to a building contractor under the provisions of Part I of the Act if defects in goods supplied as part of construction works cause death, personal injury or damage to private property other than the defective works themselves. In view of the definition of defective in the Act and of the existence of a development risks defence, many commentators believe that the scheme of strict liability it introduces adds little to the existing common law of negligence save reversing the burden of proof. This may prove a little too pessimistic. Much will depend on how the courts interpret the development risks defence.

THE CONSTRUCTION PRODUCTS DIRECTIVE

The Construction Products Directive was adopted by the European Commission on 27 December 1988. It is one of the New Approach Directives referred to in Chapter 10 and its general purpose is the achievement of uniform minima of consumer protection in relation to construction products in the Member States. Thus, in the preamble to the Directive it states:

> Member States are responsible for ensuring that building and civil engineering works on their territory are designed and executed in a way that does not endanger the safety of persons, domestic animals and property, while respecting other essential requirements in the interests of general well being.

The preamble notes the disparity throughout the EC in the way in which the Member States regulate the construction of buildings. It is thought that this disparity distorts competition in the EC and that the achievement of uniformity in this area of the law – in particular, the standards to be reached by construction products – would be a significant factor in creating a level playing field in the construction industry in the EC.

The Directive was implemented into UK law by the Construction Products Regulations 1991, which were passed under the provisions of section 2(2) of the European Community Act 1972. The main provisions of these Regulations will now be examined. In order to avoid unnecessary detail in the text of this section of the chapter, references to the individual regulations, and their corresponding articles in the Directive where appropriate, are contained in the notes.

The basic principle

The essential principle on which the Directive is based is that of fitness for use; construction products must meet certain standards in relation to the fitness for use of the *building works in which they are incorporated.* Fitness for use is defined in terms of satisfying certain essential requirements in so far as these requirements apply to the works.[17] These requirements must be satisfied for the 'economically reasonable working life' of a construction product subject to normal maintenance and foreseeable working loads and requirements. They are expressed in terms of six general objectives, viz.:

(1) mechanical resistance and stability;
(2) safety in case of fire;
(3) hygiene, health and the environment;
(4) safety in use;
(5) protection against noise; and
(6) energy economy and heat retention.[18]

These objectives will be set out in detail in interpretative documents published in the *Official Journal* of the European Communities and they in turn will lead to the formulation of harmonised standards for construction products which will be transposed into 'relevant national standards'. That task is still in hand[19] and presumably it will be some time before it is completed. Certain UK bodies will need to be designated to carry out the job of testing and certifying products. The Regulations will not be properly effective until these things are in place.

What is a construction product?

This is defined by the Regulations as any product, other than a minor part product, which is produced for incorporation in a permanent manner in works.[20] A minor part product is defined as a construction product which is included in a list of products which play a minor part with respect to health and safety drawn up, managed and revised periodically by the European Commission.[21]

The CE mark

One of the key concepts in the Directive is the CE mark. This is a mark of quality which denotes that a product achieves the standards of fitness for use with respect to the essential requirements and is therefore entitled to free circulation within the Community, unless there are reasonable grounds for suspecting that the product is unfit.[22] It is important to note that the use of a CE mark is voluntary, so that non-CE marked products which meet the essential requirements are legal.

The CE mark can be fixed to a product provided that four conditions are satisfied. These are:

(i) the product complies with an appropriate technical specification;
(ii) the appropriate attestation procedure has been followed;
(iii) an EC certificate of conformity or declaration of conformity has been used or made in respect of the product; and
(iv) the product complies with any requirements of other legislation implementing relevant EC directives applying to it.[23]

The CE mark can be:

- on the product itself; or
- on the label attached to the product; or
- on the packaging; or
- on the accompanying commercial documentation.

It must be accompanied by sufficient information to enable the manufacturer of the product to be identified. In addition certain other information has to accompany the mark, except where inappropriate. Notably this includes details of the technical characteristics of the product and (if relevant) of the independent body involved in testing or certification.[24]

The commonest ways in which products are likely to qualify for the CE mark are by conforming to a harmonised European standard or being awarded a European Technical Approval (ETA) by an approved EC issuing body. The British Board of Agrément has been designated for this role in the UK. The development of harmonised European standards is the responsibility of CEN and CENELEC technical committees. The European Organisation for Technical Approvals (EOTA) is responsible for developing the ETA system.[25]

In the case of products bearing the CE mark there is a requirement to keep available and produce the CE certificate or a copy of it. This requirement is imposed either (a) on the person who affixes the CE mark to a construction product, or (b), if that person is not established in the UK, on the person who first supplies the product in the UK.[26] If a product is not CE marked, then it may still be possible to place it on the market (e.g. in the circumstances where no 'relevant technical specification' has been produced for it). However, the supplier of such a product is required to give to an enforcement authority all the information which he has about it.[27]

The Regulations create three offences in this area. Firstly, it is an offence to make a CE declaration of conformity in respect of, or to affix the CE mark to, a construction product otherwise than in accordance with the Regulations. Secondly, where the CE mark has been affixed otherwise than in accordance with the Regulations, it is an offence to supply a construction product on the first occasion when it is supplied in the Community.[28] Thirdly, it is an offence to supply a construction product which does not satisfy the essential requirements of the Regulations.[29]

Removal of construction products from the market

The Regulations enable action to be taken to remove from the market construction products which do not satisfy their requirements. The Secretary of State may serve a prohibition notice prohibiting a person from supplying a product, or a notice to warn requiring him to publish a warning about products supplied.[30] It is an offence to contravene a prohibition notice or a notice to warn.[31] An enforcement authority may serve a suspension notice prohibiting a person from supplying a product for a period of six months from the date of the notice and, again, it is an offence to contravene such a notice.[32] It may also apply to the court for an order that a product be forfeited.[33]

Enforcement of the Regulations

Responsibility for enforcement is placed on weights and measures authorities in Great Britain and District Councils in Northern Ireland.[34]

The enforcement mechanism contained in the Regulations is closely modelled on Parts IV and V of the Consumer Protection Act 1987. Powers are conferred on the enforcement authorities to make test purchases, search premises, and examine, seize and detain products and records, and customs officers are permitted to seize and detain imported products.[35] Obstructing an officer employed by an enforcement authority is an offence.[36]

Compensation is payable to any person for any loss or damage resulting from the exercise of these powers if:

(a) there has not been a contravention of the Regulations; and
(b) the exercise of these powers does not result from any neglect or default on the part of the person to be compensated.[37]

Defences

The Regulations contain the usual defence of due diligence contained in criminal consumer protection statutes. That is, in proceedings against a person for an offence under the Regulations it shall be a defence for that person to show that he took all reasonable steps and exercised all due diligence to avoid committing the offence.[38] In addition, where the commission by any person of an offence under the Regulations is due to an act or default committed by another person in the course of his business, then proceedings can be taken against that person in addition to the first-mentioned person.[39]

Liability issues arising from the Construction Products Regulations

These Regulations impose *criminal* liability upon the *supplier* of a construction product which does not meet the essential requirements; they are not about *civil* liability as such, but arguably they do impinge on the civil liability of design professionals and builders.

Design professions (i.e. architects and engineers) will generally be under a duty to provide reasonable supervision of the building or engineering works. If it turns out that some or all of the materials used in the construction of the works do not meet the essential requirements laid down by the Regulations, then arguably the architect or engineer will not have discharged that duty.

Another task which may fall to the architect or engineer is the recommendation of the materials to be used by the contractor. In carrying out this task, these design professionals are under a duty to use reasonable care and skill, but they do not normally guarantee that any recommended product will be fit for a particular purpose. However, it seems that this aspect of the architect's or engineer's duty of care will now extend to ensuring that a product meets the essential requirements before recommending it. If a product which is not CE marked and which does not meet the essential requirements is recommended, then, arguably, the duty of reasonable care and skill will not have been satisfied. Further, it must be remembered that the architect or engineer is under a duty to ensure that any products he recommends meet any specifications laid down by the employer. If those specifications go further than the essential requirements laid down by the Regulations, then for the architect or engineer simply to satisfy those requirements and no more will not be enough to discharge his legal duty to the employer. In the event of the builder using a product which does not meet the essential requirements but which was *not* recommended by the architect or engineer, then presumably the duty of these professionals will be to warn the employer of this fact.

The builder is under implied obligations to supply materials which are of merchantable quality and fit for their purpose.[40] Arguably, these obligations will now extend to ensuring that the materials he uses meet the essential requirements. Unlike the duty owed by the architect or engineer in this respect, this duty is strict, i.e. the builder will still be liable for the use of products which do not meet the essential requirements even though he may have exercised reasonable care and skill in selecting them, e.g. by consulting with the supplier and/or an expert.

Finally in this section, it should be noted that presumably *civil* liability will also be imposed on the supplier of a construction product which does not meet the essential requirements; in these circumstances, arguably he will be in breach of his implied obligations of merchantable quality and fitness for purpose in the contract of sale with the builder.[41] Again, this liability will be strict. Indeed, it is the fact that the builder in these circumstances has what amounts to an indemnity action against the supplier which the courts have used to justify imposing strict liability with respect to materials on the builder.[42]

Summary

Recent years have seen an increasing emphasis on product safety, in both the civil law and the criminal law, and the Construction Products Regulations are a continuation of that trend. Safety in buildings until now has been largely a matter of safety in the *construction* of buildings – the law has required builders to comply with the provisions of the Building Regulations in the construction of buildings. There have been no safety requirements relating to *materials* used in the construction of buildings other than the general implied terms in a contract for work and materials that the materials be of merchantable quality and fit for their purpose.

The success of the Regulations, as with all legislation which creates regulatory offences, will depend ultimately on how effectively they are enforced. Like other recent legislation of this kind, they grant impressive, if not draconian, powers to the enforcement authorities. But how widely these powers will be used will depend on the resources available to the enforcement authorities. The Regulations themselves and their Explanatory Notes are silent on this point.

THE GENERAL PRODUCT SAFETY DIRECTIVE

The General Product Safety Directive was adopted by the Council on 29 June 1992. The Directive will be implemented into UK law by Regulations made under the provisions of section 2(2) of the EC Act 1972. They are due to come into force by 29 June 1994.[43] Like the other two directives discussed in this chapter, this Directive was part of the Commission's programme for the establishment of the Single Market. Recital 2 of the Directive states that legislation on product safety in the Member States differs in the level of protection it affords to persons, and that these disparities are likely to create barriers to trade and distortions of competition within the EC. The principal purpose of the Directive is to remove these disparities by harmonising the laws of the Member States relating to product safety. The secondary purpose of the Directive is to provide a broadly based legislative framework with a view to ensuring a high level of safety and health of persons, as required by Article 100a(3) of the Treaty of Rome.

The Directive applies to producers and distributors. Producers are required to place only safe products on the market; this is 'the general safety requirement'. Distributors are required to act with due care in order to help to ensure compliance with the general safety requirement; they must not supply products which do not comply with this requirement. It is in the capacity of distributor that a builder or construction professional is likely to be caught by the Directive.

The main provisions of the Directive will now be examined.

The general safety requirement

Article 3 of the Directive imposes a requirement on producers to place only safe products on the market. Under the provisions of Article 2(a) this will apply to all products 'intended for consumers or likely to be used by consumers, supplied whether for consideration or not in the course of a commercial activity and whether new, used or reconditioned'. Article 2(a) exempts from the general safety requirement secondhand goods that are sold as antiques or as being in need of repair or reconditioning. Further, Recital 5 of the Directive provides that 'production equipment, capital goods and other products used exclusively in the course of a trade or business' are excluded from the general safety requirement.

Article 3(2) imposes certain duties on producers as part of the general safety requirement. It states that within the limits of their respective activities, producers must:

- provide consumers with the relevant information to enable them to assess the risks inherent in a product throughout the normal or reasonably foreseeable period of its use, where such risks are not immediately obvious without adequate warnings, and to take precautions against those risks.
- adopt measures commensurate with the characteristics of the products which they supply, to enable them to be informed of risks which these products might present and to take appropriate action including, if necessary, withdrawing the product in question from the market to avoid these risks.

The above measures include, whenever appropriate, marking of the products or product batches in such a way that they can be identified, sample testing of marketed products, investigating complaints made and keeping distributors informed of such monitoring. It should be noted that provision of a warning does not exempt a producer from compliance with the other requirements of the Directive.

Article 3(2) also provides that distributors must act with due care in order to help ensure compliance with the general safety requirement. In particular, they must not supply products which they know, or should know, do not comply with this requirement and they must participate in monitoring the safety of products placed on the market, especially by passing on information on product risks.

Who is a 'producer'?

Under the provisions of Article 2(d) of the Directive a 'producer' means:

- the manufacturer of the product, when he is established in the Community, and any other person presenting himself as the

manufacturer by affixing to the product his name, trade mark or other distinctive mark, or the person who reconditions the product;
- the manufacturer's representative, when the manufacturer is not established in the Community or, if there is no representative established in the Community, the importer of the product; or
- other professionals in the supply chain, in so far as their activities may affect the safety properties of a product placed on the market.

What is a 'safe product'?

Under the provisions of Article 2(b) of the Directive a 'safe product' means any product which, under normal or reasonably foreseeable conditions of use, including duration, does not present any risk or only the minimum risks compatible with the product's use, consistent with a high level of protection for the safety and health of persons. The feasibility of obtaining higher levels of safety or the availability of other products containing a lesser degree of risk does not constitute grounds for considering a product to be 'unsafe' or 'dangerous'.

In assessing the safety of a product, Article 2(b) provides for several factors to be taken into account:

- the characteristics of the product, including its composition, packaging, instructions for assembly and maintenance;
- the effect on other products, where it is reasonably foreseeable that it will be used with other products;
- the presentation of the product, the labelling, any instructions for its use and disposal and any other indication or information provided by the producer; and
- the categories of consumers at serious risk when using the product – in particular children.

When is a product safe?

Article 4(1) of the Directive states that in the absence of specific Community provisions, a product will be deemed safe if it conforms to the national, legal rules of the country in which it is in circulation, provided that these rules are in accordance with the Treaty of Rome (in particular, Articles 30 and 36) and lay down the health and safety requirements which the product must meet in order to be marketed. Article 4(2) lays down additional criteria for assessing the safety of the product where there are no such national rules, e.g. conformity with any voluntary national standards giving effect to a European standard, or to a code of good practice in respect of health and safety. Under the provisions of Article 4(3) the Member States will retain the right to take action against a particular product where it presents a danger to consumers, despite its conformity with national rules or other criteria.

The effect of the Directive on UK law

The general safety requirement of the Directive is similar to that contained in Part II of the CPA, though wider in its application. It seems clear from the Recitals to the Directive that once it is in force then any domestic legislation which conflicts with its provisions will need to be amended. To the extent that the CPA is narrower in scope than the Directive, it will require amendment.

The question arises as to what is to be the relationship of this general safety duty to the detailed requirements of the Construction Products Regulations. It seems that where specific safety legislation is in existence then that will take precedence over the general duty, but where gaps exist or where the general duty would impose additional requirements then the general duty will apply.[44]

Liability issues arising from the General Product Safety Directive

The essence of this Directive is to impose *criminal* liability upon the manufacturer or distributor of a product which does not meet the general safety requirement. But, as in the case of the Construction Products Directive, the General Product Safety Directive will almost certainly have implications for the *civil* liability of design professionals and contractors. Thus, architects and engineers will be under a duty to take reasonable care to see that any materials they recommend comply with the general safety requirement if such products are not covered by the provisions of the Construction Products Directive. A contractor who supplies materials which do not meet the general safety requirement presumably will be in breach of his obligation to supply materials of merchantable quality and fit for their purpose.

One point on which the Directive is silent is whether or not it creates an action for breach of statutory duty in the event of an individual suffering damage as a result of a producer or distributor being in breach of his duty under the Directive. Under the provisions of section 41 of the CPA a breach of the general safety duty in Part II of that Act would enable the victim to sue for breach of statutory duty.

NOTES

1. 85/374/EEC, OJ No. L210/29.
2. This came into force on 1 March 1988.
3. 89/106/EEC, OJ No. L40/12.
4. S.I. No. 1620.
5. 92/59/EEC, OJ No. L228/24.
6. For more detailed treatment of this area of law, the reader is referred, in particular, to Bradgate, J.R. and Savage, N. (1987) NLJ 929, 953, 1025, 1049; Merkin, R., *A Guide to the Consumer Protection Act 1987*, Financial Training Publications Ltd, 1987; Clark, A. *Product Liability*, Sweet & Maxwell, 1988; Wright, C.J. *Product Liability*, Blackstones, 1992; and Geddes, A., *Product and Service Liability in the EEC*, Sweet & Maxwell, 1992.
7. [1932] AC 562.
8. The builder will also be under a duty to supply materials which are of merchantable quality and fit for their purpose under the provisions of Part I of the Supply of Goods and Services Act 1982.
9. He will, however, owe a duty of care to the employer for the completed building under the provisions of the Defective Premises Act 1972.
10. The provisions of Part I of the Supply of Goods and Services Act 1982 do not apply to this case; however, the builder does owe a duty to the purchaser under the provisions of the Defective Premises Act 1972.
11. Clark, A., *supra*, n.6, Ch. 2.
12. See, in particular, *D & F Estates Ltd v. Church Commissioners for England* [1988] 2 All ER 992, and *Murphy v. Brentwood DC* [1990] 2 All ER 908.
13. *Ibid.*, n.12, per Lord Oliver.
14. C.P.A., section 5(3).
15. C.P.A., section 4(1)(e).
16. Article 7(e).
17. Regulation 3(1), implementing Articles 2 and 3 of the Directive.
18. See Annex 1 of the Directive and Schedule 2 of the Regulations.
19. DoE Circular 3/91.
20. Regulation 2(1).
21. *Ibid.*, n.18.
22. Regulation 4, implementing Article 4(2) of the Directive.
23. Regulation 5(1), implementing Article 4(2) of the Directive.
24. Regulation 5(2).
25. See DoE (1992) *Euronews Construction*, May, p. 3.
26. Regulations 6(1) and 6(2).
27. Regulation 7.

28. Regulation 5(3).
29. Regulation 8(1).
30. Regulation 9(1).
31. Regulation 9(4).
32. Regulations 10(1) and 10(6).
33. Regulation 12(1).
34. Regulation 15, Guidance on the responsibilities of these bodies on enforcing the Regulations, is provided by DoE Circular 13/91.
35. Regulations 16–19.
36. Regulation 20.
37. Regulation 22.
38. Regulation 26(1).
39. Regulation 27(1).
40. Supply of Goods and Services Act 1982, sections 4(2)–(6).
41. Sale of Goods Act 1979, section 14(2).
42. See *Young and Marten v. McManus Childs* (per Lord Reid) [1968] 2 All ER 1169, 1172.
43. Draft Regulations were published in January 1994. At the time of writing they were not in force, and for this reason the text refers to the Directive. In terms of principal provisions, the contents of the Directive and the draft Regulations differ not at all.
44. See DT1 introduction to the Draft Directive on General Product Safety, Com. (89) 162.

12 Construction Services Liability

INTRODUCTION

At the time of writing, a number of proposals relating to liability for services are being considered by the European Commission. The most important of these proposals is a draft Directive on liability of suppliers of services. If implemented this will have an important impact on the civil liability of professional persons. The exact scope of this draft Directive had still to be determined in 1993 and it seemed likely that suppliers of construction services (i.e. contractors, architects, engineers, etc.) will be exempted from its provisions. These professions are likely to come within the scope of a proposal for harmonising construction liability.

It is the purpose of this chapter to discuss both of these proposals. However, at the outset two points must be emphasised. Firstly, as yet there is no actual proposal for construction services liability in the form of a draft Directive. Secondly, the future of the draft Directive on liability of suppliers of services is uncertain. In December 1992, the Edinburgh European Council, in considering the implementation of the subsidiarity principle, concluded that certain proposals tended to go into excessive detail in relation to the objective pursued. Accordingly, it decided to ask the Commission to revise a number of them so that they establish general principles which would be given more detailed form by the Member States. The draft Directive on liability of suppliers of services was identified as one of those proposals. It seems likely that the draft Directive in its present form will be withdrawn and replaced by a series of 'sector-specific instruments', i.e. a number of proposals governing specific services. None the less, the draft Directive in its original form is an important milestone in the debate concerning the standard of liability that the law should impose upon professional persons. Further, its provisions are bound to influence the bases of any future proposals in this area which apply to specific services.

It is from this historical standpoint that the provisions of the draft Directive are worthy of attention.

THE DRAFT DIRECTIVE ON LIABILITY FOR SERVICES[1]

The purposes of the draft Directive

There are two underlying purposes of the draft Directive. They are outlined in the Recitals. Firstly, it is intended to promote the safety of consumers as part of the Council's consumer protection policy. Secondly, it is part of the process of harmonising the laws of the Member States in order to prevent distortions of competition in the EC and in order thereby to create a Single Market. The laws of the Member States governing the liability of suppliers of services at present differ in the degree of protection provided to consumers. These differences relate primarily to the burden of proof. In some Member States the burden of proof is reversed in favour of the consumer, whereas in other States, e.g. the UK, the consumer has to prove negligence on the part of the supplier. Such differences may create barriers to trade and unequal conditions in the internal market for services. Further, they mean that there are differing degrees of protection for consumers of services throughout the EC.

The provisions of the draft Directive

It is important to note that the draft Directive does not propose a scheme of strict liability for the suppliers of services; under the proposed scheme liability for defective services will still be a negligence-based liability but the burden of proof will rest on the defendant supplier and not, as now in the UK, on the plaintiff.

The basic principle

The basic principle of this draft Directive is contained in Article 1, which provides for a scheme of liability based on a reversal of the burden of proof to the advantage of the plaintiff. Article 1(1) states:

> The supplier of a service shall be liable for damage to the health and physical integrity of persons or the physical integrity of movable or immovable property, including the persons or property which were the

> object of the service, caused by a fault committed by him in the performance of the service.

The cornerstone of this draft Directive, however, is contained in Article 1(2), which states:

> The burden of proving the absence of fault shall fall upon the supplier of the service.

This means that the supplier of a service will be liable for damage caused while supplying that service unless he can prove that he was in no way at fault in supplying that service. Article 1(3) goes on to provide that in assessing fault, account must be taken of the behaviour of the supplier of a service who, under normal conditions which it would be reasonable to presume, provides a degree of safety which it would be legitimate to expect. The fact that a better service existed or might have existed at the moment of performance or subsequently does not constitute a fault; this part of the definition of fault is a recognition that it is not possible to take a similar service and test it (as it would be a product).

The injured person is still required, however, to establish that the performance of the service caused him damage (Article 5).

The fundamental obligation imposed on the supplier of a service under UK law is now contained in section 13 of the Supply of Goods and Services Act 1982. This section provides that where the supplier is acting in the course of a business, there is an implied term that he will carry out the service with reasonable care and skill. The current duty and liability of suppliers of services in the UK are therefore based on negligence, with the burden of proof very much on the shoulders of the consumer of the service. Implementation of this draft Directive in its current form in the UK would therefore require an amendment to the 1982 Act.

There has been much debate over whether the liability of the supplier of a service should be strict in the same way that the liability of the seller in a contract for the sale of goods is strict under subsections 14(2) and 14(3) of the Sale of Goods Act 1979. As we saw in Chapter 6, for a time it was thought that the common law of liability for services was moving in that direction, but the most recent case law on this subject has re-emphasised negligence as the basis of this form of liability.[2]

Definition of service

Article 2 defines a service as:

> ... any transaction carried out on a commercial basis or by way of a public service and in an independent manner, whether or not in return for payment, which does not have as its direct and exclusive object the manufacture of movable property or the transfer of rights in rem or intellectual property rights.

The draft Directive provides for three exclusions from this definition:

(i) public services intended to maintain public safety;
(ii) package holidays; and
(iii) services concerned with waste.

The first exclusion clearly is based on policy; as for the other exclusions, package holidays are the subject of a separate Directive and waste services are the subject of a separate draft Directive. It is important to note that as the proposed Directive is concerned only with physical protection of persons and of their property and not their economic protection, then services which are unlikely to cause personal injury or damage to material goods (e.g. insurance advice, investment advice, surveys of property, etc.) are in effect excluded from the Directive. None the less, this is a much more comprehensive definition of a service than at present contained in English law. There, section 12(1) of the Supply of Goods and Services Act 1982 simply provides that a 'contract for the supply of a service' is a contract under which a person ('the supplier') agrees to carry out a service, and section 12(2) goes on to exclude a contract of service or apprenticeship from this definition.

Definition of supplier of services

The supplier is defined by Article 3 as the natural or legal person who provides a service in the course of his commercial activities or public functions. If he subcontracts all or part of these services, the independent subcontractor will be considered as a supplier of services and will be liable for damage caused by his fault.

The damage covered

Under the provisions of Article 4 damage means:

(a) death or any damage to the health or physical integrity of persons;
(b) any damage to the physical integrity of their movable or immovable property, including animals, provided that this property:
    (i) is of a type normally intended for private use or consumption; and
    (ii) was intended for or used by the injured person, principally for his private use or consumption; and

(c) any financial damage resulting from the damage referred to in (a) or (b).

The Commission's commentary on the proposal makes it clear that pure economic loss, such as loss of profit, is excluded from this definition. It should also be noted that this definition extends only to private property; it does not cover damage to commercial property.

As we have seen in Chapter 2, recent decisions of the English appellate courts concerning defective buildings have strongly emphasised the distinction between damage to other property and damage to the building itself. Damage to the building itself was classified in those decisions as pure economic loss and only recoverable in contract.[3] No such distinction seems to exist in the draft Directive. Article 1 states that the supplier of a service shall be liable for damage to the physical integrity of immovable property, including the property which was the object of the service. Thus, if an architect designs a building and there subsequently occurs subsidence in that building, then, since the building was presumably the object of his service within the meaning of Article 1, such damage will be within the scope of the directive, and in any action brought by his client he will have to establish that his design was *not* faulty.

It is not clear from the provisions of the draft Directive whether this principle applies to third parties, but in the commentary preceding it it is emphasised that consumers and injured persons should have equal rights and their actual chances of receiving compensation should be based on standard principles. If this interpretation is put on the Directive, should it become part of English law, then it will clearly result in a reversal of the principles governing third party liability for defective buildings laid down in *D & F Estates* and *Murphy*. The effect of those principles is that if an architect or engineer designs a defective, but not dangerous, building, then he will not be liable to a subsequent owner of that building because the loss suffered is classified as economic, and economic loss is not recoverable in the tort of negligence unless there is a special relationship between the parties.[4] A special relationship is very difficult to establish in such circumstances and the only construction profession who have been held, by the House of Lords, to come within its scope is surveying.[5] The law of tort, it seems, imposes more onerous duties on surveyors than on other construction professionals![6]

Exclusion of liability

Under the provisions of Article 7 the supplier of services may not limit or exclude his liability under the Directive. Bearing in mind the nature of the damage to which the proposal applies, this is already the case in English law, under the provisions of the Unfair Contract Terms Act 1977.[7]

In a practical sense the provisions of the 1977 Act are far-reaching, but it is not very appropriately named in that it does not regulate 'unfair' contract terms in general and it has left English contract law open to the criticism that it contains no general concept of 'unfairness' or 'unconscionability' which exists in other parts of the common law world. Under the provisions of an EC Directive on unfair terms in consumer contracts,[8] the use of unfair terms in a contract between a consumer and a person acting in the course of his trade, business or profession will be prohibited and rendered void. The approach which the Directive takes to the concept of unfairness in this context is to lay down a general test followed by an indicative list of the terms which may be regarded as unfair. The general test is contained in Article 3. Article 3(1) states:

> A contractual term which has not been individually negotiated shall be regarded as unfair if, contrary to the requirement of good faith, it causes a significant imbalance in the parties' rights and obligations arising under the contract, to the detriment of the consumer.

That provision is clearly intended to control the non-negotiated clause in a standard form contract which operates to the disadvantage of the consumer. Article 3(2) defines the meaning of non-negotiated in this context:

> A term shall always be regarded as not individually negotiated where it has been drafted in advance and the consumer has therefore not been able to influence the substance of the term, particularly in the context of a pre-formulated standard contract.

Article 3(2) goes on to state that if certain aspects of a term or one specific term have been individually negotiated, that will not exclude the application of this Article to the contract if it is clear that the contract as a whole is a pre-formulated standard contract.

A 'consumer' is defined in Article 2(b) as any natural person who is acting for purposes which are outside his trade, business or profession. This definition is likely to raise the same problems as the definition of consumer contained in the Unfair Contract Terms Act.[9]

Several comments may be made on this Directive. Firstly, it applies only to contractual terms, whereas the 1977 Act embraces non-contractual notices and so applies to claims in tort as well as claims in contract. Secondly, it seems clear that standard form contracts which have been negotiated in advance will not come within the scope of its provisions.

Thus, the standard form contracts used in the construction industry (JCT, ICE, etc.) will not be caught by the provisions of this Directive. In such cases, it can be argued, both parties have been able to influence the substance of the contract and therefore these will not result in any 'significant imbalance in the parties' rights and obligations arising under [it]'. In general, the effect of this Directive will be to narrow the scope for excluding or limiting liability in contracts made with consumers. In particular, terms used by professionals and the service industries to exclude or limit liability for loss or damage other than death or personal injury resulting from negligence will be prohibited rather than subjected to a statutory test of reasonableness. It should be remembered, however, that the application of the reasonableness test has already moved the English law on exclusion clauses a long way in that direction. The guidelines evolved by the courts in relation to this test make it very unlikely that a clause in a consumer contract excluding the supplier's liability will stand up as reasonable. In the case of commercial contracts, to which the EC Directive does not apply, the courts have generally tended to leave the contracting parties to allocate contractual risks between themselves as they think fit (though with some exceptions).

Joint and several liability

Under the provisions of Article 8 all the persons responsible for specific damage are jointly and severally liable. This is already the case in English law under the provisions of the Civil Liability (Contributions) Act 1978. These provisions are not affected by this draft Directive. The provisions of Article 8 mean that where two or more persons are responsible for the plaintiff's injuries, then, if the plaintiff so chooses, he can take proceedings against only one of those persons. It is a rule which has been criticised as operating unfairly in the construction industry, where many clients are large-scale companies with the means of verifying that all parties have adequate financial backing. A DTI/DoE report, *Professional Liability – Report of the Study Teams*[10] recommended that, except in the case of claims of less than £50 000 made by domestic clients, construction professionals should no longer owe 100 per cent liability to their clients where they were only partially at fault.

The limitation period

Under the provisions of Articles 9 and 10 a limitation period of three years from the date on which the plaintiff became aware or should reasonably have become aware of the damage is laid down. If no action is commenced within five years of the date on which the service which caused the damage was provided, the right to sue is extinguished. In the case of services relating to the design and construction of buildings these periods are extended to ten and twenty years.

The current position in English law regarding the limitation period in personal injury cases is governed by section 11 of the Limitation Act 1980, which provides that an action for damages for personal injuries resulting from negligence must be commenced within three years of the date when the victim knows or should know that he has been injured. The provisions of Articles 9 and 10 seem to conflict with this section. Consider a case where a factory building contains a material the dust from which results in a serious disease on the part of the factory workers but the symptoms of that disease do not begin to manifest themselves until after twenty years have elapsed. Under the EC proposals the workers' actions would seem to be time-barred, whereas under the provisions of the 1980 Act their actions would be allowed to proceed, provided that they were started within the stipulated three-year period.

Summary

In summary, three points need to be emphasised about the draft Directive. Firstly, it does not propose a scheme of strict liability for suppliers of services; under the proposed scheme liability for defective services will still be a negligence-based form of liability but with the burden of proof resting on the defendant supplier. Secondly, as the draft Directive is concerned with the physical protection of persons and of their property, then those services which are unlikely to cause this kind of loss if defective (e.g. insurance advice, investment advice, surveys of property, etc.) are effectively excluded from its scope. Thirdly, it should be noted that the precise ambit of the proposal and any future proposals in this area are still a matter for negotiation between the government and the European Commission. The government is of the opinion that the construction professions (i.e. architects, engineers and surveyors) should be excluded from the Directive because their liability will be governed by a directive on the harmonisation of construction liability.

These EC proposals must have come as a disappointment to some commentators who, in the interest of consumer protection, have argued for a model of liability for services under which the obligations of the supplier would be laid down in much more detailed terms than simply reasonable care and skill.[11] There will still be a fundamental difference in the underlying basis of liability for defective services and defective products. Liability for defective products is, of course, now strict (though with certain defences available to the supplier), following the implementation of the Product Liability Directive,[12] but under the EC proposals for services liability will contine to be fault-based. The argument for strict liability is that the damage created by an activity is a risk to society and the cost of compensating it should be distributed between the whole population of consumers of that activity. It should be remembered, however, that this is also the function of negligence-based liability. Both fault-based liability and strict liability are methods of loss distribution and therefore of spreading the risk of loss from an activity throughout society. The essence of strict liability is that it precludes the plaintiff from having to establish fault on the part of the defendant and prima facie, therefore, it strengthens his chance of success in litigation.

The EC proposal is essentially a compromise between these two systems of liability. It is based on the premise that it is extremely difficult for an injured person to prove that the supplier of a service is at fault in the case of damage resulting from the service being defective, whereas the supplier, with his technical knowledge, can provide proof to the contrary much more easily. Given the diverse nature of services in a modern economy, strict liability is not always the appropriate basis for their legal duty. Strict liability may fit in with the nature of, say, plumbing and carpentry or possibly even the functions of architects and engineers, but in other cases, principally medicine and law, the concept would seem largely inappropriate. It is no doubt for this reason that the EC seems likely to conclude that a series of measures applying to specific services is a more appropriate approach in this area of law.

THE PROPOSED HARMONISATION OF CONSTRUCTION LIABILITY

In October 1988 the European Parliament adopted a resolution calling for the standardisation of contract clauses, the harmonisation of responsibilities and the promotion of housing insurance in the construction industry. In response, the European Commission sponsored a study into these issues under the chairmanship of Claude Mathurin, the French General Engineer of Bridges and Roads. His report, known as the Mathurin Report, was published in February 1990.[13] It has largely been superseded by the work of a number of pan-European construction industry groups which have been set up by the Commission to consider the issues raised by harmonising construction liability. These groups are known as the GAIPEC working groups.[14] It is their proposals which will form the basis of any draft directive on this subject, and not those of the Mathurin Report. None the less the Mathurin Report is an important landmark in the development of this subject and it is instructive to examine its proposals.

The Mathurin Report

The Mathurin Report was the result of a survey of the general characteristics of construction liability in the legal systems of the Member States. It set out the case for harmonisation of construction liability in terms of the now familiar aims of the New Approach Directives, viz. contributing to the creation of a single market by removing legal obstacles to free trade between the Member States and protecting the consumer. It recommended three directives to achieve harmonisation:

(i) a directive defining the role of the main parties in the construction process – client, designer, contractor, building control officer, etc.;
(ii) a directive on the responsibilities of architects and engineers in the construction process; and
(iii) a directive devoted to liability, guarantees and insurance.

It was the third of these proposed directives that was the most important of the Report's recommendations. The main elements of this proposal are as follows:

(i) There should be a standardised specific liability of the builder. In particular, the Report recommended that the liability of the builder should be invoked in the event of a breach of any of the six essential requirements contained in the Construction Products Directive. This specific liability should be for a ten-year period except in two cases, where liability would be for a thirty-year period:

    (a) a collapse of the structure; and
    (b) a deterioration of the structure to the extent that it becomes impossible, functionally and economically, to use it as originally planned.

(ii) For every new structure and every renovated structure constructed by a builder or sold within five years of its approval, there should be a guarantee as to soundness of structure backed by a third party. This guarantee was to be known as 'a European guarantee', and it would have signified that the structure met certain harmonised standards – in particular, the six essential requirements of the Construction Products Directive. In the case of housing, the Report recommended that the European guarantee should, in addition, contain a guarantee of satisfactory delivery of the structure in the event of the builder's failure to perform. The Report recommended that the absence of a guarantee should be a criminal offence.

(iii) The liability of the developer and builder should be strict, but the specific liabilities of the other parties should depend upon the existence of proof of a causal link between the damage suffered and the service supplied, and also of proof of a party's negligence.

The Report was clearly much influenced by the UK's NHBC scheme, and the recommended third directive is, in effect, an extension of the principle underlying that scheme to non-residential buildings.

The GAIPEC proposals

It is the proposals of the GAIPEC working groups which are likely to form the basis of any future directive on construction liability. These proposals were published in an annex to a Commission staff discussion paper.[15] This paper reaches no conclusions and contains no recommendations. Rather, it raises a number of questions for discussion on any future harmonisation of construction law in light of the principle of subsidiarity set out in Article 3b of the Maastricht Treaty. In particular, the paper invites comments on a number of specific matters:

- scope;
- acceptance;
- liability;
- financial guarantee; and
- quality control.

The limits of space means that the range of influences which impinge on these matters cannot all be examined in this text. Nonetheless, reference to the key issues is essential. In the first place, there are two aspects to scope: material scope and legal scope. The main question which the discussion papers sees in relation to the material scope of any future action is whether it should be limited to consumer protection and include only dwellings or extend to include construction works other than housing. In relation to legal scope, the discussion paper sees the main issue as whether any community measure should apply to all liabilities borne by participants in the construction process or whether it should be confined to contractual liability. The second key issue is the conditions which should govern the liability of participants: should the liability of the participants be based on proven fault (which is the rule at present applying in most Member States) or should there be a presumption of fault, whereby the plaintiff would have to prove only the existence of damage or a causal link between this damage and the activity of the defendant. The discussion paper states that whatever definition of fault is finally adopted, it must take account of the six essential requirements of the Construction Products Directive.[16] The discussion paper goes on to point out that the GAIPEC working groups are in favour of the introduction of a financial guarantee, but it states that the principle of subsidiarity may allow the Member States to deal with the practical implementation of such a measure. Finally, the discussion paper emphasises that the aim of liability and guarantee measures is to improve the quality of construction works. In this connection, it raises the question of whether there should be a Community quality control system, with the implementation of such a system again in the hands of the Member States.

CONCLUDING COMMENT

European construction law is hardly in a settled state at present, with vital issues of liability still outstanding. However, one matter seems virtually certain: harmonisation will not mean a complete equation throughout the community of the liabilities of the parties involved in the construction process. The differences in construction law between the Member States will remain, but the effects of those differences will be greatly reduced in the event of the implementation of a future harmonisation directive.

NOTES

1. COM (90) 482 final – SYN 308, OJ 1991 C12/8. This part of the chapter is based on the author's article in (1991) 8 *Building Law Monthly* 11.
2. *Hawkins v. Chrysler (UK) Ltd* and *Burne Associates* (1986) 38 BLR 35 and *Thake v. Maurice* [1986] QB 644.
3. *D & F Estates v. Church Commissioners for England* [1988] 2 All ER 992 and *Murphy v. Brentwood DC* [1990] 2 All ER 269.
4. *Hedley Byrne v. Heller* [1964] AC 465 and *Caparo v. Dickman* [1990] 1 All ER 568.
5. *Smith v. Bush* and *Harris v. Wyre Forest DC* [1989] 2 All ER 514.
6. For a jurisprudential view of the difference between the tortious liability of surveyors and accountants, see the judgement of Hoffman J. in *Morgan Crucible Co. v. Hill Samuel Bank Ltd* [1991] 3 All ER 153, p. 155.
7. See Chapter 1.
8. 93/13/ EEC, OJ 1993 L.95/29. This Directive will be implemented by Regulations made under the provisions of section 2(2) of the EC Act

1972. These Regulations are due to come into force by 31 December 1994.

9. See section 12 and its application in *Davies v. Summer* [1984] 3 All ER 831, and *R & B Customs Brokers Co. Ltd v. United Dominions Trust Ltd* [1988] 1 All ER 847.
10. HMSO, 1989 (The Likierman Report).
11. G. Stephenson and P. Clark, *The Law and Practice Relating to the Provision of Services,* National Consumer Council (1985); cf. the Law Commission Report, *Implied Terms in Contracts for the Supply of Services,* Law Com. No. 156 (1986).
12. 85/374/EEC, OJ 1985 L 210/29.
13. It is available free of charge from Agence Qualité Construction, 30 Place de la Madeleine, Paris 75008.
14. Groupe des Associations Industrielles et Professionnelles Européennes de la Construction.
15. Commission of the European Communities, *Commission staff discussion paper concerning possible community action with regard to liabilities and guarantees in the construction sector* (1993).
16. 89/106/EEC, OJ No. L40/12.

Part III

Reform

13 Reform of Construction Law

INTRODUCTION

Construction Law at present can hardly be said to be in a satisfactory state and a number of proposals have been put forward for its reform. It is the object of this chapter to examine these proposals.

The need for reform and the adequacy of proposals for reform can be understood properly only if the structure and principles of the existing law are grasped. It is worthwhile, therefore, summarising the present law governing liability for the construction of defective buildings and recounting briefly the recent fluctuations in these liabilities. The law at present governing this area can be summed up as follows:

(1) A contract for the sale of a dwelling is subject to the maxim of *caveat emptor*, unless the seller had provided the buyer with a warranty as to the quality of the dwelling. This is very unlikely, as in most cases the buyer will be expected to survey the property to see whether it has any defects. Generally speaking, the only basis on which the seller of a dwelling may be liable to the purchaser for defects in it will be a misrepresentation on which the buyer relies, e.g. a false statement that the dwelling has been rewired recently.

(2) Where the seller is a vendor/builder or where the owner or occupier of a dwelling has employed a builder to carry out improvement works on the dwelling, then the buyer or the owner or occupier will have the protection of the implied obligations of workmanship and quality and fitness of the materials.[1]

(3) The benefit of these implied obligations do not extend to a subsequent purchaser of the building. Further, such a purchaser will have no action in tort against the builder unless either (i) he can show that he relied on the builder in the sense in which reliance is now defined by the courts, or (ii) the defective building work can be brought within the complex structure theory as now defined by the House of Lords.[2]

(4) When a local authority carries out its building control function, it is not liable in negligence to the owner or occupier of a building for the cost of remedying a dangerous defect in the building which is discovered before such owner or occupier suffers personal injury or damage to other property. The question of whether a local authority is liable in negligence to an owner or occupier of a building who does suffer personal injury or damage to other property as a result of a latent defect in the building is undecided.[3]

(5) A surveyor employed by a mortgagee to carry out a mortgage valuation survey of a low- or moderately priced dwelling house owes a duty of care not only in contract to the mortgagee, but also in tort to the mortgagor.[4]

(6) In the case of a dwelling, the builder, designer or developer will be liable for breach of the obligations contained in section 1(1) of the Defective Premises Act 1972. Such liability will be owed to the first buyer and to subsequent buyers, subject to the limitation period laid down in the Act.

(7) Where a dwelling is subject to the NHBC scheme, then the builder will be liable for breach of the warranties contained in that scheme. Again, liability will be owed to the first buyer and to subsequent buyers. The warranties cover a period of ten years from the date of completion of the dwelling.

Two legal concepts underlie these propositions: firstly, the doctrine of privity of contract, that a person cannot enforce rights under a contract to which he is not a party, and secondly, the rule that the cost of repairing a defect in a building to prevent personal injury or damage to other property is economic loss and as such is not recoverable in tort by a third party. As we have seen in Chapter 1, construction projects typically involve a number of different contracts between the developer, the main contractor, subcontractors, the architect or engineer, and financiers. In view of the doctrine of privity of contract, those not privy to a particular contract cannot rely on its provisions to found a contractual action. Further, following the decisions in *D & F Estates Ltd v. Church Commissioners for England*[5] and *Murphy v. Brentwood DC* a builder will not be liable in tort to a subsequent purchaser in respect of the cost of repair of defects in the quality of the building unless it can be shown that there is a special relationship between the parties. So far, in the area of Construction Law only surveyors have been brought within the scope of the concept of the special relationship. The result of these developments has been that developers, subsequent purchasers and tenants frequently seek to protect themselves by means of collateral warranties made with the developer, the main contractor, subcontractors and the architect or engineer. This trend has introduced considerable complexity into the legal structure of the construction process. It has been estimated that in the case of an average shopping centre, a design professional may be expected to enter into separate collateral warranties with the financiers, the purchasers and fifty or more tenants.[6]

It is hardly surprising that the law as it affects third parties in the construction process has attracted considerable criticism. Recent decisions on the duty of care issue have produced arbitrary distinctions between the liabilities of the different parties in the construction process. A buyer of a low- or moderately priced dwelling may successfully sue his surveyor for a negligent survey on which he has relied; however, if the dwelling is defective because of the negligence of the architect or of a subcontractor, it is very doubtful whether the law would say that the buyer had relied on any of these parties.

Finally in this introductory section, a comment on the effects of the decisions in *D & F Estates* and *Murphy* is called for. A distinction must be made between commercial buildings and dwellings. The former are not usually subject to any guarantees provided by the contractor or designer and in the absence of appropriate collateral warranties third parties are now left without a remedy in the event of the building proving defective (at this point it is worth remembering that even a negligent surveyor is unlikely to incur liability in tort). Virtually all new dwellings are covered by the NHBC ten-year guarantee scheme and it may be wondered, therefore, why the decisions in *D & F Estates* and *Murphy* are considered so critical from a consumer protection standpoint. There are two specific reasons. Firstly, the NHBC scheme is of no use where the defects come to light more than ten years after the dwelling is completed. In the case of defects caused by inadequate foundations that is usually the case; thus, in *Murphy* the cracks did not appear until some twelve years after the house was built. Secondly, loss or damage resulting from defects caused by subsidence and inadequate foundations are not generally covered by domestic first party insurance. It is open to a house purchaser to sue his surveyor in these circumstances but failure on his part to discover a latent defect such as too shallow foundations is unlikely to constitute negligence, even if he has carried out a structural survey.

Recent proposals for reform in the areas of third party liabilities and Construction Law have come from two sources.

(1) a study set up by the DTI and the DoE – the resulting report of which is known as the Likierman Report;[7] and
(2) an evaluation by the Law Commission of the doctrine of privity of contract.[8]

THE LIKIERMAN PROPOSALS

The Likierman Report is in effect three reports produced by independent Study Teams: the Auditors' Study Team, the Surveyors' Study Team and the Construction Professionals' Study Team. The report of the Construction Professionals' Study Team is the longest of the three reports; in addition, there are a number of annexes not included in the published report.[9] In this section the proposals made by the Construction Professionals' and Surveyors' Study Teams are examined.

Before examining the details of the Likierman recommendations it is important to remember the legal background against which the Study Teams were set up. The dominant feature of this background was an expanding law of negligence and, in particular, an expansion in the scope of the duty of care owed by a professional person to third parties. Although this expansion had come to an end by the time the report was published (1989), it greatly influenced the report's philosophy. That philosophy was concerned mainly with the interests of professional defendants and their fear of virtually unlimited liability and very high, if not prohibitively high, PII premiums. The report of the Construction Professionals' Study Team pointed out that an expanding law of tort in the period from the mid-1960s to the mid-1980s was accompanied by two further developments with implications for PII. Firstly, there was a significant growth in the volume of defects that were discovered in recently completed buildings, partly as a result of the novel designs and new building materials which were introduced into the construction industry in the 1960s. Secondly, there was an increasing readiness on the part of building owners to seek legal redress, no doubt encouraged by developments in the law of tort.

The recommendations of the Construction Professionals' Study Team

The Study Team considered a number of proposals that were made to them for reforming the law of professional liability. Those proposals were of three kinds:

(i) radical reform of risks and liabilities in the industry;
(ii) consolidation of the existing law into a Construction Industry Bill; and
(iii) amendments to legislation together with other measures to reduce uncertainty.

In effect the Study Team opted for the third set of proposals. The details of these proposals are as follows.

Limited liability

Construction professionals, along with other professionals, have under the present law unlimited liability for the consequences of any negligence on their part. Although the Study Team concluded that it would not be possible to justify legislation to limit the liability of construction industry professionals without also considering limiting the liability of other professionals, they were in sympathy with the arguments that are often put forward in favour of such a proposal. These arguments include, in the first place, the consideration that the great majority of the industry's clients are limited liability companies or public corporations, whereas consultants are frequently employed in partnerships, with each partner being jointly and severally liable for the negligent acts of all the partners. Secondly, it is argued that the liability incurred should bear some relationship to the fee charged so that a service provided for a small fee should not give rise to unlimited liability.

Neither of these arguments seem particularly convincing, though the first point may seem to have a sort of rough and ready equity to it. The second argument ignores a fundamental principle of the law, which is that liability for negligence must be seen from the standpoint of its consequences; indeed it is damage consequent upon a careless act or omission which turns that act or omission into negligence in the eyes of the law. The fee charged for a particular project has no bearing either on this question or on the degree of care and skill which the law requires of the professional in carrying out the job.

The fact that many construction professionals have only limited resources with which to meet the damages awarded against them in a negligence action may well point to any limitation clause in their contract of engagement as being reasonable under the provisions of section 11(4) of the Unfair Contract Terms Act 1977.[10]

It seems better to deal with the problem of limited professional resources in this way. Both of the above factors can be taken into account in assessing the reasonableness of the limitation clause and, moreover, the statutory concept of reasonableness is more flexible than capping, as it is known, enabling each case to be judged on its merits.

Mandatory PII

This proposal was rejected by the Study Team principally on the ground of the cost of cover required. This argument seems to ignore the primary principle of insurance, that it is a means of spreading the losses resulting from negligence over the whole construction industry instead of those losses being allowed to lie where they fall. Moreover, some professional bodies, notably the Law Society and the RICS, require their members to take out PII.

Strict liability

Not surprisingly the Study Team rejected any proposal for strict liability in the construction industry. Such a scheme would be a major departure from the duty of reasonable care and skill imposed upon construction professionals, except where they agree to design a building for a purpose made known to them in advance.

A reduction in the limitation period

As we have seen in Chapter 9, the purpose of the law of limitation of actions is to strike a balance between, on the one hand, plaintiffs, who should be allowed adequate time in which to commence an action, and on the other hand, defendants, who need to know with certainty that beyond a certain time scale claims cannot be pursued against them. The problem of striking this balance is particularly acute in the construction industry because of the problem of latent defects, i.e. defects which may not be discoverable for many years after the completion of a building. The Study Team were of the view that the present law allowed too long a limitation period and they recommended:

(i) that there should be a limitation period for negligent actions in tort and in contract (whether or not under seal) of ten years from the date of practical completion or effective occupation; and
(ii) that this ten years limitation period ahould act as a long-stop extinguishing these rights.

The aim of the Report's proposals in this respect was twofold: (i) to provide a limitation period that was common to contract and tort and that commenced at the date of completion so that there would be no need to determine the date when either the damage occurred or it was reasonably discoverable; and (ii) to bring the law of building into line with product liability, where, under the provisions of the Consumer Protection Act 1987, there is an absolute long-stop of ten years.

The proposal for a common limitation period seems a commendable one, since it would infuse some much needed simplicity into this area of the law, but the aim of equating building law with product liability in this respect is much more debatable. Defects in buildings are much more likely to take longer to manifest themselves than defects in products and that would seem to justify a longer limitation period for them if the interests of plaintiffs and defendants are to be correctly balanced.

Joint liability

Where two or more persons are responsible for the plaintiff's losses or injuries, then, if the plaintiff so chooses, he can take proceedings against only one of those persons, and, if he is successful, that defendant will be liable for the whole of his loss. This rule struck the Study Team as operating particularly unfairly in the construction industry, where many clients are large-scale companies with the necessary means of verifying that all parties have adequate financial backing. They recommended that construction professionals should no longer owe 100 per cent liability to the plaintiffs where they were only partially at fault. They did, however, go on to say that there should be an exception to this rule in the case of claims of less than £50 000 made by domestic clients.

To sum up, the Study Team's principal recommendations for reform of the law were twofold:

(1) an amendment to the Limitation Act 1980 and the Latent Damage Act 1986 in order to achieve a limitation period of ten years from the date of completion of the building, for both actions in contract and actions in tort;
(2) the abolition of joint liability in commercial transactions not involving personal injury where the plaintiff's claim exceeds £50 000 and where the defendant's actions were partly the cause of the plaintiff's damage and were not carried out jointly with another defendant.

The recommendations of the Surveyors' Study Team

Limiting liability

The report made two proposals for avoiding the uncertainties of the reasonableness test in the Unfair Contract Terms Act: (i) model clause 'certification' and (ii) capping.

Model clause 'certification' This would be a scheme whereby a statutory body such as the Office of Fair Trading would approve standard clauses submitted by professional organisations and certify that such clauses were reasonable for incorporation into a contract between a professional and a consumer. Under such a scheme the Unfair Contract Terms Act would be amended so that it would not apply to such clauses. This suggestion is unlikely to see the light of day in view of the forthcoming implementation of the Directive on unfair contract terms.[11]

Capping The Study Team examined the possibility of capping, i.e. introducing legislation to limit liability for damages resulting from negligence. However, they rejected the idea, for a variety of reasons, principally because they felt that it would be difficult to construct an equitable scheme. In any event, as we have just seen in the section on construction professionals, such a scheme seems to be unnecessary in view of the fact that under the provisions of section 11(4) of the Unfair Contract Terms Act it is possible for a small firm with limited financial resources to limit its liability for damages resulting from its negligence.

Compulsory PII

Since 1 January 1986 it has been compulsory for all chartered surveyors in private practice who are members of the RICS to take out PII. The Study Team recommended that insurance cover be compulsory, stating that it would encourage standards to rise, promote risk management procedures, give added protection to the consumer and put all practitioners on an equal footing in the market place. This seems a good recommendation based on sound reasoning. One could also add that insurance is a means of loss-spreading, i.e. it is better that the losses resulting from the negligence of surveyors be spread over the whole body of consumers of surveying services, rather than be allowed to lie on the unfortunate few. It has, however, resulted in a large increase in the number of claims and a huge rise in the cost of premiums.

Strict liability

The introduction of no-fault liability for surveying services was, not surprisingly, rejected by the Study Team, principally because of the increase in PII premiums which, they felt, would inevitably result from such a reform. The introduction of strict liability into the law concerning the supply of services would, of course, be a major departure from the law as it stands, because it would involve an implied warranty as to results on the part of the supplier, something firmly rejected by the courts.[12]

THE LAW COMMISSION PROPOSALS

The Law Commission in their consultation paper examine the doctrine of privity of contract in general. This doctrine is one of the cornerstones of the

English law of contract. It means that only those persons who are parties to a contract may sue and be sued on it. There are two strands to this doctrine. Firstly, a person who is not a party to a contract cannot take the benefit of it, even if it was intended to benefit him. Secondly, a contract cannot impose obligations upon a third party. It is the first of these strands which has attracted the most criticism and the law has created a number of exceptions to this aspect of the doctrine in order to circumvent what are considered to be its inconveniences and injustices.[13] One of the areas of law in which this rule is said to operate with most injustice is that of product liability; it is felt that the ultimate consumer of a product should have a direct right of action against the manufacturer in the event of the product proving defective, independent of any guarantee provided by the manufacturer. Indeed, some jurisdictions, most notably the US, have abolished the third party rule in this area of law.[14]

The Law Commission do not recommend the creation of further exceptions to the rule that a third party cannot take the benefit of a contract. Rather they recommend a detailed legislative scheme to allow third parties to enforce contractual provisions made in their favour.[15] The basic principle underlying their proposal is that a third party should only be able to enforce a contract in which the parties *intend* that he should receive the benefit of the promised performance and also *intend* to create a legal obligation enforceable by him. The Law Commission were at pains to emphasise that a third party should not be allowed to sue on any contract which is simply made for his benefit or which merely happens to benefit him or on which he has relied. This, they say, would create an unacceptably wide ambit of liability. The Law Commission illustrate this point with the following example. Where a contractor is employed by a highway authority to construct a new road, the road may be intended for the benefit of all road-users, but there will usually be no intention that individual road-users should have a right of action in the event of any delay in construction.[16]

The main features of the Law Commission's proposal, which is modelled on the New Zealand Contracts (Privity) Act 1982, are as follows:

(1) Rights created against a contracting party should be governed by the contract and be valid only to the extent that it is valid. These rights may be conditional upon the other contracting party performing his obligations under it.

(2) Rights which may be created in favour of a third party should extend:
   (a) to the right to receive the promised performance from the promisor where this is an appropriate remedy and also to the right to pursue any remedies for delayed or defective performance; and

(b) to the right to rely on any provisions in the contract restricting or excluding the third party's liability to a contracting party as if the third party were a party to the contract.

(3) Rights may be created in a third party even though he is not in existence or ascertained at the time the contract is made.

These proposals relate to the general law of contract, but the Law Commission consider that they would have considerable advantages for third party liabilities in the construction field. If the contract between the developer and the contractor or the contract between the contractor and the first building owner could be expressed for the benefit of subsequent building owners, tenants, etc., then this would remove the need for collateral warranties and simplify legal relationships in the construction industry.[17]

EVALUATION

The question at the heart of any discussion on the reform of Construction Law is how wide the ambit of third party liability should be drawn. Readers of this work will be aware that the recent dramatic swings in the tort of negligence have mostly involved building and construction cases. It is for this reason that Construction Law is so illuminating an area of study; it highlights the problematical areas of economic loss and negligence and the relationship between contract and tort. None of the proposals for reform discussed so far in this chapter really address these issues. The Likierman Study Teams were set up at a time when the law of negligence had become plaintiff-oriented and they were concerned to redress the balance of the law in favour of the defendant. The decisions in *D & F Estates* and *Murphy* have brought to an end the expansionist phase of negligence and the concern now is whether the balance has swung too far to the advantage of the defendant. As a result there seems to be little likelihood of any of the Likierman proposals being implemented. The proposals of the Law Commission, if implemented, will enable the benefit of a contract to extend to third parties, but only if it can be established that this is the intention of the parties to the contract. Thus, if one or more of the parties to a construction contract do not wish a third party to receive the benefit of the contract, a third party who becomes the occupier or owner of the building will still be without a remedy in the event of the building proving defective. Only a reform of tort law in the area of premises liability can substantially improve the legal position of third parties in the construction process.

In devising such reform there is clearly a balance of interests to be struck. On the one hand, there is the interest of plaintiffs. If they are subsequent purchasers or tenants of a commercial building which proves defective, they will now be without a remedy against the builder or designer of the building. A subsequent purchaser or lessee of a dwelling subject to an NHBC guarantee will be in a stronger position but only if the defects reveal themselves before the expiry of ten years following completion of the building. Many such plaintiffs will not have first party insurance to cover defects such as subsidence or heave. On the other hand, there is the interest of defendants with their (arguably quite legitimate) fear of virtually unlimited liability and very high PII premiums.[18] Arguably tort law is the proper vehicle for achieving a satisfactory balancing of these conflicting interests. Contract law is designed to give effect to the intention of the parties to the contract in question and despite statutory intervention it is largely *laissez-faire* in its philosophy. It is not essentially a regulatory mechanism for reallocating losses. Tortious liabilities, in contrast, are imposed by the law and it is just that characteristic of tort law that makes it so suitable for carrying out a regulatory role.

A new Defective Premises Act?

The English appellate courts have set their face against a regulatory or welfarist philosophy of the common law of tort. The Law Lords in *D & F Estates* and *Murphy* were adamant that it is the task of the legislature to carry out any reform of product and premises liability. Statute law reform seems to be the only way forward in this area and a new Defective Premises Act has been suggested as one solution.[19] The purpose of this statutory reform would be to replace existing duties contained in section 1 of the Defective Premises Act 1972 with a new strict liability duty for the quality of buildings. Such an Act should apply to all buildings, not just dwellings. Sections 1 and 2 of the 1972 Act would be repealed.

The key problem for such new legislation would be to define the content of the new duty. It is essential that it address the issue of economic loss and liability for defective buildings, and clarify exactly the nature of the loss to be covered, thus avoiding the ambiguity of the duty in the 1972 Act.[20] It should allow recovery for economic loss not just by the other contracting party, but also by all third parties in the construction process. Such liability would be imposed on the main contractor, subcontractor, design professionals, developers and local authorities.

The enactment of such a duty would repeal the common law rule on negligence and economic loss in relation to buildings laid down in *D & F Estates* and *Murphy*. The Law Lords in those cases saw recovery for economic loss as solely the province of the law of contract and they considered that creating tortious liability for defective buildings would lead to the introduction into English law of a transmissible warranty of quality for products. The origins of those arguments lay in the dissenting speech of Lord Brandon in *Junior Books v. Veitchi.*[21] He asked: if there were a warranty of quality in tort, by what standard would such warranty be judged? He clearly saw this as an insurmountable obstacle to any liability in tort to third parties for a defective building or for a defective chattel. It has not proved to be an insurmountable problem in other jurisdictions. Thus, in New Zealand the Consumer Guarantees Act 1993, which came into effect on April 1st 1994, has introduced liability on the part of the manufacturer of a defective chattel towards the ultimate purchaser for the cost of repairing it, where such purchaser is a consumer. The Act sets out a number of guarantees which are implied where goods or services are supplied to a consumer.[22] The consumer will have an action against the manufacturer where the goods fail to comply with the guarantee as to acceptable quality and with the guarantee as to correspondence with description where the description was applied by or on behalf of the manufacturer. In short it allows the consumer to enforce the familiar implied terms in the Sale of Goods Act[23] against the manufacturer as well as the retailer. This is clearly a consumer protection measure in the field of personal estate. However, it is suggested that its provisions could form a basis for a new English Defective Premises Act, where such guarantees of quality could apply to real estate and to commercial buildings as well as dwellings.

A new Defective Premises Act of this kind is unlikely to conflict with the provisions of any future EC directive on construction liability. Until such a reform is put in place, that elusive balance between the interests of plaintiffs and defendants in the construction process is unlikely to be achieved.

NOTES

1. *Hancock v. Brazier* [1966] 2 All ER 901 and sections 4 and 13 of the Supply of Goods and Services Act 1982.
2. *Murphy v. Brentwood DC* [1990] 2 All ER 908, p. 919 (per Lord Keith), p. 928 (per Lord Bridge) and p. 932 (per Lord Oliver).
3. *Murphy v. Brentwood DC, ibid.*, n.2.
4. *Smith v. Bush; Harris v. Wyre Forest DC* [1989] 2 All ER 514.
5. [1988] 1 All ER 992.
6. Bates [1990] EG 57 and referred to in Law Commission Consultation Paper 121 (1991), p. 78.
7. *Professional Liability – Report of the Study Teams,* HMSO, 1989.

8. *Privity of Contract: Contracts for the Benefit of Third Parties*, Consultation Paper No. 121 (1991).
9. These can be obtained from the Construction Directorate of the Department of the Environment.
10. Section 11(4) provides that where a person seeks to restrict his liability in this way the court shall have regard to (a) the resources which he would expect to be available to him for the purpose of meeting the liability; and (b) how far it was open to him to cover himself by insurance.
11. 93/13/EEC, OJ 1993 L.95/29.
12. See *Greaves v. Baynham Meikle* [1979] 3 All ER 99; and *Thake v. Maurice* [1986] QB 644.
13. For a detailed account of this doctrine, see any of the contract law texts.
14. See Harvey, B.W. and Miller C.J., *Consumer and Trading Law: Cases and Materials*, Butterworths, 1985, pp. 26–31.
15. *Supra*, n.8, paras 5.8–5.15.
16. *Supra*, n.8, para. 2.19.
17. The particular area of third party liabilities in the construction process is discussed at pp. 76–78 of the report.
18. The problems facing owners of defective dwellings are highlighted in the report of the National Consumer Council, *Murphy's Law* (1991); the problems facing owners and occupiers of commercial buildings under the law as it now stands are described in the NEDO BUILD report; for a forceful presentation of the difficulties facing defendants, see the Inaugural Lecture of the Centre for Professional Law and Practice, University of Leicester, given by Lord Oliver and published in [1988] 4 PN 173.
19. See Nicholas Brown (1990) 6 PN 150.
20. See *Thompson v. Alexander* (1992) 59 BLR 77.
21. [1983] 1 AC 520.
22. For a more detailed account of the provisions of the Bill, see Todd [1993] 9 PN 54.
23. In this case, the New Zealand Sale of Goods Act 1908.

BIBLIOGRAPHY

PRIMARY SOURCES

The primary sources of Construction Law are, as in any other area of law, case law, UK statutes and European legislation. They are to be found in the tables at the beginning of this work.

SECONDARY SOURCES

The following are the texts in Construction Law and related areas to which the author has principally referred in the preparation of this work. Other texts and journal articles are referred to in the notes.

Allen, D.K., *Latent Damage Act 1986*, Current Law Statutes Annotated, Ch. 37, Sweet & Maxwell, 1986.

Consumer Council, *Murphy's Law* 1991.

Cornes, D.L., *Design Liability in the Construction Industry*, 3rd edn, Blackwell Scientific Publications, 1989.

DTI/DoE, Professional Liability – *Report of the Study Teams* (The Likierman Report), HMSO, 1989.

Emden's Construction Law, 8th edn, Sweet & Maxwell, 1990 (Issue No. 28 – February 1993), Binder 1.

Furmston, M.P., *Cheshire, Fifoot & Furmston's Law of Contract*, 12th edn, Butterworths, 1991.

Geddes, A., *Product and Services Liability in the EEC*, Sweet & Maxwell, 1992.

Hepple, B.A. and Mathews, M.H., *Tort: Cases and Materials*, 4th edn, Butterworths, 1991.

Holyoak, J.H., *Negligence in Building*, Blackwell Scientific Publications, 1992.

Holyoak, J.H. and Allen, D.K., *Civil Liability for Defective Premises*, Butterworths, 1982.

Jackson, R.M., and Powell, J.L., *Jackson & Powell on Professional Negligence*, 3rd edn, Sweet & Maxwell, 1992, sections 1 and 2.

…s, M.A., *Textbook on Tort,* 3rd edn, Blackstone Press, 1991.
…ay, Sir Anthony, *Keating on Building Contracts,* 5th edn, Butterworths, 1991.
Morgan, D., *Limitation Act 1980,* Current Law Statutes Annotated, Ch. 58, Sweet & Maxwell, 1980.
Rogers, W.V.H., *Winfield & Jolowicz on Tort,* 13th edn, Sweet & Maxwell, 1989.
Speaight, A. and Stone, G., *The Law of Defective Premises,* Butterworths, 1982.
Speaight, A. and Stone, G. (eds.), *AJ Legal Handbook,* 5th edn, The Architectural Press, 1990.
Uff, J., *Construction Law,* 5th edn, Sweet & Maxwell, 1991.
Weir, T., *A Casebook on Tort,* 7th edn, Sweet & Maxwell, 1992.
Winward Fearon & Co., *Collateral Warranties,* Blackwell Scientific, 1990.

Index

Note: Page numbers ending with an 'n' indicate that the title of the legislation appears in an endnote on the page in question